TURNING WOOD
WITH RICHARD RAFFAN

TURNING WOOD

WITH RICHARD RAFFAN

COMPLETELY REVISED AND UPDATED

The Taunton Press

Publisher: James Childs

Associate Publisher: Helen Albert

Associate Editor: Jennifer Renjilian

Copy Editor: Diane Sinitsky

Indexer: Harriet Hodges

Cover Designer: Anne Marie Manca

Interior Designer: Rosalind Loeb Wanke

Layout Artist: Suzie Yannes

Photographer: Richard Raffan assisted by Les Fortescue

Illustrators: Lisa Long, Michael Gellatly

Taunton
BOOKS & VIDEOS
for fellow enthusiasts

Printed in the United States of America
10 9 8 7 6 5 4 3 2 1

The Taunton Press, Inc.,
63 South Main Street, PO Box 5506, Newtown, CT 06470-5506
e-mail: tp@taunton.com

Distributed by Publishers Group West

Library of Congress Cataloging-in-Publication Data
Raffan, Richard.
    Turning wood with Richard Raffan.—Completely rev. and updated
        p. cm.
    Includes index.
    ISBN 1-56158-417-7
    1. Turning. 2. Lathes. I. Title.
TT201 .R34 2001
684'.08—dc21   00-061557

ABOUT YOUR SAFETY

Working with wood is inherently dangerous. Using hand or power tools improperly or ignoring safety practices can lead to permanent injury or even death. Don't try to perform operations you learn about here (or elsewhere) unless you're certain they are safe for you. If something about an operation doesn't feel right, don't do it. Look for another way. We want you to enjoy the craft, so please keep safety foremost in your mind whenever you're in the shop.

Acknowledgments

Woodturning has been very good to me and taken me across the world to all manner of out-of-the-way places. It's put me in the way of interesting people from all walks of life whom I would not otherwise have had the chance to meet. And from them I've gained wonderful insights into not just woodturning but art, design, communication, and a mass of other bits and pieces that make life and the world so interesting. Thank you one and all.

Contents

Introduction

Since I wrote *Turning Wood* in the early 1980s, the craft of woodturning has undergone a reformation. And that was after it developed in leaps and bounds in the very late '70s. In the early to mid-'70s, it was difficult to find another woodturner, and the range of tools and equipment available was extremely limited. Today there are numerous woodturning clubs all over North America, Europe, and Australasia as well as a number of national associations.

Woodturning symposiums run by clubs and associations have disseminated information, while specialist woodturners' stores offer a bewildering array of stuff pertaining to the lathe. New chucks make life a whole lot easier, and lathes are better than ever. And while most turners are content to make a fairly conservative range of traditional forms and objects, others are not. Some are determined to get their turnings accepted as serious works of art that will make their way into art galleries and into the hands of woodturning collectors, who in turn (so to speak) have their own association. The craft is now a long way from its mass-production origins.

I took to woodturning as a practical means of earning a living, fearing that technology would eliminate me as a middle manager. I was probably wrong about that, but at the time I felt that the sooner I learned to do something practical the better—but it had to be something that couldn't be done by machine. So on January 1, 1970, I drove west with the dawn of a new decade, leaving London big-city life and a very well-paid job for an uncertain but hopefully more fulfilling life as a craftsman. I never once regretted the decision.

I chose to be a woodturner totally on a whim. When discussing with my sister (an established potter) how I might earn a living, she suggested woodturning and a place where I might be able to learn just up the road from the studio where she trained. For no good reason, the idea appealed to me and I decided to give it a go, knowing that if I didn't like the craft after a couple of months, or if I was totally inept, I could try something else. I had absolutely no knowledge of the craft other than it involved lathes and tools with rather long handles. I chose woodturning not because of some long-standing love affair with wood or trees, but because I felt intuitively that I could learn the basics of turning more quickly than almost any other hand skill. And an internal voice told me it was the right thing to do.

My intuition proved correct. During five months in a country workshop, I was not taught as such. I had to learn by watching and listening, as the skilled journeyman Rendle Crang cranked out the workshop's production on the other side of the tiny dusty workshop. Using the monkey-see-monkey-do approach, I got to know the rhythm of production turnery, what my shavings should look like, and which noises I should be making and which I should not. And I learned enough to produce well-made bowls, lamp bases, plates, and scoops, which were destined to pay all my basic bills. I did not have the skills to turn enough merchandise for a decent living, but I cobbled together enough of a livelihood by selling to small craft and gift stores.

It was a time of relative poverty for me. My income plunged 90% as it dropped a zero, but I'd prepared for this in the earlier times-of-plenty by ensuring I owned a small house and everything in it. Debt free, I exchanged my sports car for a more practical vehicle in which I could carry timber and from which I could hawk my wares. My major concern had been to find an alternative way of earning a living, so the immense enjoyment and satisfaction I gained as I developed the skills of my craft came as a surprise. The long hours of a self-imposed apprenticeship were no hardship, and eventually I developed the speed to get a good return on the hours I spent at the lathe.

If I had a problem, it was working alone with no mentor from whom I could get advice. I discovered almost everything the hard way—buying poor lots of wood, ruining nearly completed bowls, and so on. But on the positive side, there was nobody telling me I was doing things the wrong way. Despite the fact that I'd been told that real turners don't use scrapers, I adopted an uninhibited approach in search of my own solutions to what I later discovered were all the classic woodturning problems.

If one technique failed, I tried another, and I reckon I've experienced every conceivable way of cutting, hacking, and scraping wood on the lathe. Pieces often flew off and bounced about the workshop (and still do occasionally), but I learned a great deal in the process. In particular, I learned that real turners do use all manner of scraping techniques but not for spindle work. Some instruction undoubtedly would have helped me get started, and this book aims to make life easier for novice turners than it was for me.

No matter what you want to turn on a lathe, you need to have a good set of technical skills if the work is to be enjoyable and fluent. And fluency always makes for a better object. The techniques set down in this book show the way I go about turning wood. They are the result of an odyssey of 30 years in which I meandered the highways and byways of woodturning. They serve me well, but they are subject to instant alteration should anything better come along.

In the 18 years since I wrote the first edition of this book, I've been exposed to a lot of ideas as I've traveled the international woodturning circuit teaching and demonstrating. Fresh insights have been tested, adapted, and refined during my normal production work, and as a result many of my techniques have changed considerably since the mid-'80s.

This is a manual of hand techniques. I have tried to explain how to cut any internal or external surface and what problems and hazards to expect. I've tried to keep in mind the difficulties students commonly encounter, and if I repeat myself in the text, it is because I know these things tend to be forgotten in the mass of stuff to remember. To make the book comprehensible to readers everywhere, measurements are both imperial and metric. For the sake of expediency, most measurements have been rounded to the nearest 5mm.

Novices should be able to work through the exercises in centerwork and facework, practicing the cuts and enjoying the shavings while developing tool control. Even if you're not remotely interested in making spindles, do the skew chisel exercises. You will learn all the basics of the craft and tool control, and the time spent will be richly rewarded. Further skill-building projects are in *Turning Projects* and *Turning Boxes* (both from The Taunton Press) if your interest lies in that direction. *Turned Bowl Design* (also from The Taunton Press) will help you make better bowls.

Those who know a little more should find much that is useful here, whilst gaining an insight into one professional's approach.

If you have never turned wood before, I'm sure you'll enjoy it. Shapes develop in seconds as the shavings fly away, and I have a hunch that the ability to remove so much wood so quickly satisfies some basic destructive urge and gratifies the vandal in us all.

1

THE LATHE

A BRIEF GUIDE TO THE LATHE,
THE ESSENTIAL TOOL OF THE WOODTURNER

I WILL BEGIN BY EXAMINING the qualities you'll want to look for, or avoid, when you purchase a lathe. I'll suggest ways of modifying commercially available models to enhance their performance and offer advice on purchasing a lathe that meets your needs rather than your wants. My comments are based largely on my own experience and those of the several hundred students I have helped in hands-on workshops over the past 20 years.

The wood lathe is the machine that spins the wood, so it is the heart of the turner's craft. The care you take in choosing (or making) this most important tool of the trade will return endless dividends of satisfaction. It's very frustrating to struggle against the limitations imposed by an ill-conceived or poorly constructed lathe.

This chapter covers just the lathe and its standard parts. Attachments for the lathe—drives, faceplates, and chucks—are described in chapter 2. Cutting tools, such as gouges, scrapers, chisels, and parting tools, are examined in depth in chapter 3, and safety gear is dealt with in chapter 4. As you read through these chapters, refer to the illustration on the facing page to locate the various elements as they are discussed.

How It Works

Although lathes have been endlessly adapted to suit the specific requirements of many trades, there are characteristics common to virtually all of them. The business end of the lathe is called the headstock, which is a stationary housing containing a step-pulley on a drive shaft (see the illustration on p. 9). Power from an electric motor is transmitted to the headstock by a V-belt running in pulleys—one on the motor, one on the drive shaft. The motor is normally mounted below or behind the headstock and is securely bolted to the frame or base of the machine. The motor rotates the shaft in a counterclockwise direction, and a drive center, faceplate, or chuck mounted on one of the threaded ends of the shaft transmits power to the work.

Lathe speeds can be adjusted in one of three ways. The simplest is to adjust the drive belt on the pulleys manually. There are also two variable-speed options—electronic and mechanical—the latter operated by a lever that places tension on split pulleys.

The tailstock assembly slides up to the headstock along the horizontal lathe bed to provide tail-center support, and it can be locked at any point along the bed's length (see the illustration

THE LATHE

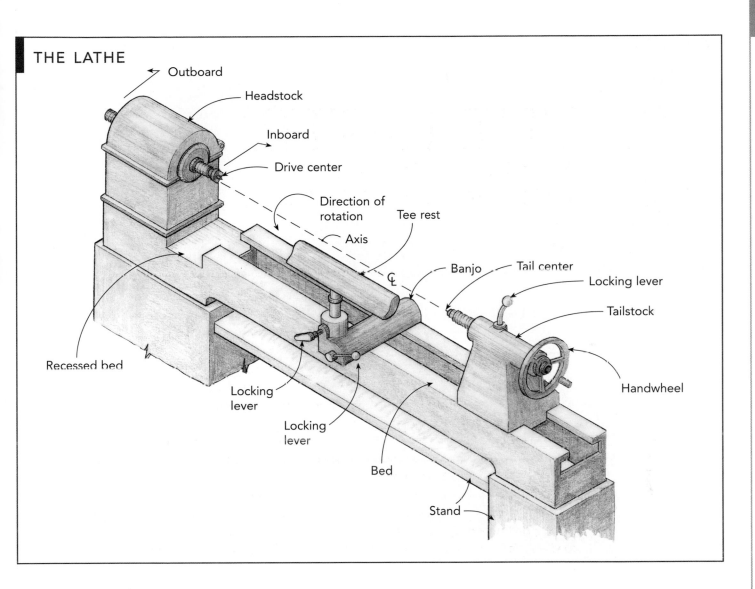

Outboard

Headstock

Inboard

Drive center

Direction of rotation

Tee rest

Axis

C̶L

Banjo

Tail center

Locking lever

Tailstock

Recessed bed

Locking lever

Locking lever

Bed

Handwheel

Stand

above). Lathes are designed so that as you stand facing the front of the lathe, the headstock will be on your left, the tailstock on your right. It's a right-handed world to which left-handers generally adapt, although a few left-handed lathes have been built with the headstock to the right.

The maximum diameter that can be turned on any lathe is determined by the distance between the point of the drive center (on the headstock) and the bed. This distance is the maximum radius of any work you can mount on the lathe, or half the maximum diameter. Turners describe this distance in terms of what

a lathe will swing. For example, a lathe with a center height of 6 in. (150mm) will swing 12 in. (300mm). The length of work that can be turned is determined by the distance between the drive center and tail center when the tailstock is moved to its outermost position at the end of the bed.

Woodturnings fall into two categories—centerwork or facework. A job is defined as centerwork or facework by the orientation of the grain of the wood in relation to the lathe axis, rather than by the way in which the wood is held on the lathe. In centerwork the grain runs the length of the work and lies parallel to the

Pod Boxes

After the turning of these boxes was completed, the asymmetric finials/stems were carved using a range of abrasive discs. Seed pods provided the inspiration for these pieces.

MATERIAL: Cocobolo

SIZE: About 3 in. (75mm) diameter

rotational axis of the lathe, while in facework the grain lies at a 90° angle to the axis (see the illustration on the facing page).

Most people think of centerwork as chair legs and rungs, newel posts, or other long, thin projects turned between two centers. Bowls, platters, and other large-diameter work turned on a faceplate or chuck are considered standard facework. While this is often the case, there are frequent exceptions, which I will describe in greater detail in chapter 2.

My lathe, a long-bed Vicmarc 300, is ideal for just about any production work I'm likely to do (see the photo on the facing page). It's very heavy, at just less than 880 lb. (400kg). It will swing 23½ in. (600mm) inboard, which is much more than I commonly need even for my

This short-bed lathe, with its mechanical variable-speed adjustment, is ideal for facework and short centerwork. Speed is adjusted by moving the lever below the headstock. It will swing 23½ in. (600mm) and accept 15¾ in. (400mm) between centers.

CENTERWORK AND FACEWORK

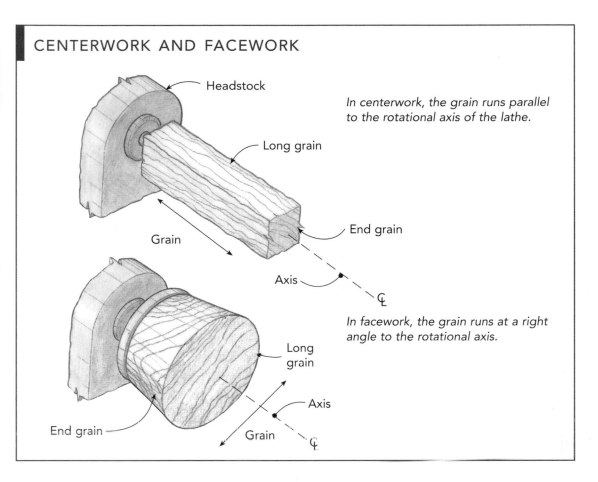

Headstock

Long grain

In centerwork, the grain runs parallel to the rotational axis of the lathe.

End grain

Grain

Axis

℄

In facework, the grain runs at a right angle to the rotational axis.

Long grain

Axis

End grain

Grain

℄

This Vicmarc long-bed lathe will swing 23½ in. (600mm) and accept 51 in. (1,300mm) between centers. It's heavy, weighing just less than 880 lb. (400kg).

Elm-Burl Bowl

Because of the uneven rim, the blank was mounted initially between centers and the profile turned with a foot so that the form could be mounted in a chuck for hollowing. Finally, the bowl was mounted into a deep jam-fit chuck so the foot could be turned away and the base finished.

MATERIAL: Elm burl
SIZE: 8 in. (200mm) diameter

The type of lathe you need depends on the kind of work you do.

large bowls, and it will handle work up to 51 in. (1,300mm) between centers. Until recently, I preferred the short-bed version of the same machine, shown in the photo at right on p. 6, but I like having the tailstock at the end of the bed ready to slide up any time I need it. I keep the short bed for enclosed forms such as the elm bowl shown in the photo at left.

The type of lathe you need depends on the kind of work you do, but there are certain features to look for in any lathe.

The Headstock

The headstock houses the drive shaft, which transmits power to the wood (see the illustration on the facing page). I recommend a drive shaft at least 1¼ in. (30mm) in diameter, mounted in 3-in.- (75mm) to 4-in.- (100mm) diameter ball bearings or tapered roller bearings. When powered by a 1-hp motor, this combination of drive shaft and bearings will easily handle a 75-lb. (34kg) block of wood.

The smallest drive shaft I would consider using would be 1 in. (25mm) in diameter, mounted in 3-in. (75mm) bearings. A drive shaft larger than 1½ in. (38mm) in diameter is heavier and requires a larger motor (2 hp to 3 hp), which is slower to start and stop and involves a higher energy cost.

A drive shaft of less than 1 in. (25mm) mounted in small bearings, a combination typically found on inexpensive lathes, is seldom satisfactory, especially when the bearings are solid bronze. Such combinations of narrow drive shaft and small bearings tend to flex and rarely eliminate all play, especially on facework. Robust ball or roller bearings are needed to cope with the stress and vibration of unbalanced blocks of wood and the force of knocks against the axis or end of the shaft occurring as centerwork blanks are mounted.

The shaft and bearings should be mounted in a heavy casing, similar to the cast-iron

THE HEADSTOCK

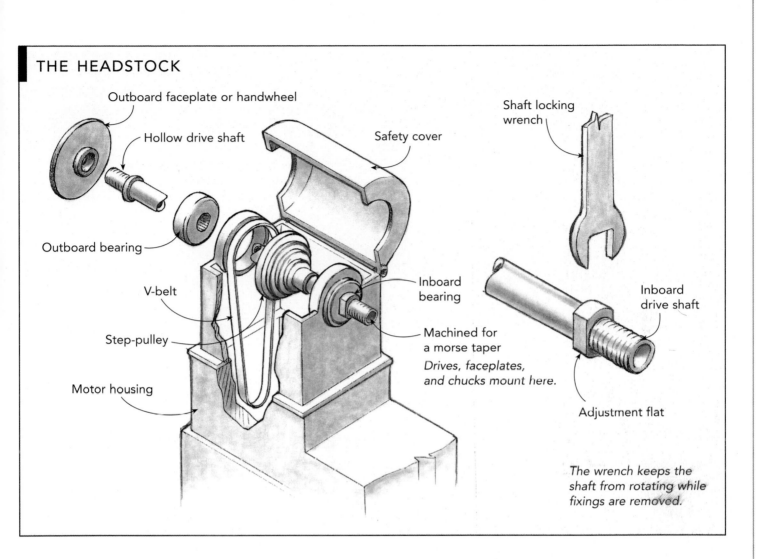

Outboard faceplate or handwheel

Hollow drive shaft

Safety cover

Shaft locking wrench

Outboard bearing

V-belt

Inboard bearing

Step-pulley

Machined for a morse taper
Drives, faceplates, and chucks mount here.

Motor housing

Inboard drive shaft

Adjustment flat

The wrench keeps the shaft from rotating while fixings are removed.

machines seen throughout this book. If the shaft does not run true or if it is not secure in its bearings, any play will be magnified at the point where the tool is cutting. Not only does this make fine work impossible but it also leads to dangerous vibration and tool catches. When bearings become worn, they must be replaced to ensure safety. (You will find that new ones run more quietly, too.)

The drive shaft should be hollow and machined to accept morse-taper drives. Some solid shafts are designed to accept a morse-taper drive, which is removed by unscrewing a collar that has been previously wound onto the drive shaft. A hollow drive shaft is preferable because

you can use a rod to knock drives from the spindle quickly and easily.

Drive shafts are typically threaded at both ends to accept faceplates and chucks. Look for a handwheel on the outboard (left) end or a thread where you can attach one. I use it to rotate a job for close inspection while the motor is switched off, and I need it to slow the lathe to a stop rapidly. Each year a handwheel saves me hours of standing around waiting for the lathe to slow down. I regard a 4-in.- (100mm) diameter handwheel on the outboard end of the shaft as essential.

Because lathes rotate in a counterclockwise direction, the threads on the outboard end of

On this Vicmarc lathe, the indexing pin, which doubles as a spindle lock, is located just behind the handwheel.

The cam-action locking lever to the left allows you to lock this tail center at any point along the bed with minimal fuss.

the shaft must be opposite to the ones on the inboard end, which are right-handed, so that attachments will screw on tighter with the machine's rotation. If the threads are both right-handed, attachments on the outboard end of the shaft will unscrew. (Some lathes are equipped with a reversing switch that aids in sanding and finishing, but care must be taken to ensure that the chuck or faceplate doesn't become unscrewed.)

You must be able to lock the drive shaft to aid in the removal of lathe attachments. Manufacturers offer various locking devices. A wrench on a flat or octagonal section of the shaft is best (see the illustration on p. 9), but most manufacturers now seem to opt for a pin that slots into the drive shaft or into holes on the largest pulley. The pin also acts as an indexing head. Many are awkward to use and most are easy to abuse inadvertently, which leads to excessive wear.

An indexing head allows you to fix the lathe in a number of positions at regular intervals for such jobs as fluting spindles or applying other decorative patterns to a turned form. Those interested in such work will find whole books on the subject.

Some headstocks with integral motors swivel to allow you to swing large diameters on small lathes. This was a feature of my first lathe, and it always sounds like a nice option because it gives you better access to a job—when hollowing a bowl or goblet, for instance—but I never found this arrangement satisfactory because the rests never are firm enough to eliminate vibration. If you have such a lathe, consider supporting the rest from the floor using lengths of timber wedged beneath the rest assembly.

The Tailstock

The tailstock slides along the lathe bed and is locked in position before the tail center is wound in to support the work (see the illustration on the facing page). The locking operation should be quick and easy. A locking lever that remains attached to the unit is better than a nut and bolt assembly that requires separate wrenches.

A handwheel is turned to adjust the tail center. It's useful to have the tail center wind out at least 4 in. (100mm) so that work may be mounted or unmounted without moving the tailstock. The handwheel should be at least 6 in. (150mm) in diameter and have a handle on its rim to make it easy to use.

The shaft should be the same size as the one in the headstock and also hollow and machined to accept morse-taper centers and chucks. Check that these can be removed easily, either by winding the handwheel or by using a knock-out bar.

Centers

The headstock and tailstock centers should be in exactly the same plane. In my experience, this is uncommon on most woodturning lathes. It is not essential when the wood is held between two points (as between a drive and a tail center), but it is when you want to provide tail-center support for work mounted on a faceplate or chuck. When the wood is held firmly in one plane, an off-center center will work it loose from faceplate screws or a chuck.

To check if your tail center is correctly aligned with the drive shaft, move the tail center in so that the point just touches a trued blank mounted on a faceplate or in a chuck. An untrue tail center will make a circle on the wood; a true center will leave a dot. Use shims to adjust the tailstock until the point of the center is aligned with the center of the circle.

The Bed and Stand

A common source of vibration, especially in small lathes, lies in the substructure of the machine. The best headstock and tailstock are no good unless mounted on a substantial bed of

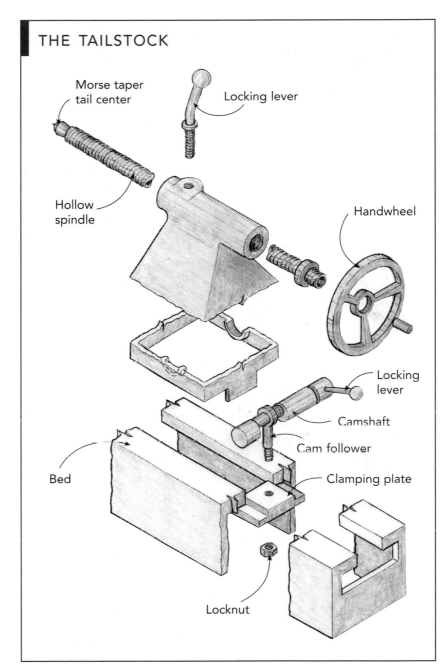

THE TAILSTOCK

Morse taper tail center

Locking lever

Hollow spindle

Handwheel

Locking lever

Camshaft

Cam follower

Clamping plate

Bed

Locknut

IMPROVING A LIGHTWEIGHT LATHE STAND

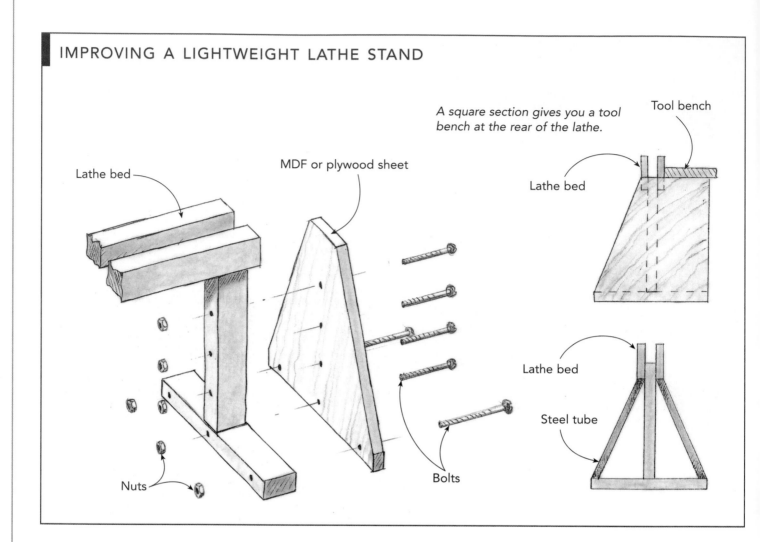

A square section gives you a tool bench at the rear of the lathe.

Tool bench

Lathe bed

Lathe bed

Steel tube

Lathe bed

MDF or plywood sheet

Bolts

Nuts

When turning off-balance work on a small lathe, it's a good idea to stabilize the machine. Bags of concrete mix work well.

cast iron, on steel or wood beams fixed to a heavy frame, or, perhaps best of all, on a large block of concrete. A solid, well-built lathe eliminates all vibration, and the job of turning becomes much easier. Greater precision is possible, and the scope of what you can achieve is broadened.

Most good-quality lathes have beds of cast iron and stands made of ³⁄₁₆-in.- (5mm) thick sheet steel or heavy angle iron that provide excellent, rigid support. Buy these with confidence.

The stand footprint should be at least as wide as the base of the lathe bed and preferably wider, with lugs enabling you to bolt it to the

Mounted on a custom stand made of 3-in. (75mm) angle iron, this mini lathe will swing 9 in. (230mm) and accept 13¾ in. (350mm) between centers.

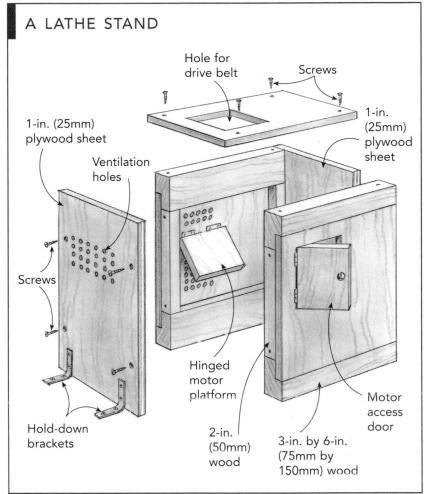

A LATHE STAND

Hole for drive belt

Screws

1-in. (25mm) plywood sheet

1-in. (25mm) plywood sheet

Ventilation holes

Screws

Hinged motor platform

Hold-down brackets

2-in. (50mm) wood

3-in. by 6-in. (75mm by 150mm) wood

Motor access door

floor. Lathes mounted on single pillars rising from the floor are not worth considering as is, but you can beef them up using sheet material or steel tubes at an angle (see the illustration on the facing page). This is a useful way to firm up any lathe, and commercial versions are available. A lathe cannot be too heavy or too well anchored.

Many good small lathes are sold on light-weight sheet-metal stands, which can vibrate enough to render the lathe nearly useless. These stands should be weighted down as shown in the photo on the facing page. You may also consider removing the lathe from its manufactured plinth and mounting it on a heavier custom base or big lump of concrete.

You can buy a lathe without its stand—known as a bare lathe—and make a solid base yourself using 3-in. (75mm) angle iron (see the photo above left). Or you can make one from wood and sheet material as shown in the illustration above.

Switches and Motors

It is vital to be able to turn off the lathe quickly if something goes wrong. Have a switch box with a big red off button. A button or bar, both seen in the photo on p. 14, should need be touched only lightly to stop the motor, which is essential when things go wrong. You can get

It is vital to be able to turn off the lathe quickly if something goes wrong.

Every lathe should have a big red off button that will cut the power instantly, even if touched only lightly. A bar running the length of the lathe bed, like the red bar shown here, is even better. This lathe also has a reverse switch (left), recessed start button (green), and a dial for the electronic variable-speed control (right).

foot-operated and remote safety switches, but a better option is a magnetic control switch that you can locate wherever is most convenient. I prefer to have fixed switches so I always know where they are. In an emergency you might forget where you put a moveable switch. It is prudent to locate switches where you won't have to cross the firing line of the work (see "Workshop lighting and layout" on p. 65) in the event of a problem. The red bar on my big lathe is ideal, and I can nudge it with my knee so both hands are free to be occupied elsewhere.

As for motors, I have always used a single-phase 1-hp electric motor sealed against dust. It provides enough power to cope with blocks up to 75 lb. (34kg). If you are unlikely to turn anything larger than a 12-in. (305mm) by 4-in. (100mm) bowl or a newel post, you could get

by with ¾ hp, but I would still suggest opting for the larger motor. My lathe, with its 1⅜-in.-(30mm) diameter shaft and 1-hp motor, gets up to speed within 1 second, and I can stop it almost as fast. Many lathes with bigger motors take 10 to 12 seconds to reach full speed and almost as long to slow, which is time-consuming and costly if you're stopping the lathe frequently to inspect progress on a job.

Speeds

Another consideration with any lathe you buy should be the ease with which you can change speeds. On occasion, you may need to slow the lathe down if you're working with unbalanced wood or if you're changing from one type of work to another. On most lathes, the drive belt is moved by hand to change speeds, so be sure that the belt and any tensioning devices are accessible and easy to operate. Usually, there are four or five speeds available within the 400 rpm to 2,500 rpm range, which should be more than adequate for most turners who do not need to change speeds often. Specific speeds are recommended on p. 102 for centerwork and on p. 142 for facework.

Variable-speed systems are better (and they're more expensive). The advantages of the variable-speed systems are that you can change speeds without stopping the lathe, and you can select the exact speed that you want, rather than having to choose between one speed that's too high and another that's too low.

Variable-speed systems can be mechanical or electronic. With a speed range varying between 300 rpm and 2,500 rpm, mechanical systems are based on floating or sprung pulleys that allow you to change lathe speed simply by moving a lever like that on the Vicmarc 300 shown in the photo on p. 7. Electronic systems are commonly connected to pulleys with two or three steps, largely for reasons of torque, and most allow you to start from 0 rpm. However, for safety when using an electronic speed control, set the drive belt on the pulleys to ensure you'll work within the safe maximum speed for the diameter you are turning. For instance, you'd turn a large bowl when the maximum possible speed is 1,000 rpm, not 2,500 rpm. Otherwise you might inadvertently start at too high a speed and risk a very serious and maiming injury.

Remember to ensure safety by keeping all belts covered while the lathe is running.

Center Height

I like to be able to see what's happening without bending double, so I prefer to have a center height no lower than my elbow or even 2 in. (50mm) to 3 in. (75mm) above. If a number of people are going to use the same machine, it's better to fix the center height high—at, say, 55 in. (1,400mm) from the floor—and build up platforms or stack chipboard sheets for the shorter people rather than give the taller ones backaches. For some facework, I prefer the center to be 1 in. (25mm) to 2 in. (50mm) lower than for centerwork, so I stand on 1-in. (25mm) or 2-in. (50mm) green boards that I have seasoning.

Tool Rests

The tool rest is an integral and very important part of the lathe. It absolutely must provide solid support for the tool as it cuts the wood. It is a two-part assembly with a heavy adjustable banjo (or base) supporting an adjustable tee rest.

The banjo must lock down securely when tightened, and you should be able to adjust the tee rest at least ½ in. (13mm) above and below center height and at any position along the bed. The rest assembly must be easy to adjust because it is frequently moved as close to the work as possible in order to minimize leverage

To ensure safety, keep all belts covered while the lathe is running.

A range of tee rests makes life at the lathe easier. Never use a longer rest than you need.

as cutting proceeds (see pp. 68–70 for more on leverage). Rest assemblies should have only two quick-action locking levers—one to lock the height and angle of the tee rest, the other to lock the banjo in position on the bed. (Avoid systems that require wrenches and often three hands and a tail. Life is too short.) The rests on my lathes can be positioned well above and below center height and can be readily moved to work on both the outside and inside of a large bowl held at its base (see the photos on p. 16). This isn't possible on many lathes but is worth looking for.

Tee rests should be of heavy construction, ideally of cast iron. The most useful tee rests are tapered and set at an angle on top of a solid post. The tool post must be at least 1 in. (25mm) in diameter for stability; anything

Ensure that the
rest can reach all
around a large job.
This is not possible
on many lathes.

smaller will flex and lead to a severe loss of tool control as you cut, increasing the likelihood of an accident.

The illustration on the facing page shows four rests in profile. In Fig. 1, leverage is reduced to a minimum, affording the turner the maximum control. With the rests shown in Fig. 2 and Fig. 3, the fulcrum moves back across the rest as the tool is angled up to cut, increasing leverage against the edge. The advantage of the rest shown in Fig. 3 is that the groove provides a useful guide along which to slide a finger, which helps control the distance of the cutting edge from the rest. Avoid the square, flat-topped rest shown in Fig. 4 because the moment the tool is angled up to cut, the fulcrum is moved to the edge farthest away from the work. This increases the leverage, making any tool more difficult to control.

For each lathe, I have rests ranging from 4 in. (100mm) to 12 in. (305mm), which are ideal for small general work and bowls. You can manage with one rest 5 in. (125mm) to 7 in. (180mm) long, but be prepared to move it more often. A long rest the length of the lathe with two banjos is convenient if you are intending to turn large runs of long spindles (see the photo on the facing page). There are also specialized rests available that are curved to fit bowl curves. These are typically flat-topped and are fine to use with scrapers when the tool is held flat on the rest, but I've never found them easy to use with gouges. My standard rests have always served me well, so I have never bothered to acquire a curved one.

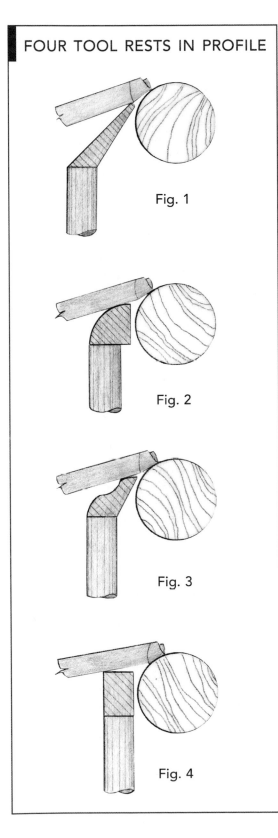

Fig. 1

Fig. 2

Fig. 3

Fig. 4

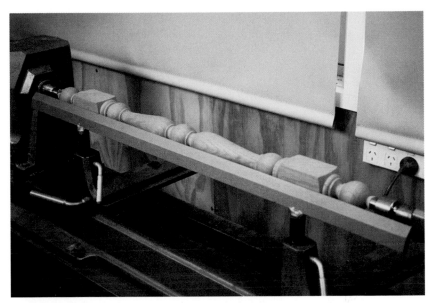

For making a number of similar spindles, a long rest makes life a lot easier.

Choosing a Lathe

It is a sad fact that most would-be woodturners start out with the wrong lathe, as I did. And there must be many souls who never pursue the craft thinking themselves totally inept when, in fact, it was the machine that never allowed them a proper start. I know now that my experience as I jumped into lathe ownership back in 1970 was not unusual. I failed to heed advice offered at the time as I endeavored to save money, then I had to upgrade within months, losing money on the first lathe.

The type and size of lathe you choose should depend on the sort of work you are interested in, modified, of course, by your budget. I think it is a mistake for any beginner to acquire some monster lathe whose capacity might never be used. The best way to learn woodturning techniques is to work repetitively on a small scale. As a novice you should buy as good a machine as you can afford and learn on that, then graduate to a larger machine when you feel the need. Chances are you won't, unless you start with a mini lathe. Most good small lathes will

Wavy Bowls

These were turned from green wood (the small tree had been felled less than an hour before). Speed is essential when turning green wood so finely because the wood warps almost as soon as it's turned. These bowls were microwaved for 80 seconds on full power after which they were steaming and distorted. To obtain a symmetrical distortion, blanks should be evenly grained with the pith of the tree aligned across the top of the blank.

MATERIAL: Casuarina

SIZE: 5½ in. (140mm) diameter

enable you to turn up to 12 in. (305mm) in diameter and 36 in. (910mm) in length, dimensions that have long been established as best suited to the needs of most amateur and professional woodturners. On such a lathe you can make a good-size family salad or fruit bowl, dinner plates, table lamps, spindles for furniture, and a host of smaller projects such as drawer knobs and goblets.

For most centerwork, a 12-in. (305mm) swing is sufficient and a 3-ft.- (915mm) to 4-ft.- (1,220mm) long bed is desirable. For facework, a center about 10 in. (255mm) above the bed, giving a 20-in. (510mm) capacity, is nice to have, but the fact is that few turners ever need in excess of 16-in. (400mm) capacity. A short bed, about 18 in. (455mm) long, will allow you to move with the tools and work from all angles across the face more easily than a long bed.

A top-quality lathe is made from material that goes clunk rather than ping when hit with a hammer. Best is cast iron, which will absorb most vibration, unlike aluminum or steel, which can ring like a bell. Solidity is essential in a lathe, so it is for these reasons that lathes constructed of steel beams or tubing are generally best avoided unless very substantial. Well-constructed lathes with cast aluminum headstocks and tailstocks on steel bars are typically fine for small projects but rarely adequate once you test their advertised capacity.

If you are short of workshop space, there are a number of tremendous small lathes (see the photo on p. 13), which enable you to swing about 10 in. (250mm) in diameter and to do short spindles.

If you want to go larger, the lathes developed in the late 1980s specifically for craft professional and serious hobby turners will enable you to tackle just about any turning job except really large pieces that are well beyond the skills or desires of most turners, let alone novices. These will swing between 16 in. (400mm) and 24 in. (600mm) and accept from 14 in. (360mm) to 52 in. (1,320mm) between centers, depending on the model.

Whichever lathe you choose, make sure it measures up to the standards I've discussed. Beware of the many lightweight lathes competing for the vast amateur market and of good-looking cast machines with small-diameter drive shafts made by manufacturers who seem to have overlooked the stresses involved when turning wood as well as the vibrations arising from off-balance blanks spinning at speed.

Finally, if you are hesitating about committing more cash to a lathe than you anticipated, remember that a top-quality machine will always maintain its value and be easy to sell. Several times in recent years I have been offered way more than I paid for a lathe years before.

Acorn Boxes

For the most part, standard 1¾-in. (45mm) chuck jaws were used to grip these boxes. The bases were jammed over a small spigot so the bases could be rounded.

MATERIALS: Huon pine (left) and goldiewood (right)

SIZES: 2 in. to 2¾ in. (50mm to 70mm)

A top-quality machine will always maintain its value and be easy to sell. Several times in recent years I have been offered way more than I paid for a lathe years before.

CHAPTER

2

FIXINGS:
DRIVES, FACEPLATES, CHUCKS & ADHESIVES

B EFORE A PIECE OF WOOD can be turned, it must be securely mounted on the lathe so that power is transmitted to it efficiently. There should be no play or chatter in the headstock connection or tailstock support. Above all, you want methods that are quick and easy to use and that do not impose too many restrictions on the design of an object. I'll discuss the pros and cons of each method and show you ways of making the best use of the techniques and chucks at your disposal.

Devices for holding wood on the lathe are divided into three categories: drives and centers, faceplates, and chucks. **Drives,** or centers, support the wood from either end, with the power transmitted through a spur drive that bites into the wood at the headstock end, while the tail center (at the other end) keeps the job pressured against the spur drive. **Faceplates** are flat metal discs that screw on to the drive shaft. Wood is attached to the faceplate by using one or more screws. **Chucks** come in many forms. Mechanical chucks grip by expanding into, or clamping around, the work. Jam-fit chucks hold by friction and are mostly turned as needed to fit work that is jammed into or over them. Vacuum

chucks hold the job by suction. **Adhesives** can be used to stick a blank to a waste block attached to a faceplate.

Most of the fixings I describe in this chapter have applications for a wide variety of work. For example, there are several chucks that can be used to hold centerwork by only one end so that the other can be worked. (This is helpful for jobs like egg cups, goblets, and small boxes.) And it is often desirable to turn bowl profiles between centers, rather than on a faceplate.

As a rule, centerwork, where the grain lies parallel to the lathe axis, is mounted on the lathe between centers or held by a chuck. Facework, where the grain lies at 90° to the lathe axis, is held by a faceplate or chuck. Do not attempt to hold centerwork on a faceplate because screws don't grip well in end grain (see the illustration on the facing page). Faceplates should be reserved for facework, where the grain alignment is ideal for screws. Always ensure that any chuck or faceplate is wound fully onto the drive shaft before switching on the lathe. Failure to do this can lock a chuck or faceplate on so tightly that removal will take a great deal of time, effort, and ingenuity.

It is always advisable to cut any wood as close as possible to its end shape—or at least to a symmetrical and balanced form—prior to mounting it on the lathe. Cut discs for facework and squares or octagons for centerwork. If you don't have a bandsaw or hand-held electric jigsaw, cut facework with a series of flat edges so that the blank is as near to round as possible. Square blocks for facework sound like propellers and are about as dangerous.

Before starting the lathe, always rotate the wood by hand to ensure it swings clear of the tool rest and bed. With large blocks, check for balance. If one side gravitates to the bottom when the lathe is stopped, the block should be trimmed and a slow speed selected to cope with the vibration. If you have an electronic variable-speed control, develop a habit of setting it near zero rpm before you turn on the lathe. Mechanical variable speed controls only work with the lathe running, so be sure to set a low speed before mounting any large job on the lathe.

Drives

The simplest way to mount wood on a lathe is between centers. Spur drives and tail centers work together, with the tail center supporting the job as it pressures the wood against the spur drive. The main disadvantage of mounting work between centers is that you can't turn the wood at the points where it is supported. This won't matter for such work as chair rails, where each end fits in a mortise and can remain rough. If you want a smooth finish on a spindle end, you'll have to do it by hand.

Drives and centers each have a morse-taper shank that fits into the end of a shaft machined to accept them. Drive and tail centers are available with morse tapers in sizes ranging from No. 1 to No. 3 (small to large). If your spur drive has too small a morse taper for your shaft, you can buy a sleeve to make it fit. Drives and

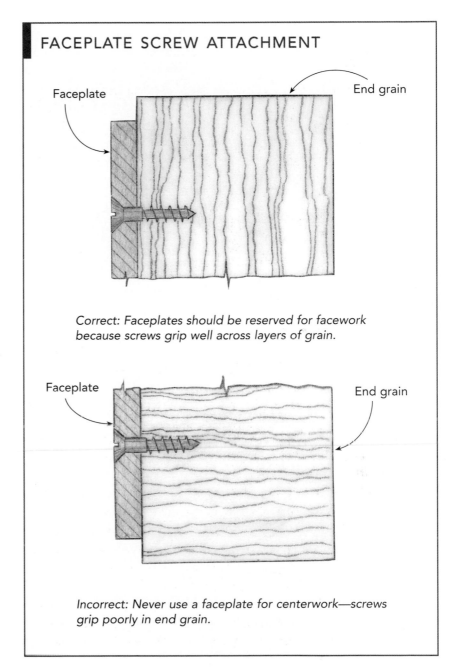

FACEPLATE SCREW ATTACHMENT

Faceplate

End grain

Correct: Faceplates should be reserved for facework because screws grip well across layers of grain.

Faceplate

End grain

Incorrect: Never use a faceplate for centerwork—screws grip poorly in end grain.

Always ensure that any chuck or faceplate is wound fully onto the drive shaft before switching on the lathe.

At left are typical spur drives. Those in front are for spindles smaller in diameter than the standard upper drives. At right are four types of tail centers. From the top right: two live cup centers, a live center, a dead center, and a hollow center for use with an auger or drill.

Two-spur drives (TOP RIGHT) work well on most surfaces, but four-spur drives (BOTTOM RIGHT) need a flat surface to grip properly.

centers are typically removed by using a knock-out bar through the hollow shaft. If your lathe has a solid drive shaft but no collar to aid removal of a spur drive, lock the shaft and rotate the spur drive with Vise-Grip pliers to loosen it.

SPUR DRIVES

Spur drives come with two or four flat spurs arranged around a central cone, which locates center and supports the work. The cone should be sharp and stand proud of the spurs by about ⅛ in. (3mm). The edges of the spurs should be kept sharp, ground on one side only at about 45°. If the angle is too long and chisel-like, you risk splitting the wood when applying tailstock pressure. A four-spur drive requires the blank to have a flat surface at 90° to the axis of the lathe to grip satisfactorily, while two-spur drives will bite into almost any kind of surface. A two-spur drive is very handy when rough-turning a bowl between centers because it enables you to tilt the wood around the spur to expose certain grain patterns or adjust the plane of a free-form or bark rim.

TAIL CENTERS

The job of a tail center is to support the end of the job while keeping it pressured against the drive center. Tail centers are basically a 60° cone, but a preferable variation is a cup center, which has a supporting ring just behind the point (see the top photo at left) that prevents the cone from splitting the wood and spreads the load if too much tail-center pressure is applied. A hollow center, which is like a cup center but without the cone, is used in conjunction with an auger for drilling long holes down the axis, as in lamp bases.

Tail centers come as either live (revolving) or dead (solid) centers. The heat generated through friction when using a dead center wears away the wood, loosening the fixing and often causing a good deal of smoke. These problems are greatly increased if the tail center is not aligned on the lathe axis. Traditionally this friction was reduced by daubing a little tallow on the tip of the cone, but the wood still tends to wear away, which means that the tailstock needs to be wound in constantly.

A live center, which has the cone mounted in a bearing, is much easier to use because it allows the center to revolve with the work, thus preventing the burning and loosening that occurs with dead centers. Some centers (including drive centers) have removable cones, which have a nasty habit of staying attached to the wood (rather than the tail center) when the work is removed from the lathe. They are easily lost, so I stick them in place with cyanoacrylate adhesive (also known as Super Glue). If you need to remove the cone later, just heat the metal with a gas torch to melt the bond.

MOUNTING THE WOOD

To mount a length of wood between centers, you tap it against the drive center to wedge the spurs into the wood. Present one end of the wood to the drive center and tap the other end with a mallet (see the top photos on p. 24). Use the tool rest as a support for the hand holding the wood. Wind in the tail center as tightly as possible by hand, then ease off a fraction. Lathe sounds can tell you when the tail center needs adjustment; if the pitch changes, it may only mean that the center needs winding in slightly or backing off.

Production spindle turners often have their lathes running continuously and have developed methods of mounting stock on a spinning lathe. The end of the spindle blank is rested against the center cone of the spur drive and the tail center is wound or levered in to support the other end lightly. With the blank held lightly between the two centers, the slight friction will cause the wood to revolve, even though it doesn't contact the spurs of the drive. (When doing this, it's important that the drive cone protrudes at least ³⁄₁₆ in. [5mm] beyond the spurs.) If the wood is off-center at this stage, it

Mulga Bowls

The blanks for these bowls were initially mounted between centers. I did that so I could pivot each around the spur drive to align the two highest points and two lowest points of the rim in their respective horizontal planes.

MATERIAL:	Mulga
SIZES:	4 in. and 6 in. (100mm and 150mm) diameter

can be stopped easily with one hand and tapped true. Once centered, the tail center is wound in, forcing the wood into the spurs. When the spindle has been turned, the tail center is unwound to release pressure and the finished piece is jerked off the spur drive by hand.

One problem with spur-drive fixings, particularly when turning heavy blocks, is that the drive can revolve faster than the wood when the motor is started so, instead of gripping, the spur drive bores into the end grain. To avoid this, cut

(RIGHT) **To mount centerwork on a spur drive, present one end of the blank to the spur drive and tap the other end with a mallet. Use the tool rest to support your hand as you manipulate the blank, then wind in the tail center to support it (BOTTOM RIGHT).**

A bandsawn ¹⁄₁₆-in.- (2mm) deep slot improves the grip while keeping the spur drive from boring into the end grain.

a ¹⁄₁₆-in.- (2mm) deep slot in the drive end of a spindle to accommodate the flat edges of the spur (see the bottom photo at left). Two-spur drives require only one saw cut; four-spur drives require two. Alternatively, spin the stock by hand as you switch on the motor so that the wood is revolving as the motor picks up speed. Make sure to pull your hand well clear of the wood. It is easier for the spurs to grip the wood when you remove the inertia of a static block at the start.

Often I mount bowl blanks between centers for rough-turning prior to seasoning. The disadvantage of not being able to work the tail-center face freely is outweighed by the advantages. It's quick and easy to mount a block of wood between centers, especially if it has natural bark edges or is rough and uneven. And such irregular blocks are more securely held between centers than balanced on a faceplate, no matter how many screws are used to fix one to the other.

Another major advantage is that the block can be aligned precisely so that as you shape the profile, you can manipulate the grain patterns. It's easy to stop the lathe and adjust the axis of a block just by shifting the base in relation to the tail center. Once the rough exterior form has been turned with a foot, the piece can be transferred to a chuck for hollowing. To ensure a good grip for the spur drive in facework and to prevent the spurs from boring into the wood, I cut a shallow V slot across center using a carver's chisel and mallet. My chisel and spur drive are the same width.

Alternatively, I have a 6-in.- (150mm) diameter steel faceplate with two sharpened bolts protruding about 1 in. (25mm). The bolts are set on the diameter, equidistant from the center and 4 in. (100mm) apart. To locate the points accurately and easily on the blank, I draw a line through center, then drill two holes on the line 2 in. (50mm) from each side of center. The

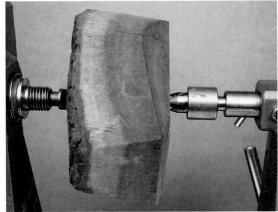

When mounting heavy facework blanks between centers, cut a V slot the width of the spur to prevent it from boring into the wood.

modified faceplate works like a big spur drive (see the photos at right).

FRICTION DRIVE TECHNIQUE

Here is a useful technique for turning a bowl foot or rounded base without any obvious chucking or fixing points, or for turning a larger piece for which you don't have a suitable jaw chuck such as the grass-tree bowl shown on p. 26. It's an ideal technique if you are working burl wood that cannot be mounted on a vacuum chuck (because it has holes) or on a natural edge bowl.

I complete the bowl as much as possible using a chuck, then remount the bowl between centers (see the illustration on p. 26). The tail center pressures the bowl against a rounded form covered with thin foam or soft cloth to protect the finished surface of the bowl. I will usually have finished the base along with the profile, so to preserve the finished surface I use a flat tail center and avoid using any conical detail at center. If you don't have a flat center, turn one in to fit over your cup center. (Now there's a nice little project!)

On larger, heavier, or off-balance pieces, I use a cup center for greater security, then remove the spigot retained for the cup center by hand using a power sander.

A spur-drive faceplate is excellent for mounting blanks with uneven surfaces.

Grass-Tree Bowl

Having an uneven rim, this bowl was turned initially between centers, then gripped by a chuck for hollowing. To remove the chuck marks, I finally put the bowl over a friction drive as shown in the illustration at right and added the heavy beads up from the foot for decoration.

MATERIAL:	Grass-tree
SIZE:	16 in. (400mm) diameter

You can use the same technique to finish off a sphere, except that both the drive and tail chucks should be turned with concave ends to fit the convex surface of the sphere to provide firm drive and support.

Faceplates

Faceplates come as standard or center screw. Standard faceplates are flat metal discs with symmetrical holes for attaching turning blanks with screws. Center-screw faceplates, often known and marketed as screw chucks, have a single center screw and blanks are attached while the faceplate is on the lathe. They are much faster and easier to use than standard faceplates. Most modern woodturning chucks

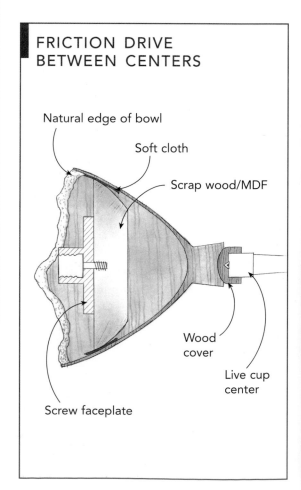

FRICTION DRIVE BETWEEN CENTERS

Natural edge of bowl

Soft cloth

Scrap wood/MDF

Wood cover

Live cup center

Screw faceplate

convert to a screw faceplate. At least one standard faceplate is supplied with most lathes, and although center-screw faceplates (see the photo at right) and chucks have increasingly superseded them, they remain very useful for mounting blanks with an uneven face.

For mounting centerwork, I always use chucks rather than faceplates because screws do not grip well in end grain (see the illustration on p. 21). Screws grip well across the grain, so facework can usually be held securely by just one face without tail center support, allowing free access to the remainder of the blank.

Because a blank is attached to a faceplate by only one face, there are dangers that relate to a basic law of physics: Every force has an equal and opposite reaction. When you sit on one end

The faceplates in the foreground came standard with my lathes. The screw centers to the rear and on the lathe are easier to use.

FACEPLATES AND LEVERAGE

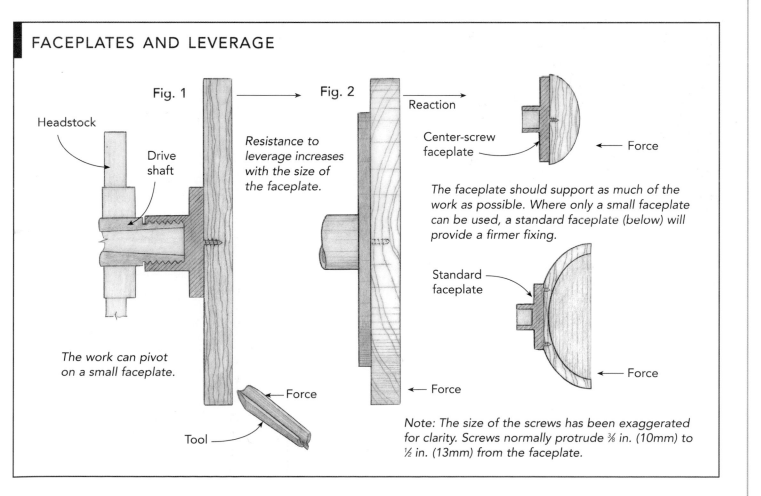

Fig. 1

Headstock

Drive shaft

The work can pivot on a small faceplate.

Tool

Force

Fig. 2

Resistance to leverage increases with the size of the faceplate.

Force

Reaction

Center-screw faceplate

Force

The faceplate should support as much of the work as possible. Where only a small faceplate can be used, a standard faceplate (below) will provide a firmer fixing.

Standard faceplate

Force

Note: The size of the screws has been exaggerated for clarity. Screws normally protrude ⅜ in. (10mm) to ½ in. (13mm) from the faceplate.

MOUNTING IRREGULAR SURFACES

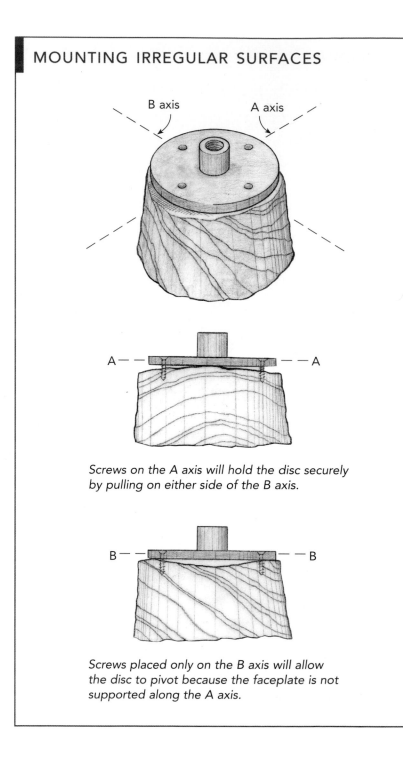

Screws on the A axis will hold the disc securely by pulling on either side of the B axis.

Screws placed only on the B axis will allow the disc to pivot because the faceplate is not supported along the A axis.

The basic rule is to use a faceplate that supports as much of the work as possible.

of a seesaw, for example, the other end will go up just as quickly as you go down. In wood-turning, if a tool is cutting with strong forward pressure parallel to the axis on the edge of a large blank mounted on a small faceplate (see Fig. 1 in the illustration on p. 27), the blank is certain to come loose as it pivots, seesaw-like, on the small faceplate.

If you increase the diameter of the faceplate, there is much more support for the blank and less danger of its coming loose (see Fig. 2 in the illustration on p. 27). The basic rule is to use a faceplate that supports as much of the work as possible. A 10-in.- (255mm) diameter by 2-in.- (50mm) thick blank can be held quite easily on a 7-in.- (180mm) diameter center-screw face-plate with only a ⅜-in. (10mm) to ½-in. (13mm) screw. A 4-in.- (100mm) diameter faceplate would be much less effective and would require longer and heavier screws.

STANDARD FACEPLATES

The most secure method of attaching facework is to use a standard faceplate. You must remove the faceplate from the lathe to insert two or more screws through its back into the wood. Sheet-metal screws penetrating the wood ½ in. (13mm) to 1 in. (25mm) are ideal, and they should fit the faceplate holes exactly, otherwise the blank can shift slightly on the faceplate. Normally, I find two screws sufficient, even on blocks up to 15 in. (380mm) in diameter by 6 in. (150mm) thick or 18 in. (460mm) in diameter by 4 in. (100mm) thick. When roughing-down larger pieces, I use the tail center for extra security.

A flat face on a blank is less critical with standard faceplates than with center-screw face-plates because on standard faceplates the screws can lie on either side of any high point (see the illustration at left). Screws on the A axis will hold the blank securely by pulling on either side of the B axis. Screws on the B axis only, with no support on the A axis, will not secure the blank to the faceplate.

If the weight or shape of a blank makes it unbalanced, it's safer to use more screws and err on the side of caution. Always check a heavy or irregular block by rotating it first by hand. Rotate it toward you and let it swing freely through a couple of revolutions to see where it comes to rest. If the uneven weight of the block brings it rapidly to the same position, use a very slow lathe speed and check that the screws are tightened. Large flying blocks are an unpredictable hazard.

When turning seasoned wood, place the screws across the grain to reduce the risk of splitting (see the illustration at right). However, if you are turning green wood that will be remounted when dry (as when rough-turning bowls), the screws must be placed along the grain, where the shrinkage will be the least, so they will fit into the same holes at a later date.

Remember that you can always use the tail center with any faceplate to provide extra support, provided that it's aligned true on the axis. Using the tail center will restrict the use of many tools, but with heavy blocks it is safer, at least until some of the bulk has been removed.

CENTER-SCREW FACEPLATES

There are two common methods of mounting a blank on a center-screw faceplate, and each requires that you first drill a pilot hole the same diameter as the screw shank in the center of the blank (see p. 88 for finding centers). With the lathe turned off, lock the drive shaft to keep it from rotating and screw the blank onto the center screw. Or you can hold the blank to the screw with one hand and use your other hand to rotate the drive shaft. Either way, rotate the blank until it rests tightly against the surface of the faceplate. I tend to combine the two methods, starting with the latter, then lock the drive shaft so I can use both hands to ensure the wood lies snugly against the faceplate.

A flat or slightly concave surface on the face of the blank is essential to prevent it from pivoting on the screw of a center-screw faceplate.

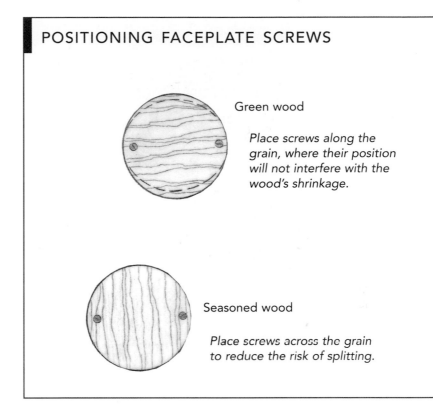

POSITIONING FACEPLATE SCREWS

Green wood

Place screws along the grain, where their position will not interfere with the wood's shrinkage.

Seasoned wood

Place screws across the grain to reduce the risk of splitting.

Friction between the bottom of the blank and the faceplate will help keep the wood in place. Where there is a gap and the wood can rock on the faceplate, use tail-center support.

Experienced turners often mount blanks on a center-screw faceplate with the lathe running. Although this is a quick method and I use it frequently, it's not a technique for novices to use at higher lathe speeds. Present the blank to the faceplate, lining up the pilot hole with the screw. Don't grip the blank with your fingers but rest it on your flat, open hand (as you would feed a horse), and give a slight push with the heel of your palm as the revolving screw bites into the hole (see the photos on p. 30). The weight and inertia of the wood and pressure from your hand will cause the blank to rotate more slowly than the faceplate, so the screw will feed right in, drawing the blank tight against the faceplate.

With practice, blanks can be flicked onto the revolving screw in a moment, but the largest

To flick the work onto a spinning lathe, present the predrilled hole in the blank to the screw (RIGHT), then give a slight push with the heel of your open hand as the revolving screw bites into the hole (FAR RIGHT).

blank I would ever mount this way at speed—say, 1,500 rpm—would be 12 in. (305mm) in diameter by 2 in. (50mm) thick. At such speed, the weight of a larger blank will typically cause the screw to spin in the hole and fail to grip. If you have a variable-speed lathe, you'll have few problems if you keep the lathe running about 300 rpm, but if you don't have the variable-speed option, larger blanks must be screwed on with the lathe at rest. Very small, light blanks can be flicked on the lathe, but they require more pressure from your hand. They can be held on with a very short screw—only ⅛ in. (3mm) long.

Woodturners formerly made their own center-screw chucks by mounting a disc on a faceplate and using a fat wood screw or carriage bolt (see the sidebar on the facing page). If a screw thread stripped or some other problem occurred, it took only a few minutes to make

another. They did me very well until Jerry Glaser introduced his screw chuck with its hardened stainless-steel screw and a parallel shank (see the photo on p. 27). Much copied but rarely emulated, the screw is so superior in its ability to grip that shop-made screw chucks pale by comparison.

CHUCKS AS SCREW FACEPLATES

Most modern woodturning chucks come with 2-in. (50mm) jaws and a center screw, but in this setup, the jaws don't offer much backing support for any blank wider than 6-in. (150mm), as shown in the illustration on p. 27. These screws need to be mounted in larger jaws, but if you don't have any, either turn a large washer to fit around the chuck jaws or use tail-center support. Better yet, fit the screw in a dedicated screw faceplate so your chucks remain fully accessible at all times.

Manufactured screw chucks are about 4½ in. (115mm) in diameter at most. Although modern screws grip incredibly well, a smaller and shorter screw in a larger chuck is more effective for production items, such as cutting boards. It's easy to make your own if you have a standard faceplate.

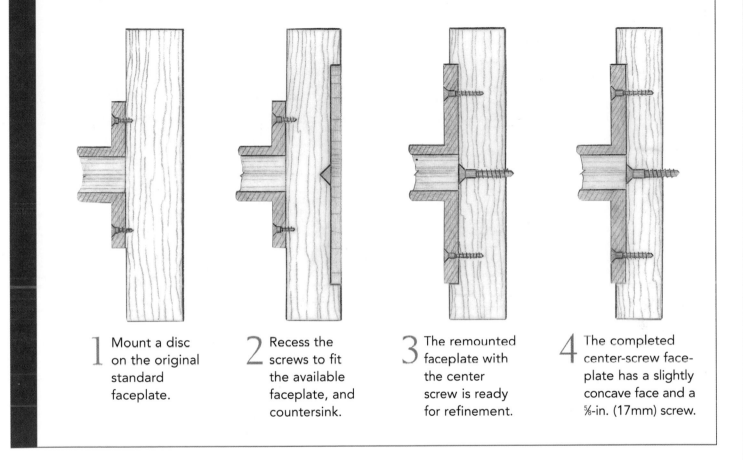

1 Mount a disc on the original standard faceplate.

2 Recess the screws to fit the available faceplate, and countersink.

3 The remounted faceplate with the center screw is ready for refinement.

4 The completed center-screw faceplate has a slightly concave face and a ⅝-in. (17mm) screw.

For all jobs but large bowls—14 in. (355mm) by 4 in. (100mm) and heavier—I don't need the full length of the screw, so I reduce its effective length by using a plywood disc between the work and the faceplate as shown in the far left photo on the facing page. If I have a catch and the job loosens, I transfer it to a fatter screw or carriage bolt mounted in a chuck. I also have an elderly three-jaw chuck (shown in the rear of the photo on p. 27), whose three jaws will provide firm support against just about any undulating surface.

Chucks

When I started to turn wood in 1970, wood lathes came with drive and tail centers and a faceplate or two, usually one big and one huge. Some manufacturers offered a cup chuck (into which blanks are driven with a mallet) as an accessory, and that was it. If you needed a chuck, you got an engineer's scroll chuck and, after a few bloody and painful encounters, learned to keep your knuckles out of the way of the jaws.

Self-centering chucks can be used to grip either blanks or partially completed work in dozens of ways. Here we see just a few of the many commercially available jaws being used in typical situations. In each case you could use a different type of jaw set to do the same job.

Standard 2-in. (50mm) jaws grip a small centerwork blank. Square or cylindrical blanks should be seated right into the chuck, ideally with squared end grain that can sit firmly against the base of the jaws.

Here 5-in. (130mm) dovetail jaws grip a bowl by the foot in preparation for hollowing and completion.

The largest of a set of step jaws grips a completed 3½-in. (90mm) bowl by the rim in preparation for re-turning the base.

(TOP) The 3½-in. (90mm) step jaws close around a decorative groove near the foot of a vase. As hollowing proceeds, the vase is supported by a three-point steady. (ABOVE) To remove bruise marks inflicted by the steady, I use the tail center to support the vase neck for a final sanding and finishing.

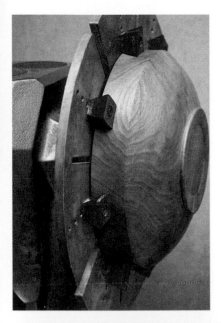

Vicmarc Adjusta jaws are designed to grip bowls around the rim so the base can be refined.

For the best grip on long or heavy centerwork or where there might be a lot of stress on the fixing as hollowing proceeds, heavy serrated or grooved jaws like these Vicmarc Shark jaws are the best option. The rim of the jaws must abut a shoulder on the blank for maximum support.

Long-nose jaws are ideal for gripping small centerwork blanks.

Small blanks can be gripped quite securely on as little as 1/16 in. (2mm), provided the rim of the jaws abuts a shoulder. (These are Vicmarc Shark jaws.)

Long-nose jaws are far superior to a Jacobs chuck for gripping drills or sanding discs because their clamping action is at 90° to the lathe axis.

Large step jaws expanded into a 3/16-in.- (5mm) deep recess on a 16-in.- (400mm) diameter cutting board. When using these chucks in the expansion mode, ensure there is at least a 3/4-in. (20mm) ring of material to support the pressure of the jaws.

Citadel Box

The base of this container was held by jaws gripping either side of each corner. The eight jaw marks were lost during the finishing process, which included scarring the square base with saw cuts and charring the surface with a propane gas torch. The base was held against a 360-grit abrasive disc for sanding.

MATERIAL: Charred jarrah burl
SIZE: 4 in. (100mm) square

Since the mid-1970s when the woodturning revival began, many optimistic manufacturers have marketed all manner of chucks designed specifically for woodturners. Most demanded an accuracy tedious to hobby and professional turners alike, were often inaccurate, and frequently imposed severe restrictions on the design of the turnings they held.

I shall make no attempt to analyze each weird and wonderful device because in the mid-'80s a New Zealand company, Teknatool, developed a self-centering four-jaw scroll chuck called the Nova. This chuck revolutionized the way woodturners mount wood on a lathe, spawning a load of similar chucks internationally, so that today there are many versions commercially available. These chucks are multifunctional, with all manner of interchangeable jaws designed for specific tasks.

SCROLL CHUCKS

A self-centering four-jaw scroll chuck should be regarded as an essential element on any wood lathe, much as a chuck is on a metal-working lathe. I, like most turners I know, cannot imagine working without these wonderful tools, and I have a number of chucks set up with different jaws. The chucks have a wide range of adjustment, offering exceptional flexibility combined with ease of use and a reasonable margin for error.

The jaws I use are, with one exception, all smooth. My business is turning bowls and boxes, and the smooth jaws enable me to take finished pieces straight from the chuck. The serrated jaws standard on some chucks don't allow you to do this. If this ability is important to you, look for a brand with smooth jaws or make sure you can have a set of plain jaws fitted. Serrated jaws do have their uses, though. They are excellent for gripping big or long end-grain projects such as tall vases where you are hollowing deep into end grain.

Some scroll chucks are operated by keys and others by a pair of levers. With each, the work is

You can't have too many chucks. Having a range of different jaws all ready to go beats having to change them every time you start a new project. On the lathe, to the rear, and at the center left are step jaws, which can grip several diameters without marking the wood.

mounted while the chuck is on the lathe. The lever-operated chuck is faster and less frustrating to use if you are expanding and contracting the jaws over a wide range, but you need both hands free to operate it and, consequently, you must be able to lock the drive spindle. Many spindle locks are sprung, and you have to hold them in place, supposedly for safety reasons. (If you switch the lathe on with the spindle locked, all that happens is that you burn a bit of rubber as the drive belt screeches.) Key-operated chucks were developed for lathes with sprung spindle locks and for the few lathes without any spindle lock.

To extract maximum value from a self-centering four-jaw chuck while keeping your frustration levels to a minimum, you need to remember a few points about the jaws and about the structure of wood.

Vase

The grooves at the base located the chuck jaws and added visual interest to an otherwise stark form.

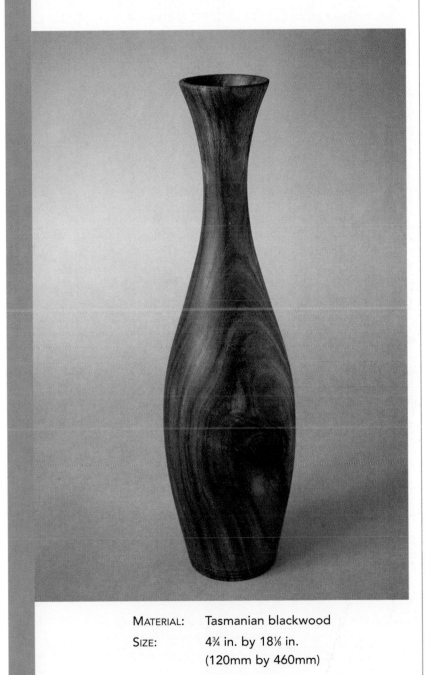

| MATERIAL: | Tasmanian blackwood |
| SIZE: | 4¾ in. by 18⅛ in. (120mm by 460mm) |

CROSS-GRAIN AND SELF-CENTERING FOUR-JAW CHUCKS

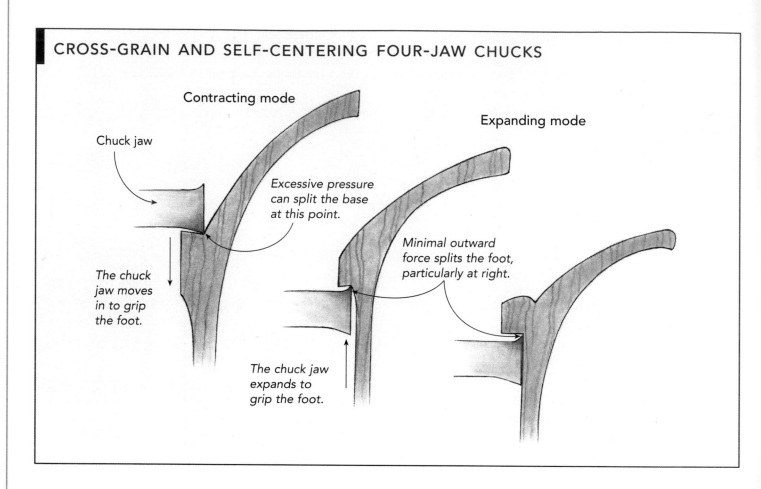

Contracting mode

Expanding mode

Chuck jaw

Excessive pressure
can split the base
at this point.

Minimal outward
force splits the foot,
particularly at right.

The chuck
jaw moves
in to grip
the foot.

The chuck jaw
expands to
grip the foot.

The chuck jaws are machined as a cylinder then cut into four. While the jaws can grip a wide range of diameters, they do so without leaving a discernable mark only when adjusted to their original machined diameter or less. On larger diameters, the jaw corners bite into the wood, leaving eight indentations (often considered decorative by those who don't know what they are). On diameters smaller than the machined diameter, only the center of the jaw contacts the wood, leaving barely a mark. There will always be some compression of the fibers, but this is usually difficult to see, particularly if you obscure it by having the jaws locate in a groove as shown in the photo on p. 35.

The other major point concerns the structure of wood and the way it splits under stress. When a job flies out of the chuck, turners tend to blame the chuck for not gripping properly,

but chances are that too much is being asked of the wood. All woodturners' chucks with collet-type jaws were originally designed to grip short lengths of wood so you could work the end grain unhindered by a tail center as shown in the top left photo on p. 32. Used this way, the chuck grips well, hanging on even if a catch pulls the job off-center because the grain runs parallel to the lathe axis and into the chuck jaws. Overtighten the jaws and the wood is compressed and marked, but it doesn't split.

The situation is different for facework because the grain lies at 90° to the lathe axis. As the jaws are tightened, they act as little wedges against the end grain, which can split the wood if you overtighten the jaws (see the illustration above). A catch, especially on the outer diameter of the bowl (see the illustration on p. 27) will cause the wood to split where the jaws contract. Thus extreme care must be exercised when using woods known to split easily. You gain very little by having a deeper foot or flange because the inherent weakness is in the structure of the timber where the jaws bite into end grain.

If you expand the jaws into a recess on end grain or facework—typically a bowl—the chances of the foot splitting are greatly increased. I only use the expanding mode on a base (see the bottom right photo on p. 33) where there is a wide rim of material for the jaws to expand against. It is better to clamp around a foot for hollowing a bowl, then eliminate it if required by using larger jaws such as Vicmarc Adjusta jaws (see the top left photo on p. 33).

When turning a rebate for expanding jaws, you don't need any more than a wide groove slightly dovetailed on the outer rim (see the illustration at right). I rarely cut the recess deeper than ⅛ in. (3mm) unless the wood is particularly heavy or I'm using jaws that are small in relation to the diameter of the job. Rather than have a wide flat recess, I decorate the center, partly to decorate but also to disguise the fact that this is a fixing. However, it is important to keep a wide rim of material around the recess that can absorb the pressure of the expanding jaws.

To ensure a secure grip, the jaws should abut a turned shoulder, groove, or flat surface for maximum support. As a professional turner, I tend to push the holding capacity to the limit, and I soon learned that the jaws will grip on the hint of a groove on the foot of an outflowing bowl. Always ensure that the chuck is wound on tight against the spindle.

Basic self-centering four-jaw chucks typically come with 2-in. (50mm) jaws and a screw for conversion to a screw chuck, but the screw set in the 2-in. (50mm) jaws offers only limited support for a blank more than 6 in. (150mm). Each manufacturer offers a wide range of jaws that, in a few minutes, can be interchanged with the ones provided. If you do a variety of turning, this can get tedious, so ideally you'd have a number of chucks, each set up with different jaws. Few people, apart from tool junkies, will need all of them.

If your interest is in long-stemmed goblets, you might prefer long and heavily serrated jaws to the standard 2-in. (50mm) set, but I find the latter will hang on to just about anything. And

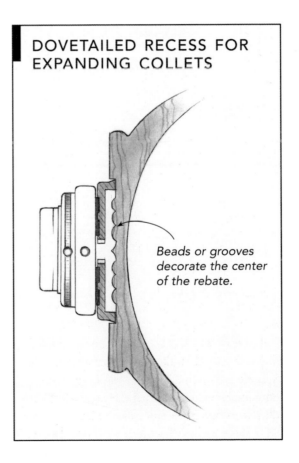

DOVETAILED RECESS FOR EXPANDING COLLETS

Beads or grooves decorate the center of the rebate.

To ensure a secure grip, the jaws should abut a turned shoulder, groove, or flat surface for maximum support.

Red-Gum Bowls

These production bowls were rough-turned and left to season for eight months before being completed on two fixings. The roughed bowls were initially mounted over the expanding jaws of large step jaws for completion of the profile. I used the same jaws to grip the bowl by the foot for final hollowing and completion.

MATERIAL: River red gum

SIZES: About 10 in. to 18 in. (305mm to 460mm) diameter

why buy, say, 4-in. (100mm) expanding jaws when for a few dollars more you can buy step jaws, which allow you to grip three different diameters (see the left photo on p. 35).

Ensure that you get the right thread for your lathe. Manufacturers make a range of inserts to fit most popular thread sizes, but if none fit your lathe you can always have an adapter made. The great thing about these chucks is that once you have the body you can purchase accessory jaw sets as you need them. Alter-

natively, most manufacturers offer flat jaws to which you can attach wood, MDF, or nylon blanks from which you can turn your own custom jaws.

JAM-FIT CHUCKS

I, like professional woodturners the world over always have, make chucks from odd lumps of wood as needed, often fixing the job over the chuck as it spins on the lathe. The work is jammed into or over the chuck, which is held on a screw or self-centering chuck. While largely replaced by the chucks I have discussed, jam-chucking techniques remain very useful and are essential in any woodturner's bag of tricks.

I still have a boxful of jam-fit chucks and use them most frequently for turning the bases of boxes, ends of scoop handles, and such. Occasionally I need one for finishing bowls despite the availability of vacuum chucks and self-centering bowl jaws. For facework chucks, I use offcuts scrounged from a small joinery works. The one shown in the photos on the facing page is typical: It's a bit of very scruffy fir, but it does the job and would be little use for anything else. Bowls or platters never finished due to some defect also make good jam-fit chucks. And it means earlier work isn't entirely wasted.

When fitting work into a chuck, try to fit the rim of the work tightly to a shoulder turned in the chuck (see A in the illustration on p. 40). The flanges, or rebates, on these chucks are turned with a very slight taper (ideally of 1° or 2°) to ensure a good fit. Although I occasionally jam-fit work over a taper because it is quicker, it is preferable to fit the piece inside a chuck because the wood is less likely to split.

In the illustration on p. 40, the facework bowls at A and C and the centerwork forms at E and F have the grip around the form, rather than pushing out from within, so the work is securely contained. The forms fitted over a taper (B and D) can easily split if the work is pushed on too firmly. In addition, there is

(FAR LEFT) **Outflowing forms are most safely gripped when inserted into a slightly tapered rebate. The slight vacuum created as the bowl is pressed into the rebate helps keep the bowl in place while the base is refined. However, it's good insurance to use tail-center support and a small waste block to prevent the center point from damaging the job (LEFT).**

always a risk that work will come loose during cutting or sanding if the taper is too steep. If enclosed, the rim of the work may rattle around within the chuck and possibly sustain surface damage, but it should remain intact. (Such damage can be repaired easily by hand-sanding.) If fitted over a taper, however, there will be no such external restraint on the rim and the work can fly outward and, with the centrifugal force, possibly disintegrate. For extra security with facework, you can support the job using the tail center with a pad to prevent damaging the job (see the top photo at right).

My facework jam-fit chucks mostly attach to a screw chuck so they can be removed easily. This is especially useful if a bowl is jammed in tightly and a tap on the chuck rim fails to dislodge the bowl. When this occurs, unscrew the chuck, turn it over, tap its rim against the lathe bed, then catch the bowl as it drops out. With a really good fit, a vacuum is created when the bowl is pressed onto the chuck, so what appears

An enclosed internal form is most easily chucked over a tenon. Use the tail center and a waste block when possible for added security.

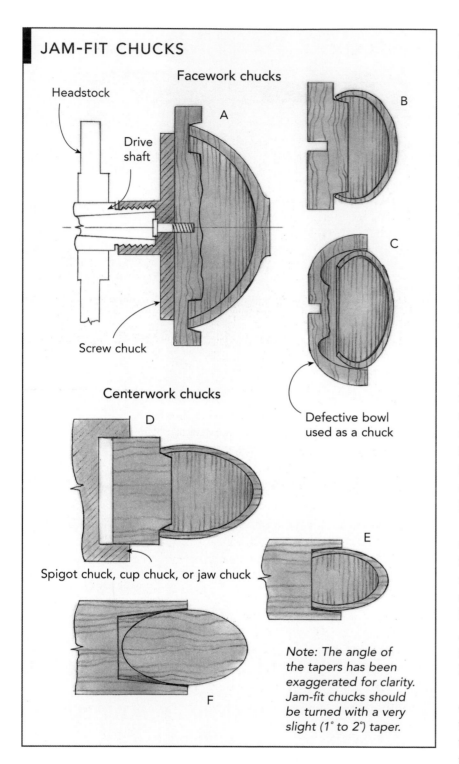

JAM-FIT CHUCKS

Facework chucks

Headstock

Drive shaft

A

B

C

Screw chuck

Defective bowl used as a chuck

Centerwork chucks

D

Spigot chuck, cup chuck, or jaw chuck

E

Note: The angle of the tapers has been exaggerated for clarity. Jam-fit chucks should be turned with a very slight (1° to 2°) taper.

F

Remember that the best jam-fit always occurs when the taper is very slight.

to be a risky fitting is in fact usually quite strong. Remember that the best jam-fit always occurs when the taper is very slight. Too steep a taper will allow the job to jam in quickly—and, just as quickly, pop out.

To make a small centerwork chuck for something like a 2-in.- (50mm) to 3-in.- (75 mm) diameter goblet or boxes like those shown in the photo on p. 42, mount a waste block in 2-in. (50mm) jaws as shown in the photos on the facing page. First, turn a tapered spigot, then, with the lathe running, ease the work over the taper to get a slight burnish mark. This gives you the precise diameter. Turn a very shallow taper from the burnish mark back toward the headstock, then ease the work over the taper until its rim abuts the shoulder on the chuck.

Being a professional in a hurry, I do all this with the lathe running, but you are less likely to mess things up if you stop the lathe to test the fit. If you get the rim of the work against a shoulder on the chuck, it should run true. If it doesn't, rotate the lathe slowly by hand, watching the top edge of the work. When the base is farthest away from you, tap the nearest portion of the base rim to true the job as shown in the illustration on the facing page.

When you have problems mounting an object in a jam-fit chuck so it runs true rather than wobbling off-center, be assured that, as usual, it's all a matter of practice. It should go easily into the chuck at first and gradually become tighter as it is pushed gently forward. As you ease the work into or over the chuck, rotate the lathe by hand and keep tapping the high point until it runs true.

Larger objects, such as salad bowls, are more difficult to center. If you can get the rim to abut the shoulder of the chuck (see A, B, D, and E in the illustration at left) it should run true, but this is difficult to achieve if you can't see what's happening inside. Such jobs (A, C, E, and F) must be fitted with the lathe stopped. I rotate the chuck by hand once the job is fitted and note any eccentricity by watching the top of the

Jam-fit chucks can be made from short bits left over from previous turnings. (TOP) Ease the job (here a box base) over the spinning chuck so you get a slight burnish mark. (CENTER) Then use the skew chisel to turn a shallow taper (1° to 2°) from that line and (BOTTOM) ease the job onto the chuck. Make the rim of the box base abut the shoulder on the chuck to ensure it runs true.

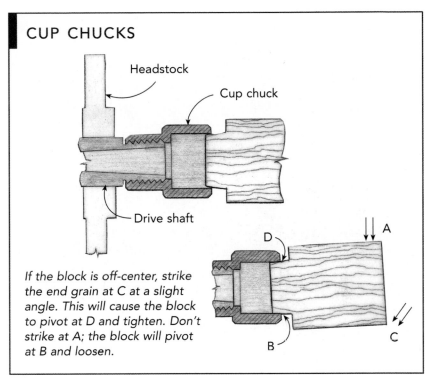

If the block is off-center, strike the end grain at C at a slight angle. This will cause the block to pivot at D and tighten. Don't strike at A; the block will pivot at B and loosen.

form. I tap any higher portion with the heel of my hand to bring that part farther into the chuck. Sometimes this will cause another part to ease out, so I have to tap that section. Eventually, the whole form runs true.

Another problem can occur when a bowl that has been finished, except for the base, is mounted in a jam-fit chuck. Sanding will often have made the form slightly oval because the long grain is removed faster than end grain. Such a bowl will never fit the chuck properly or run absolutely true. Get it trued as well as you can, then blend the new surface into the old as you cut and sand it heavily. The slight eccentricity will be difficult to discern, even when you know it's there.

CUP CHUCKS

A cup chuck is little more than a heavy tube with a cylindrical hole into which slightly tapered blanks are driven (see the illustration above). It is strictly a centerwork fixing, used to

Boxes

These boxes, inspired by my interest in architecture and buildings, look good clustered together as a sculptural entity that can be rearranged at will.

MATERIAL:	Huon pine
SIZE:	2¾ in. (70mm) diameter (largest)

grip grain running parallel to the lathe axis and into the chuck. Until the 1980s, this was the standard production chuck for small center-work such as door knobs or goblets involving hollowed end grain, and I used one for the thousands and thousands of scoops I made (see p. 110). Since then it has been superseded by the more flexible self-centering four-jaw chucks.

The main drawback of a cup chuck is that blanks have to be turned or machined to fit them, adding an extra step to production, but they remain an inexpensive option if you are strapped for cash and are handy with a welder. At their most basic they can be a 3-in. (75mm)

length of heavy steel pipe welded to a nut that fits your drive shaft. Some old chuck bodies also make good cup chucks; they just need to be round with a straight-sided hole about 2 in. (50mm) wide in the center and, for safety, smooth on the outside.

VACUUM CHUCKS

Vacuum chucks are wonderful for finishing work without leaving any obvious chuck marks or fixing points, but you do need solid wood. Most decorative splits, defects, or burl will mean you won't be able to achieve the vacuum that sucks the job onto the chuck, although small gaps can be sealed temporarily using masking tape or clingwrap. There are commercial vacuum chucks available, but these tools are so easy and inexpensive to make for yourself by utilizing an old vacuum cleaner and a faceplate that this is what most turners do.

The illustration on the facing page shows a typical shop-built vacuum system based on a standard faceplate. The chuck consists of 1-in.-(25mm) thick MDF or wood screwed to a standard faceplate, with the face slightly dished and covered with a thin layer of neoprene, which provides a better seal than a harder surface. The hollow face means that you can hold flat jobs like chopping boards.

The air is extracted through the hollow drive shaft. You need a bearing at the outboard (left) end so the tube to the vacuum doesn't try to rotate with the drive shaft. The connections can be turned, but using standard PVC pipe is easier. Fix a small bearing over a pipe, which can jam into the spindle. Next, fix another pipe over the bearing, making a small, removable connection unit. The tube from the vacuum cleaner then fits over the outer pipe.

Some vacuum pipes have a small sliding hatch that allows you to spill air to reduce the vacuum. This hatch is worth incorporating if you have one. Otherwise you can spill air by easing the tube away from the pipe. My vacuum is very noisy, so it's located outside my workshop

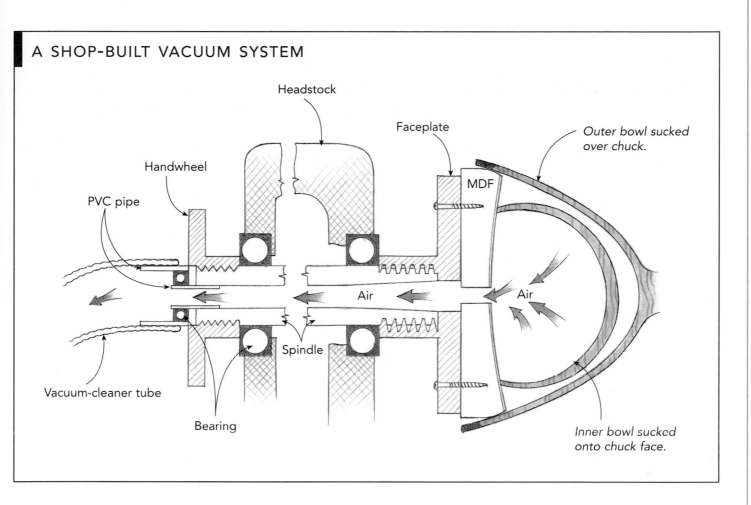

A SHOP-BUILT VACUUM SYSTEM

Headstock

Faceplate

Outer bowl sucked over chuck.

Handwheel

MDF

PVC pipe

Air

Air

Vacuum-cleaner tube

Spindle

Inner bowl sucked onto chuck face.

Bearing

at the end of a 23-ft. (7m) hose, in with the dust collector.

To locate work quickly and accurately on the chuck, mark center on the base of your bowl or vase when you initially turn the profile, then use the tail center to align the work correctly on the faceplate.

Adhesives

An expensive but effective way of securing blanks on the lathe is with adhesives to a metal faceplate. Two strips of double-sided tape will stick a 16-in. (400mm) disc to a metal faceplate provided the face of the blank is flat and smooth. On rougher surfaces, hot glue is very effective, especially in cool conditions. Work fixed with hot glue can generally be pried away,

but failing that, you can melt the glue using a heat gun or a small gas torch to warm the faceplate.

The adhesive most widely used by wood-turners these days is cyanoacrylate, commonly known as Super Glue. Mostly kept handy for repairs, it is ideal for attaching small blanks like tagua nuts or bits of bone and exotic hardwoods to a waste block. The finished object is parted off with a parting tool without wasting whichever valuable material you have.

I've also seen cyanoacrylate used extensively for securing large vases to waste blocks, but at many dollars per fixing, I regard this as a flagrant waste of money that might be better put to charitable purposes or to the purchase of a suitable chuck.

3 CUTTING TOOLS:
SELECTING & SHARPENING

THERE ARE FOUR MAIN GROUPS of wood-turning tools: gouges, scrapers, skew chisels, and parting tools. Within each group the shape of the edges, the bevels, and the cross sections of the tools vary because each is designed for a specific job. Accordingly, they are selected for specific qualities and sharpened differently. In this chapter I'll introduce the cutting tools, offer guidance as to which to buy or avoid, and finally describe how to sharpen them. How they are used will be described in chapters 6 and 7.

Selection

All four groups of cutting tools are available in either long-and-strong or standard strength. The long-and-strong tools, as their name implies, are longer, thicker, and altogether more robust than the standard, which are about ³⁄₁₆ in. (5mm) thick and less than 6½ in. (165mm) long, excluding the tang. Because of their increased mass, the long-and-strong tools flex less than standard tools when the edge is cutting well away from the tool rest. Standard tools are fine for cutting close to the rest.

When I began to turn wood in 1970, the only tools available were made of carbon steel. But since the late '70s high-speed steels (HSS) have become increasingly popular and are now universally preferred. High-speed steel holds an edge longer and is better where the tool is heated during use. The name refers to the steel's resistance to softening when used at high speeds (as in jointer knives and drill bits). Unlike carbon steel, which will lose its hardness at about 300°F (150°C), high-speed steel maintains its hardness up to about 1,050°F (570°C). This means that enthusiastic grinding that would "blue" and ruin a carbon-steel edge has little effect on a high-speed steel. Although HSS tools are nearly twice the price of similar carbon-steel tools, they hold an edge five or six times longer and so are worth the extra money. High-speed steel tools have HSS etched on the blade.

While many manufacturers produce similar ranges of tools, the market is dominated by companies based in Sheffield, the traditional home of fine steel and edge tools in England, where the leading names continue to be Henry Taylor, Ashley Iles, and Robert Sorby. Most of the tools I prefer are from these companies.

The best place to purchase woodturning tools and equipment is from specialist woodturners' supply companies or fine woodworking stores. These companies tend to be staffed by people

Basic tools, clockwise from left: 1¼-in. (32mm) long-and-strong round-nose scraper; 1-in. (25mm) shallow roughing gouge; ½-in. (13mm) skew chisel; 1-in. (25mm) round-nose scraper; parting tool; ¾-in. (19mm) standard skew chisel; ¾-in. (19mm) square-edge scraper; ⅜-in. (9mm) shallow gouge; ½-in. (13mm) shallow gouge; ⅜-in. (9mm) deep-fluted bowl gouge; 1¼-in. (32mm) long-and-strong radius scraper; 1¼-in. (32mm) long-and-strong radius scraper; ½-in. (13mm) deep-fluted bowl gouge; and 1-in. (25mm) spear-point scraper.

who have used their products and who can often offer sound advice on getting started and tuition.

To start, a basic set of turning tools will enable you to undertake just about any run-of-the-mill project on the lathe. When you first buy tools, start with a shallow gouge or two and a square-edge scraper. Then, depending on your interest and budget, you can add more. A ⅜-in. (9mm) bowl gouge and big scraper will serve you well on bowls up to 10 in. (250mm) in diameter. When you want bigger shavings, get the bigger bowl gouge and the slightly radiused scraper. The spear-point is good for getting clean surfaces around detail.

If your interest is purely spindle turning, you will need a skew chisel and parting tool (see the photo above). You will find a square-edge scraper useful for end-grain work such as lidded boxes, and a round-nose scraper enables you to undertake goblets or similar rounded internal forms. A narrow skew chisel is excellent for detailing, cutting small beads and grooves, and a number of other things beginners aren't supposed to know about such as scraping in small corners. A wide gouge, or its half-round relative, is best for roughing centerwork. And the weight of the big scraper is just what you need for finishing end-grain hollows.

Avoid two groups of tools. First, don't waste your hard-earned cash on the cheap sets of carbon-steel tools available through discount stores; poor-quality steels rarely hold an edge for more than a few seconds, making it impossible for you to experience the joys of the craft. It is better to own three good individual tools than a fancy boxed set of six or more that cannot hold an edge. And second, avoid scrapers with only a short section of HSS and gouges with a short, replaceable HSS tip. You'll soon grind your way

Cocobolo Bowl

This classic bowl sits on a small foot that lends the form a floating quality. Note how the curve swings up to the underside of the softened bead at the rim.

MATERIAL: Cocobolo
SIZE: 9 in. (230mm) diameter

Don't be misled into thinking that spindle gouges can be used only for spindles or bowl gouges only for bowls.

through the harder steel and find they are not cheap options as you replace the tips. On the gouges there is rarely enough flute for a finger-nail ground edge, and such a short flute soon jams with shavings, which is very irritating.

I will cover only the basic tools below. The interest in hollow turnings (enclosed forms with very small openings) has spawned a whole range of specialist hollowing tools that I don't review here. However, the tools I describe and use enable me to turn forms enclosed enough to challenge most beginners.

GOUGES

Gouges come in many shapes and sizes, but the preferred HSS tools are machined from round bars. For centerwork, they are used mainly for roughing large, square spindle blanks to round and for cutting shallow coves or twisted grain. Gouges are in almost constant use for facework and for cutting bowls of all shapes and sizes. Woodturning gouges have a curved cutting edge with a bevel ground on the outside of the tool. They are made either shallow or deep-fluted (see the illustration on the facing page). To confuse the issue, manufacturers tend to call shallow gouges spindle gouges and the deep-fluted tools bowl gouges.

Manufacturers are interested in selling tools, so don't be misled into thinking that spindle gouges can be used only for spindles or bowl gouges only for bowls. Although any gouge can be reground and used for any purpose, I keep my bowl gouges just for deep bowl hollowing and working well beyond the rest until they are pretty well worn down. I do this because they are so much more expensive than shallow gouges, and there's no point in using costly steel when a less-expensive shallow gouge or shorter tool serves just as well. When only 2 in. (50mm) of the flute remains, I will begin to use a deep-fluted gouge on bowl profiles and cuts close to the rest.

Shallow gouges are available from 2 in. (50mm) wide down to ⅛ in. (3mm), but the

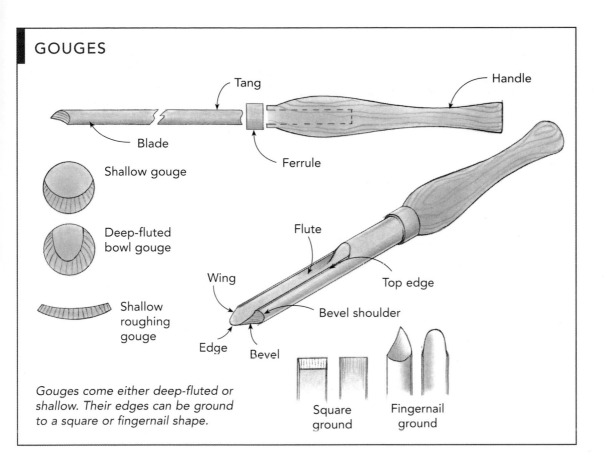

GOUGES

Tang
Handle
Blade
Ferrule
Shallow gouge
Deep-fluted bowl gouge
Flute
Wing
Top edge
Shallow roughing gouge
Bevel shoulder
Edge
Bevel

Gouges come either deep-fluted or shallow. Their edges can be ground to a square or fingernail shape.

Square ground
Fingernail ground

most useful are ⅜ in. (9mm), ½ in. (13mm), and 1 in. (25mm). The widest is used only to rough centerwork squares to round. The ½ in. (13mm) can do just about anything, but because it's not as substantial as a deep-fluted gouge, it tends to flex if the cutting point is more than 1½ in. (40mm) from the rest. For cutting close to the rest, such as spindle work detailing of coves and beads, or for rough-shaping bowl profiles it is unbeatable. Use it also for hollowing end grain. A shallow ⅜-in. (9mm) gouge is unrivaled for fine detailing of beads on any surface (see the photo on p. 49).

Gouges can be ground anywhere between straight across (square-ground) and a long, fingernail shape (see the illustration above). Square-ground edges (either deep-fluted or shallow) are best for roughing-down and for fine cutting of cylinders or tapered spindles in centerwork. To cut coves or beads in center-

work and for the shearing and scraping cuts used in facework, you'll need a long, symmetrical fingernail edge (shallow for centerwork and either deep-fluted or shallow for facework), with no corners to catch the work and a point to get into small spaces. If your budget, and consequently your range of tools, is limited, start with shallow, fingernail-ground gouges.

SCRAPERS

Scrapers are flat tools of square section with a cutting edge any shape you like: round, square, skew, or even ground to match the shape of a molding or to cut several beads at once, like a cutter on a spindle molder (see the top illustration on p. 48). Scrapers should have squared or very slightly undercut sides but should not be rounded unless they are designed for shear scraping. A sharp corner on a scraper is often useful for getting into corners on the work,

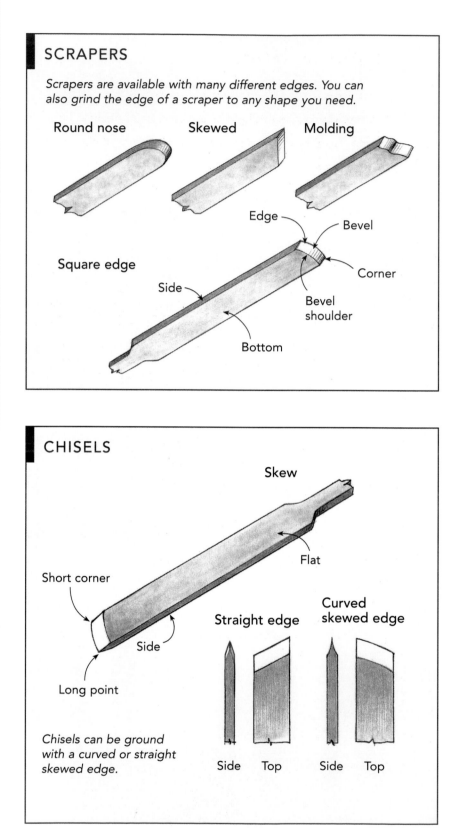

SCRAPERS

Scrapers are available with many different edges. You can also grind the edge of a scraper to any shape you need.

Round nose

Skewed

Molding

Square edge

Edge

Bevel

Corner

Side

Bevel shoulder

Bottom

CHISELS

Skew

Short corner

Flat

Side

Long point

Chisels can be ground with a curved or straight skewed edge.

Straight edge

Curved skewed edge

Side   Top

Side   Top

such as the base of a bead or the square inside a container; you cannot use a scraper with rounded sides for such tasks.

In my experience, scrapers are not generally suited for roughing down, especially for center-work. The finish they leave when used force-fully is very poor. I regard scrapers mainly as tools for fine finishing. To use them effectively requires a smooth, flowing, and delicate touch that removes only fluff and very small curly shavings. Some hardwoods—mulga, African blackwood, and cocobolo—can come up like glass off the scraper and hardly need abrasives for finishing. Scrapers can also be used to make very heavy internal cuts in some facework where gouges can't easily reach.

Because scrapers are ground with only one bevel and are always used with the bevel down, they are not always made of solid high-speed steel. Instead, the cutting edge may be made of a layer of high-speed steel laminated to a lower grade of less-expensive carbon steel, which reduces the cost of the tool. When buying such a tool, be sure that the high-speed steel runs the length of the tool (you can usually see the lami-nation seam on the top and side of the tool blade).

If I need a scraper to cut more than 2 in. (50mm) away from the tool rest, I use a heavy, ⅜-in.- (9mm) thick long-and-strong tool. For general work close to the rest, such as small boxes, I prefer a ½-in. (13mm) square tool. If you want to make really deep vases, you'll need much heavier tools, at least ½ in. (13mm) square and with a very substantial handle.

Spear-point and skewed shear scrapers have been developed to shear-scrape while the tool is tilted on edge. These tools have rounded sides to enable them to move easily and smoothly along the rest.

If you can't find a manufactured scraper the shape you require, you can always purchase steel by the bar and make your own. Grinding the edge is time-consuming because you must be careful not to overheat the steel, and grinding the tang will be tedious, but it is sometimes the only way to get what you want. I do not recommend the common practice of using old files as scrapers. The steel in files is too hard and brittle and could break easily from the shock of a sudden catch.

SKEW CHISELS

A skew chisel (commonly known as a skew) is the supreme tool for working along the grain, where the grain lies parallel to the axis. It is the main tool used in centerwork and should never be used for facework. It functions best on absolutely straight-grained, knot-free wood and can leave a near-perfect finish with its shearing cut, so that abrasives are needed only when the smoothest of surfaces is desired.

Skew chisels are square section, like scrapers, but ground with a bevel on both the top and bottom with the edge set at an angle or skewed, hence the name. For any job up to 3 in. (75mm) in diameter, I prefer my chisels thinner than the scrapers, at about 3/16 in. (5mm) thick. This creates a shorter bevel, which is easier to grind. For larger centerwork, I like a heavier tool with a cross section similar to that of the heavy scrapers.

Skew chisels are generally manufactured with straight edges, but I regrind mine to a very slight curve, as shown in the bottom illustration on the facing page. The curve allows a wider range of use for the tool. The bevel is best ground flat to slightly concave. The bevel shoulder can mark the wood as cutting proceeds, so you should soften the shoulder with a slipstone if this is a problem.

Some skew chisels are manufactured with rounded sides so they move more easily along the rest. However, rounded sides reduce the sharpness of the corners, so you need to grind each end of the bevel so that both the long point and the short corner are the product of three facets (see the top photo on p. 50). This

Rounded Bowls

These bowls with rounded bases were conceived as personal nut or potato chip bowls to be held by the user. Each was held by a small foot for hollowing, then mounted over a jam-fit chuck for the base to be rounded.

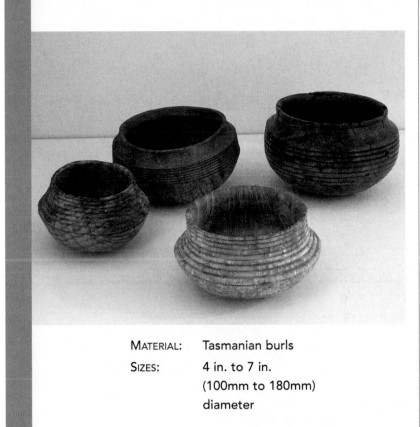

MATERIAL: Tasmanian burls
SIZES: 4 in. to 7 in. (100mm to 180mm) diameter

A skew chisel is the supreme tool for working along the grain.

To get a sharp corner or long point on a skew chisel with rounded sides, grind the end of the bevel.

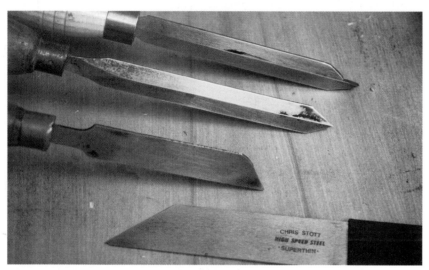

The most efficient parting tools are diamond shaped (upper two) or thicker at the bottom (third from top), all designed to prevent the tool from binding. The top tool has been ground back to the maximum width to make sharpening easier. The deep and narrow Stott Superthin (with the red handle) is ideal for small-diameter work.

reduces the width of the skew chisel, which in turn demands more precision when cutting. The square-section skew chisels I use have their short corner sides slightly rounded with a coarse diamond hone or sander, which enables them to slide along the rest easily but doesn't affect the absolute sharpness of the short corner.

Oval-section skew chisels (called oval skews) have been aggressively marketed as the answer to cutting beads and cylinders and indeed just about all centerwork. They are difficult to grind but do work very well except in areas where a skew chisel becomes really good fun—the fast

peeling cuts (see p. 123) and fine detailing using a peel/scrape cut for which square-section skews are essential (see p. 124).

PARTING TOOLS

Parting tools are narrow, chisel-like tools used primarily on centerwork when setting diameters on spindles, getting into odd corners, and cutting, or parting (as in split asunder), turned pieces from the lathe while it's running. The most popular and useful is the diamond parting tool, so named because of its shape. Traditionally, the best parting tools have had a cutting edge wider than the blade to prevent the tool from binding. The diamond parting tool is the best for beginners. To make them easier to grind, many turners remove the top half of the end to the maximum width.

A number of new narrow parting tools such as the Stott Superthin (see the photo bottom left) have been developed to reduce the width of a cut on small projects or when using expensive timbers or matching grain when making boxes.

HANDLES

Beyond deciding which tools you need, you also need to give tool handles careful consideration. Those provided by manufacturers come in all shapes and sizes and are made of wood, aluminum, or plastic-coated aluminum. They vary in length from about 12 in. (305mm), and often the length bears scant relation to the probable use of the tool. There is no point in having a long handle on a short or lightweight tool that should not be used more than ½ in. (13mm) to ¾ in. (19mm) from the rest. Likewise, I would never put an 8-in. (205mm) handle on a long-and-strong tool that might be used to cut 6 in. (150mm) or more from the rest. Not only would it feel wrong, but it also would lack the length to provide the required leverage.

My handles range from 4 in. (100mm) long on small tools used for miniature centerwork to

12 in. (305mm) for standard-strength tools. For the heaviest scrapers, handles can be as long as 20 in. (510 mm) to 24 in. (610 mm). An evenly balanced tool with the weight distributed equally on either side of the ferrule is the most comfortable to use, but of course the balance alters as the blade shortens through grinding. I will grind away an HSS bowl gouge in about 14 to 18 months of regular use and, with a new tool installed in the handle, wonder how I managed with its predecessor or why I used such an unbalanced tool for so long. I get used to whatever I'm using even though something else might be better. (Isn't that typical of life in general?)

A few manufacturers use extruded aluminum handles, which are hollow and filled with lead shot to dampen vibration. These are wonderful handles, especially on big tools used

Different handles make the tools easier to identify among the shavings, and they make a good project for any beginner. Also, it's easy to rechuck any manufacturer's wooden handle. Just grip the ferrule end in a chuck, use the tail center to support the other end, and away you go.

FITTING A TOOL HANDLE

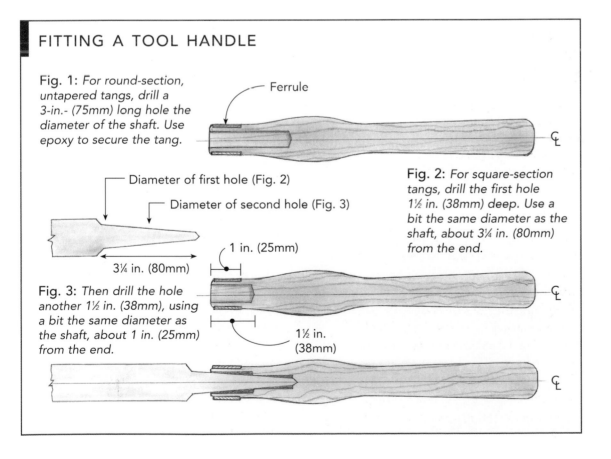

Fig. 1: *For round-section, untapered tangs, drill a 3-in.- (75mm) long hole the diameter of the shaft. Use epoxy to secure the tang.*

Ferrule

Diameter of first hole (Fig. 2)

Diameter of second hole (Fig. 3)

Fig. 2: *For square-section tangs, drill the first hole 1½ in. (38mm) deep. Use a bit the same diameter as the shaft, about 3¼ in. (80mm) from the end.*

3¼ in. (80mm)

1 in. (25mm)

Fig. 3: *Then drill the hole another 1½ in. (38mm), using a bit the same diameter as the shaft, about 1 in. (25mm) from the end.*

1½ in. (38mm)

for deep hollowing, and they don't roll about on the bench. For light gouges, I remove the lead shot for a more balanced tool.

Although I use some handles attached to new tools, I prefer to re-turn the wooden ones so they fit my hands, which are on the small side. To make your own handle, choose a straight-grained, knot-free hardwood such as hickory or ash and ensure that the grain runs the length of the blank. A cross-grained handle can easily snap in use. Blanks need not be more than 1¾ in. (45mm) square. The length will depend on which tool it will be used for. Turn the handle between centers and fit the ferrule before drilling the hole for the tool.

To drill the hole, mount a suitably sized twist drill in a chuck, then mount the handle between the drill and the tail center. Grasp the handle with your left hand to prevent it from rotating, then switch on the lathe and wind in the tail center so the handle is forced onto the drill. You can let go at any time and the handle will spin, driven by the drill bit (see the illustration on p. 51).

When making your own handles, vary them. Tools with matching handles look impressive on a rack, but they're infuriating when you want to pick one from a bunch on a bench covered in shavings. So, incorporate slightly different shapes, colors, or decoration.

Light reflecting off the edge of a damaged skew chisel indicates the chisel's dullness. Typically, though, damage appears in the form of mere nicks, which are difficult to see, even in the light.

Sharpening

Sharp tools are essential and much easier and safer to use than blunt ones. Every woodworker should be able to identify a good edge and, more important, whether a sharp tool is sharp enough for a particular job. In this section I detail my approach to sharpening without going into scientific detail, fascinating though it is. For more detail, I refer you to Leonard Lee's wonderful *The Complete Guide to Sharpening* (The Taunton Press, 1995).

Obviously, an edge should be free of chips or nicks and should not reflect light because that indicates dullness (see the photo at left). But, in woodturning, there is more to it than that. The shape and quality of the edge depends on which tool you are using and for what, as well as the species and quality of wood being turned. For instance, a shallow gouge ground for detailing a softwood spindle would probably chip when used for roughing down a hardwood burl bowl. You need to be prepared to adjust the angle of the bevel for different situations.

Woodturning tools can remove enormous amounts of wood very quickly, and the finest slicing edge soon dulls on many timbers. I see no point in doing five minutes of sharpening for 30 seconds of cutting, especially if the edge you so meticulously achieve is not overly superior to one straight from the grinder. Skillful grinding, allowing you to use the tool directly from the wheel, is the answer. I rarely hone my edges, although I do polish the flute of any gouge and the top of my scrapers before grinding.

Sharpening is usually done on a grindstone with wheels of between 5 in. (125mm) and 8 in. (205mm) in diameter. My high-speed dry-wheel grinders have 36-grit and 80-grit aluminum oxide wheels designed for HSS. My wheels are white, but there are similar wheels available in various pinks through specialist woodturners' supply stores. The gray wheels supplied with most grinders will do the job, but they clog up faster, reducing their efficiency.

Diamond-wheel dressers are by far the best tools to keep your grinding wheels clean and running true.

All grinding wheels need to be kept dressed so they are clean and running true, and these days the only tool for the job is a diamond-wheel dresser (see the photo above). These amazing tools will seem expensive for what they appear to be, but they make all dressing sticks and wheels or single point dressers obsolete—and they last a lifetime.

For most of my turning life, I have used fast-cutting, dry grinding wheels, and I generally use the newly sharpened tool straight from the 80-grit wheel. You have to be very careful not to overheat the steel. I also keep a can of water handy to cool the tool should it become too hot.

An excellent, although more expensive, alternative is to use a water-cooled wheel, which runs at about 90 rpm. The heavy grinding involved in reshaping an edge obviously takes quite a bit longer, but you won't burn the edge. Once the bevel is established, touching it up takes only a little longer than on a high-speed wheel. The major advantage is that you cannot burn, or "blue," the steel. These days I do all my heavy grinding on a faster-cutting high-speed grinder, then transfer to the water-cooled wheel for the final edge (see the top right photo).

On this water-cooled wheel you cannot burn the cutting edge. The wheels on the left side are for honing and polishing.

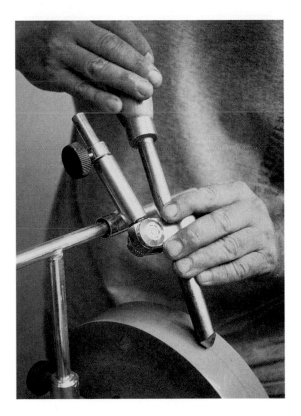

Grinding jigs ensure a perfect edge every time, here on a shallow gouge.

A used 120-grit sanding disc wrapped around doweling honed this flute smooth in preparation for grinding.

To prepare scrapers for grinding, I rub them on a used 100-grit sanding disc stuck on the bench close to the grinder.

Since the 1990s any number of grinding jigs have been marketed that promise to give you a "perfect" edge every time. The problem is that one turner's perfect edge is not the same as another's, let alone a manufacturer's, and many jigs produce an edge on bowl gouges that severely limits their use. Most require you to fix the tool within some sort of clip, which is far too time-consuming for most professionals. Others feature a very wide tool rest that cannot accommodate short tools. Overall, I think it is worth trying to master freehand grinding for all-around speed, efficiency, and general satisfaction with being able to do it. But if you find it all too much and can afford the time, a jig such as the one shown in the bottom photo on p. 53 is a good investment.

PREPARING A TOOL FOR GRINDING

An edge is defined as the line in which two surfaces of a solid object meet. In a cutting edge, the angle between the two surfaces typically lies between 10° and 45°. The smoother the two surfaces are, the sharper the edge will be, which is why cutting edges are usually honed. New tools and abused tools frequently have less than smooth surfaces (see how the polished end of the flute contrasts with the remainder of the blade in the top photo at left). If such blades are left unpolished, no matter how smooth you hone the bevels, the quality of the edge will always be affected by the roughness of the upper surface.

To polish a gouge flute, I wrap 120-grit abrasive around a short length of doweling and use it as I use my slipstone (see the top photo at left). Better still is a buffing wheel. I polish the flat surfaces of scrapers and skew sides on an old 100-grit sanding disc stuck to the bench near the grinder (see the bottom photos at left). Where you want a sharp corner, as on a scraper or skew chisel, you need to ensure the sides are similarly polished.

GRINDING THE BEVEL

I grind most of my gouges and scrapers with the bevel set at an angle of 30° to 45° from the flat surface of the blade. Ideally, the arc of the bevel matches the circumference of the grinding wheel, so a larger wheel will give you a longer bevel. The precise angle of the bevel isn't critical. Ideally you want a single facet, like the near-perfect bevel shown on the right in the photo at right, but if you don't get it and end up with the sort of multifaceted bevel seen on the left, don't worry, because it'll cut just as well even though it doesn't look as pretty.

The secret to successful freehand high-speed grinding is to have the tool touching the grinding wheel as lightly as possible, barely in contact. The tool should be cool enough so that, straight from the wheel, you can hold it ¾ in. (20mm) back from the edge for at least five seconds. Let the grinding wheel come to the tool; don't force the tool against the wheel. You should be able to use edges straight from the

The secret to successful freehand high-speed grinding is to have the tool touching the grinding wheel as lightly as possible.

The bevel on the left was ground on a high-speed dry grinding wheel. It will cut well, but it doesn't look as pretty as the bevel on the right, which was ground on a larger water-cooled wheel.

To grind a skew chisel, set the rest at the correct angle, then keep the tool blade firmly against it as you ease the edge into the wheel. (ABOVE) On the dry wheel you know the edge is sharp when sparks appear over the edge and there is a minute color change along the edge. (RIGHT) Because water flows over the edge on the wet wheel, you have to remove the tool to assess the edge.

(TOP) **To grind a gouge freehand, hook your forefinger under the rest and place your thumb and other fingers on each side of the blade to keep the tool firmly under control. (CENTER AND BOTTOM) For a fingernail edge, you need to simultaneously rotate the blade and swing it sideways, always being careful not to press it hard against the wheel. Let the wheel come to the tool.**

80-grit wheel and find that the small burr on the edge cuts superbly most of the time. On very hard woods, hone the edge because almost any burr is too aggressive and likely to catch. A honed edge also works better on very soft wood when a burr can pull the wood fibers out in tufts.

On my grinder, I have the rest set for skew chisels and parting tools, which demand a much longer bevel than other tools. To grind a skew chisel, I ensure the blade remains fully in contact with the rest as I ease the edge forward against the grinding wheel (see the bottom photos on p. 55). On a dry wheel, you know the job is done when you see sparks come over the edge of the tool. There is also a telltale slight discoloration along the edge. I like my skew chisels with a very slight curve (see the bottom illustration on p. 48) and a good, long point, so as I grind the short corner I roll the handle very slightly to ease the short corner further into the grinding wheel.

Grinding gouges and scrapers requires a swiveling and rolling of the tool. I get a firm grip on the tool blade, hooking my forefinger under the rest while my thumb and fingers grasp the sides of the blade to control its rotation (see the photos at left). Think of grinding tools in two stages. First, bring the bevel shoulder into contact with the wheel (see the illustration on p. 58). Sparks will fly from under the tool. Then raise the tool handle until the sparks come over the top, at which point the tool should have a single-facet bevel from the shoulder to the cutting edge. The bevel shoulder should remain in contact with the wheel throughout the process. Keep the tool moving and the movements flowing, side to side for scrapers, rolling and swiveling for gouges and round-nose scrapers (see the photos on p. 58).

As you strive for the perfect bevel, remember that in reality the tool wavers somewhat on the rest and you get a multifaceted bevel even grinding something as simple as a scraper (see the photos on p. 59).

A Fingernail Shape

A fingernail edge should be convex all the way, but frequently it gets messed up, especially if you're not very good at grinding. Photo 1 is a classic example where the sides have been over-ground and you could put a straight ruler on the nose and wing of the tool and see a gap beneath. It needs reshaping. The method looks pretty drastic, but here's what to do.

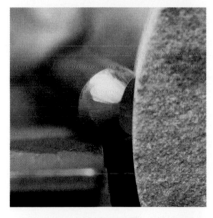

1 This edge has been over-ground on the wings and needs reshaping.

2 Begin by presenting the tool on its side with the flute near parallel to the face of the grinding wheel so both wings are ground at the same time.

3 Swing the handle so the end is curved when viewed from above. Within two light passes you should have light reflecting all around the edge as shown in photo 4.

4 The inside edge of the glinting facet will be the eventual cutting edge.

5 Grind away the flat surfaces until you are left with a perfect fingernail grind.

6 The edge is reshaped and ready for final sharpening.

GRINDING

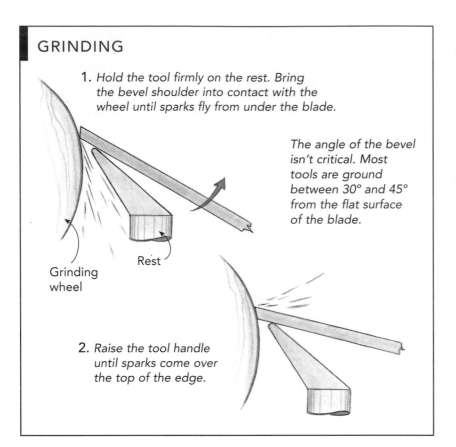

1. *Hold the tool firmly on the rest. Bring the bevel shoulder into contact with the wheel until sparks fly from under the blade.*

The angle of the bevel isn't critical. Most tools are ground between 30° and 45° from the flat surface of the blade.

Grinding wheel

Rest

2. *Raise the tool handle until sparks come over the top of the edge.*

Gouge edges can be ground either straight across or to a fingernail shape. Whichever way you do it, ensure that the wings are square with, or slightly behind, the center of the flute (see the illustration on the facing page). It is easy to over-grind the center of the edge so it lies within the plane of the wings. On a deep-fluted bowl gouge with a fingernail grind such an edge gives you a useful wing, but it renders the nose of the tool all but useless. The most useful gouge edges are convex all the way. If you place a flat surface to any portion of the edge, there should be only one point of contact.

You should do major grinding on a coarse, 36-grit wheel. If you see the end of the tool changing color as you grind, dip it in water to cool and use less pressure against the grinding wheel. If you have only a high-speed grinder, you can finish grinding turning tools on an 80-grit wheel and then use them without honing. But to do that you must have the edge barely resting on the wheel. It's common practice among beginners to grind too long and too

When you grind a round-nose scraper, swing it from side to side for the nose (RIGHT AND CENTER), then pitch it up to grind the steep, long left side (FAR RIGHT).

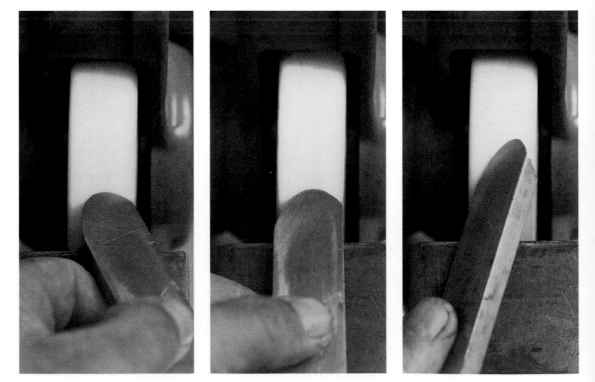

(LEFT) The position of my fingers indicates the tool is not overheating as I grind a ¾-in. (20mm) square-edge scraper. (BELOW) The bevel is not a single facet but is concave nevertheless, and it will cut well straight from the 80-grit high-speed grinding wheel.

GRINDING: THE SHAPE OF THE EDGE

Skew Chisels and Parting Tools

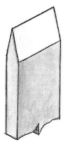

Correct: *Bevels should have a single facet.*

Incorrect: *A secondary bevel will prevent the usage of the bevel shoulder as a fulcrum.*

Square-Ground Gouges

Correct: *The edge should be straight or have the bottom of the flute slightly proud of the wings.*

Incorrect: *Beware of grinding the center of the edge back within the wings.*

hard. If you happen to grind an edge right in a few seconds, just be grateful. Don't feel you have to carry on for some regulation half minute.

WORKING WITH BURRS

When you grind an edge, no matter how delicate your touch, there will be a buildup of metal, called the burr, on top of the edge of the tool where it contacts the rotating wheel. The burr resembles a small hook running the length of the cutting edge. On scrapers, the burr does the cutting and is left on, while on gouges, skew chisels, and parting tools, it is often removed using a slipstone so that the tool will cut exceptionally cleanly. Most of the time, I use my tools straight from the fine wheel and still obtain a smooth, clean cut.

There are no hard and fast rules concerning burrs, and judging a suitable one is tricky. You can see it but that doesn't tell you enough. It has to be felt by stroking your thumb across the edge (see the photo below). Stroke across the

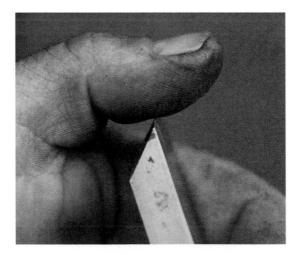

Test the burr by stroking your thumb gently *across* the edge, never along it. With experience, this critical test should become a quick indicator of the quality of an edge and become automatic every time you pick up a tool.

There is no quick route or shortcut to proficiency—any action is perfected only after being executed thousands of times.

edge, not along it, or you risk getting cut (though you'd know the tool is sharp). Because we all have a different sense of touch, you can learn how a burr should feel only from experience. I feel the edge habitually before using any tool and this almost subconscious spot check lets me know when it's time to sharpen.

As you turn, experiment with different edges. Try cutting with burrs that come from the lightest touch on the wheel and burrs from the heaviest grind and see what happens. Try honed edges. In turning, as with any other skill, there is no quick route or shortcut to proficiency—any action is perfected only after being executed thousands of times, and you must take time to experiment and compare.

Be careful not to press too hard when grinding; you'll risk not only burning the tool but also the burr will be too big. This renders gouges, skew chisels, and parting tools useless and scrapers almost so. For these occasions I keep a small softwood log or block of wood near the grinder—end grain up—into which I plunge the edge of the tool to remove the burr. This usually chips the edge slightly and I have to start the whole grinding process again, losing a bit more metal than I'd like.

Once you've achieved a good edge, it should be fairly easy to maintain by passing the tool lightly across an 80-grit grinding wheel when absolute sharpness is lost. This leaves a small, even burr. With all but the lightest of cuts, the pressure of the wood being turned removes this burr in an instant, leaving a good edge. For delicate scraping, which requires a light touch, this fine burr remains and works well. If you have a water-cooled stone, the edge off the wheel will be much the same.

Honing

Since high-speed steel is now used almost universally for woodturning tools, the demise of traditional natural stone slipstones has been hastened in favor of harder man-made versions in silicone carbide or diamond whetstones and diamond round and flat files (see the photo at right).

I tend to hone any gouge flute using 120-grit abrasive wrapped around a dowel rod rather than a diamond round file. (I lost my file and the interim measure continues to work.) Mostly in preparation for grinding, I do this dry, without any oil or water for lubrication (see the top photo on p. 54).

To remove the burr from the inside of a gouge, keep the honing file or rod flat on the inside of the blade and avoid rounding the edge. I use diamond flat files for honing all bevels. In order to hone, I tuck the tool handle under my left arm and move the file across the tool with my right hand. If the bevel is hollow ground, the tool should contact the flat file only at the bevel shoulder and at the edge. If you lift the hone off the bevel shoulder, you'll either round the edge or create a secondary bevel, which will make the tool very difficult to use. The hone should rub only two or three times on each side of the tool.

A razor edge is relatively easy to recognize once you've got it: You can't see any light flashing from flat spots on the edge and you won't feel a burr.

Afterword

Remember that woodturning tools remove a great deal of wood very quickly and consequently need attention more often than a joiner's chisel might. Don't worry if you seem to be going back to the grinder every few minutes. A fine edge can be lost very quickly regardless of the steel. With very hard woods it is not unusual to regrind after every three or four cuts, and I can recall keeping the grinder running when turning pieces of teak and elm with silica in the grain.

Too many of my students worry about their inability to achieve a so-called perfect bevel, when the shape of the edge (and the way it is

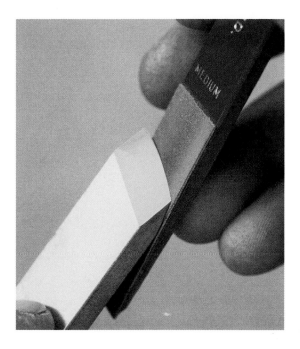

The hone must maintain contact with the bevel shoulder so you avoid rounding the edge.

presented to the wood) is usually much more important. You will note that some tools in the photos throughout this book are ground less than perfectly—but they all cut well.

I would like to dispel the myths still hawked by some woodturning gurus that there are perfect tools, steels, bevels, and so on, and that little else works. I feel that I'm fairly typical of many professional turners who temper their quest for perfection in these matters with a need to earn a living. Watch any master woodworker producing magnificent shavings and you will find work suddenly stops while the edge receives a quick hone or grind. The master knows when to resharpen from experience gained during thousands of hours of work.

In lieu of that experience, you would do well to find someone who will sharpen tools for you in the beginning so that you can glimpse the joys of cutting with a good edge. You will then know what to aim for and should recognize it when you do it yourself.

Sharpening, as I've described it, is neither mysterious, nor lengthy, nor difficult. It just takes practice.

4 SAFETY, TOOL HANDLING & CUTTING

WOODWORKING MACHINES ARE dangerous, and the lathe is no exception. If you doubt this, compare insurance quotes for woodturning against almost any other occupation. The machinery is fast moving, and you are dealing with sharp tools (or the sometimes more hazardous dull ones). The risks are real and can't be overemphasized. It's easy to become complacent and careless—especially when you think you have a machine and techniques under control. So, as you approach any machine, hesitate a second to remind yourself that it is potentially dangerous. Always think about what you are about to do and advance with care from the right direction.

Overall Safety

Here are some specific safety precautions to keep in mind and incorporate into your routine.

- Always wear eye protection. It is essential to prevent chips from flying into your eyes—secondhand eyes are still in short supply. If you wear spectacles, use shatterproof lenses. Less myopic turners can wear nonprescription safety spectacles working on very small jobs, but the best protection is a Plexiglas face shield. With the shield in place, you are less likely to require cosmetic surgery when a block flies off the lathe and hits you in the face (as it will). Over the years I've had four lots of stitches mending my face and forehead and a big hole in my left forearm.

- Never wear loose clothing. Short sleeves are best, but long sleeves with elastic cuffs are an acceptable option.

- Do not allow ties, chains, or pendants around the neck to hang free. Remove them or tuck them away.

- If your hair is long, tie it back. Or, even better, stick it under a hat and keep the dust off as well. If you do a lot of turning, you are gambling with the odds if you wear a long beard. (It has happened.)

- Remove all jewelry and watches from your hands and wrists. They might catch or simply be worn away when you are sanding.

- Keep your fingernails cut short so they are less likely to catch on the work or chucks.

- In hot weather, wear shoes or strapped sandals rather than slip-on sandals.

- When you wear a face shield, remember to put the visor down. It's there to protect your face and fend off shavings, not catch them. I know it sounds basic, but I have to remind students of this a dozen times a day.
- Keep the floor clear of loose cables, blocks of wood, etc.
- Store solvents, finishes, and steel wool away from any potential sparks and particularly from the grinder. Steel wool can catch fire.

DUST PROTECTION

Dust is a serious fire and health hazard. Fine dust and small shavings ignite easily. In particular, beware of sparks landing in the dust beneath your grinder or steel wool. I know it's impossible, but aim for a dust-free workshop.

Quantities of inhaled dust may lead to allergies or bronchial problems such as asthma. In your workshop you have to battle more than wood dust. Beware also of the insidious dusts from abrasives, grinding wheels, and the bonding agents used in their manufacture. All these substances produce extremely fine particles that can pass through most filtration systems. The dust you can't see is a real hazard. Also, the chemicals used to treat timber against insects or fungus are bound to be harmful if inhaled, as is the dust of the very popular spalted woods. I stopped turning pressure-treated and spalted wood years ago when I found they affected my breathing.

If you have any woodworking machinery, you should have a dust collector to go with it, sucking up the dust at its source. The dust collector can easily be the most expensive machine in a workshop. For 20 years I used the small dust collector shown in the photos at right. Mostly it's been bolted down in a corner attached to fixed ducting. In my new workshop (just built as I write), the dust collector is mobile because I am installing a much larger central collection unit and one of the air-filtration units now

This battered dust extractor served me well for 20 years. This latest in a long line of collection hoods, which is about 12 in. by 10 in. (250mm by 300mm), can be adjusted in any direction to catch dust as it leaves the job.

I can remove the collection hood at the front of the lathe with ease when I need to, usually when nesting bowls.

 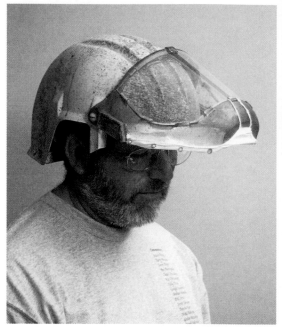

(RIGHT) **This Airstream helmet has saved me from severe head injuries several times.** (FAR RIGHT) **A visor that flips up is essential: You can get a better look at what you're doing and don't have to shout during a conversation.**

marketed through woodturning supply stores. These improvements will make a lot of difference, but I will continue to wear my Airstream helmet as well.

Really good dust extraction will cost you a small fortune, but chances are you will still inhale dust on its way to the intake, especially when sanding larger work on the lathe. You need personal protection in addition to the collection unit. You can wear a facemask, but the really fine particles go through many of these, and if the mask is worn over a beard, the dust creeps around the sides and through the whiskers. Also, a mask worn with an ordinary face shield tends to trap moisture, creating a misting problem, particularly if you wear spectacles.

The best solution is to wear one of the various respirators commercially available. For years I have spent my turning days in an Airstream helmet (made by Racal Safety Ltd. of England). It combines an effective air-filtration system with a face shield. It incorporates a small axial fan, which draws the dust-laden air through two filters. (The fan is powered by a battery

pack worn at the waist.) The air then flows down across the face behind the visor and out at the bottom. A seal around the face prevents unfiltered air, shavings, and dust from entering. Despite its apparent bulk, the helmet is comfortable to wear for extended periods. These helmets are not cheap, but they are the most effective protection I have found. Several times mine has fended off exploding bowls and I've been thankful I made the investment.

Less-expensive versions have a belt-mounted fan that delivers air to the helmet via a hose pipe up your back. Before you purchase one, though, be sure that the visor is designed for impact so you'll be protected from bits flying off the lathe.

On any helmet ensure that the visor can tilt up so you can get a clearer view of things without having to remove the whole helmet or face shield (see the photo above right).

Dust collection is a science with an industry of its own. If you are spending serious money on a fixed system, I recommend reading *Woodshop Dust Control* by Sandor Nagyszalanczy

(The Taunton Press, 1996) and consulting your local experts who can help calculate the size ducting you need.

WORKSHOP LIGHTING AND LAYOUT

Good general light, either from a window or a fluorescent tube, is an important safety consideration. In addition, it's essential to have one or two strong sources of light that can be easily moved around the job at hand. I have an antiquated articulated lamp that can be positioned anywhere around any job. It's on all the time and moved frequently so there is always light on the surface being turned and shadows highlighting the ridges, curves, bumps, and dips. An articulated or otherwise adjustable lamp that's easy to move is essential.

Convenient storage also improves the safety of your shop because you won't be distracted looking for tools. Old filing cabinets make wonderful shavings-free storage units for abrasives, chucks, and other lathe stuff. Mine is steel, so I keep a magnetic bar on it for the things that need to be close at hand such as all the tommy bars, C-wrenches, and a surgical clamp. On the top of the cabinet is nonmagnetic stuff such as dental tools and an old toothbrush, earplugs, cyanoacrylate adhesive, and a drinking straw, which is for blowing dust out of corners and hollows. The straw is very effective and much less expensive than a compressor, but you do need a flip-up visor on your face shield.

When placing your machinery, keep the following points in mind and refer to the illustrations on p. 66 and p. 67.

- Position your machines so that you can see anybody coming. If necessary, lock the door and install a bell or a light. It is dangerous to have anyone creeping up on a concentrating machinist.
- If you share your workshop with other workers, machine operators should be out of the line of fire of other machines. You don't

An old filing cabinet makes an ideal shaving-free storage unit for abrasives and chucks.

want offcuts from a circular saw or shavings, wood, or oil from a lathe showering or hitting anyone.

- Do not have a polished floor in machine areas. Floors should be nonslip. Be aware that the wax used to prevent checking on bowl blanks falls to the floor with the shavings and will build to a dangerously slick surface. If this happens, throw down sand or sprinkle water on the floor.
- Position the lathe tools you are using so that you don't have to lean over work spinning on the lathe to pick them up.
- Mount the grinder near the lathe. You will regrind often, so the grinder should be only a pace away.
- Locate the lathe so that when you look up there's a view. Sanding is boring, and who wants to see a brick wall upon looking up?

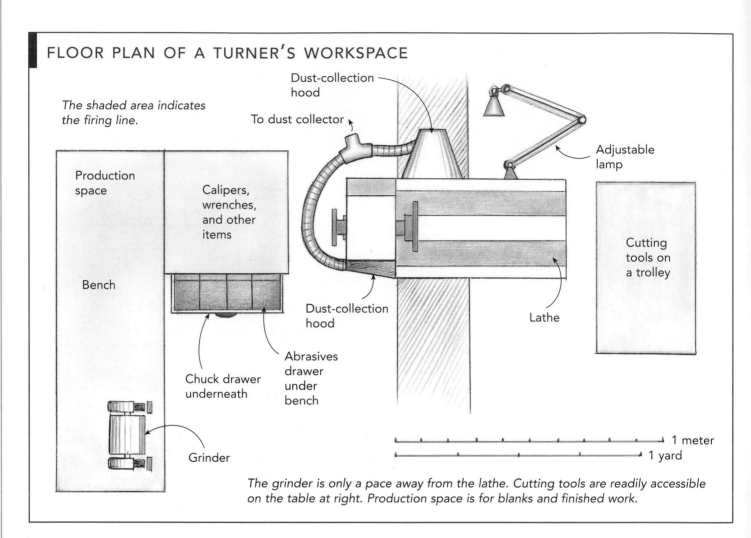

FLOOR PLAN OF A TURNER'S WORKSPACE

The shaded area indicates the firing line.

Dust-collection hood

To dust collector

Adjustable lamp

Production space

Calipers, wrenches, and other items

Bench

Cutting tools on a trolley

Dust-collection hood

Lathe

Abrasives drawer under bench

Chuck drawer underneath

Grinder

1 meter

1 yard

The grinder is only a pace away from the lathe. Cutting tools are readily accessible on the table at right. Production space is for blanks and finished work.

OPERATING THE LATHE

You can always tell if a woodturner has been turning by the state of his or her hands. There will be a multitude of tiny nicks and scratches in various stages of repair resulting from the abrasive effects of wood chips or occasional contact with chucks. Nothing serious. Beginners might boast larger and more colorful injuries resulting from pinched flesh or jammed fingers, which are usually more tiresome than dangerous, though often painful. You need to beware of several main dangers that come with turning wood.

- Always check the machine and work area before you begin. Check that all guards are in place and secure, that no wrenches or keys are left in shafts or chucks, and that no tools or materials will interfere with the lathe's operation. A quick visual examination should become a regular work habit.
- Check that speeds are set correctly for the work you are about to do.
- I've said this before, but it's worth repeating. Wear a face shield, and remember to put the visor down. It's there to protect your face and fend off shavings, not catch them.
- Always remove chuck keys or locking bars from any chuck on the lathe when you are not actually using them.
- Before starting the lathe, rotate the wood by hand to see that it revolves freely. Check that the tool rest is immobile with all locking

levers tightened. Stand clear of the firing line of the lathe when switching it on because blocks are bound to come off now and then. When an object comes off the lathe, it is usually at 90° to the axis (see the illustration at right).

- Never lean over machines, even when switched off. They might suddenly leap into action and grab you or your clothing.
- Never wrap a polishing cloth, sandpaper, steel wool, or anything else around your hands or fingers. Any of these can wrap around a rough spindle in a fraction of a second, and it's not worth being attached to the other end and risking a finger.
- Stop the lathe before adjusting the rest. If you move the rest carelessly and it makes contact with the rotating work, you are likely to damage the work or jar it from the lathe. You might even shatter delicate or fragile jobs. In any case, your hands will be perilously close to the action.
- Beware of sharp edges, corners, and rims on the work. Razor-sharp edges can develop rapidly and are just as efficient as bacon slicers in cutting you to the bone—often without pain but with a lot of blood (and that stains the wood). Develop the habit of softening edges either with coarse abrasives or a tool.

Beyond the main dangers, noise can also be a problem if a lot of machinery is running at once. Worn bearings make more noise than new ones, and three or four motors running at the same time will make it hard to hear the radio. Some woods, like jarrah burl, are very noisy to turn, so whenever I find the pitch uncomfortable I use ear protection. When wearing my helmet, I use small earplugs on a string so if I need to remove one or both they hang round my neck but never near enough to spinning wood to be a hazard. Otherwise I have a good pair of ear protectors for when I use chain, table, or band saws.

Check that speeds are set correctly for the work you are about to do.

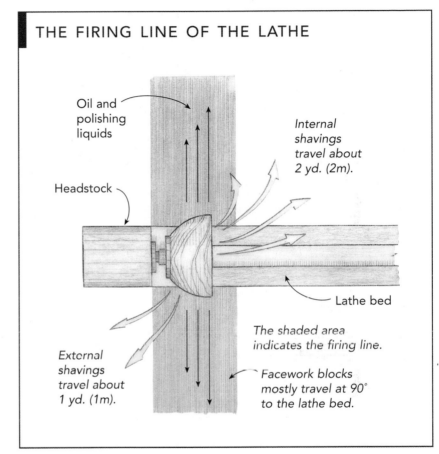

THE FIRING LINE OF THE LATHE

Oil and polishing liquids

Internal shavings travel about 2 yd. (2m).

Headstock

Lathe bed

The shaded area indicates the firing line.

External shavings travel about 1 yd. (1m).

Facework blocks mostly travel at 90° to the lathe bed.

Sounds from the lathe are among your best diagnostic tools. Any turner with a well-tuned ear can judge the thickness of a bowl wall, hear splits and loose knots before they become dangerous, and know when a job is coming loose on the lathe. If you train yourself to listen, you'll be able to avoid most accidents before they happen.

Although time-consuming at first, you should stop the lathe every time a new sound comes along and investigate. You'll soon recognize all the basic noises. Turning sounds should be a series of crescendos and decrescendos resulting from smooth, flowing cuts. Students

Sounds from the lathe are among your best diagnostic tools. Train yourself to listen; you'll be able to avoid most accidents before they happen.

or apprentices frequently find it unnerving that skilled turners can tell exactly what is going on by sounds alone. You can't get away with anything in a turner's workshop.

With experience comes an inevitable change in attitude towards safety. It no longer takes several minutes to approach your machine. What might appear to be shortcuts taken by an old pro should, hopefully, indicate internalization—not relaxation—of safety consciousness. There are procedures that simply should never be attempted by a novice but would be absurd for an expert to avoid, such as adjusting the tool rest with the lathe running. As you become more competent (and confident), try to remain aware of the limits of your skills and venture beyond only with extreme caution.

I consider myself lucky to have escaped serious injury since I began turning in 1970. But those years have not been without incident, and my hands are covered with small scars that serve as constant reminders not to be so careless in the future. On my left hand, I have a scar across two fingers from a bandsaw and one on my thumb from jamming it between the lathe bed and a large platter. On my right hand are three broken knuckles from sanding a large platter (this happened twice), I had a broken nose from a shattering burr-elm bowl and a permanent lump from the time I headed a piece of flying teak back toward the lathe.

A flying bowl smashed my shatterproof spectacle lens, leaving me with cuts and a black eye. One piece of an exploding, 10-in.- (250mm) diameter, nearly completed burl bowl took a lump of flesh out of my left forearm, while another hit my face shield and left me dazed (or was that shock?). These were major accidents

that stopped me working for a few days each time. All happened at the end of the day when I was tired and not concentrating fully or I was showing off. You have been warned: Proceed with caution and remember that when anything happens on the lathe, or on any other woodworking machine, it happens fast.

Tool Handling

There is more to woodturning than simply maintaining the correct angle of the cutting edge to the wood. The angle is important, but you must also be aware of what is happening behind the edge, how the tool is held, and how to position your body to support it while still approaching the lathe safely. In this section, I'll discuss general principles of tool handling. If these are not applied, it will be difficult to control the cutting edge, and the wood will dictate the path of the tool. Beginners should read this section before proceeding to the chapters on centerwork and facework.

Consider yourself apprenticed to the lathe. You can't just stand before it and produce excellence. As a musician practices scales, so the turner should practice routine exercises until mastered. When you begin turning, try to resist the temptation to make something; it is more important at this early stage to develop good work habits than it is to produce objects. Practice cutting the spinning wood, and enjoy the sounds and shavings that result as you develop basic tool-handling skills.

LEVERAGE
When turning wood, you have to be in control of the leverage and use it to your advantage.

Whenever you move a cutting edge against wood spinning on a lathe, you have to balance the force exerted by the wood against the tool edge, otherwise the handle will kick up and hit you in the face. In this section, I'll look at leverage before moving on to ways to hold and manipulate the tools.

When a block of wood revolving on the lathe comes in contact with a tool, it exerts considerable downward pressure on the cutting edge of the tool. As the downward force is applied to the cutting edge, there is an opposite reaction on the handle at the other end—your end. The farther the point of cut is away from the fulcrum (where the tool sits on the rest), the more pressure the revolving wood exerts on the unsupported tip of the tool and the more difficult it will be to control.

For example, when the rest is about ½ in. (13mm) away from the work, you will have no problem controlling the tool. But move the rest about 4 in. (100mm) away from the work, and the force exerted on the edge of the tool acts like a heavy weight dropped on one end of a seesaw. You must grasp the handle with grim determination to control the cutting edge. Gain control of the leverage by keeping the rest close to the point of cut, even though sometimes, as in turning the outside of a bowl, this can mean moving the rest every few seconds. But be aware of moving the rest too close, particularly with long bevel scrapers: You don't want the bevel on the rest, just the bottom of the blade.

While your primary preoccupation as cutting proceeds will be preventing the tool handle from kicking up, you will also be concerned with horizontal leverage as you move the tool edge sideways. The tool can be manipulated in two basic ways. First, you can simply pull or push the tool along the rest, but this requires some effort and makes no use of the leverage opportunity shown in Fig. 1 in the illustration on p. 70, where you have far more control of the cutting edge with much less effort.

Rounded Bowl

This bowl was jam-chucked for the removal of the foot. The base is rounded but flat enough towards the center that the bowl doesn't rock or spin on its axis.

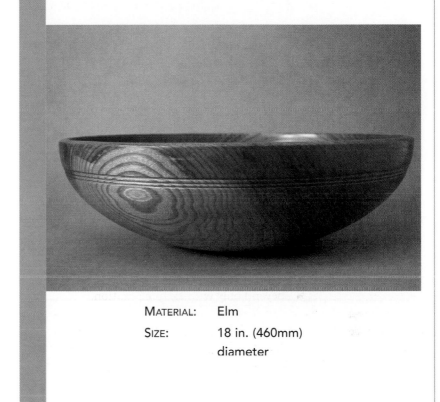

MATERIAL:	Elm
SIZE:	18 in. (460mm) diameter

When turning wood you have to be in control of the leverage and use it to your advantage.

LEVERAGE

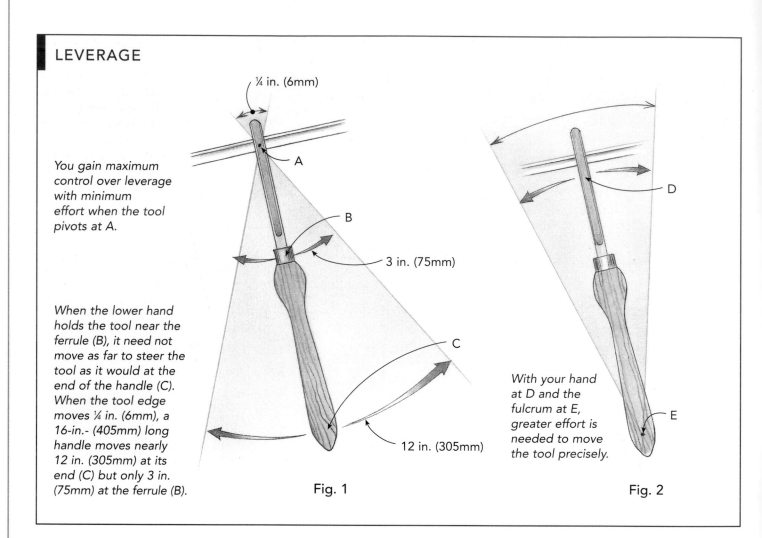

¼ in. (6mm)

A

You gain maximum control over leverage with minimum effort when the tool pivots at A.

B

3 in. (75mm)

C

When the lower hand holds the tool near the ferrule (B), it need not move as far to steer the tool as it would at the end of the handle (C). When the tool edge moves ¼ in. (6mm), a 16-in.- (405mm) long handle moves nearly 12 in. (305mm) at its end (C) but only 3 in. (75mm) at the ferrule (B).

12 in. (305mm)

Fig. 1

D

E

With your hand at D and the fulcrum at E, greater effort is needed to move the tool precisely.

Fig. 2

You have the most control when the tool pivots on the fulcrum (as in Fig. 1). The edge is swung through an arc by moving the handle, giving you a great mechanical advantage with comparatively little effort. I usually hold the tool near the ferrule (at B) so that as the tool swings through an arc, my hand doesn't have to move as far as it would if on the end of the handle (at C).

If you swing the tool using your upper hand at D (in Fig. 2), the fulcrum effectively moves to the end of the handle (E). Such a position requires more effort on your part and, in some situations such as the end of a broad sweeping cut, much less fine control of the edge.

STANCE

To move the cutting edge precisely where you want, you must get your weight behind the tool and guide it through space on a predetermined trajectory, regardless of the wood or space lying in its path. On metal lathes, you control the cutter by winding it in on a rack-and-pinion system. In woodturning, you hold the tools, replacing the rack and pinion. You'll need all the support for the tool you can muster, and you'll get it from the tool rest, the lathe, and your body.

Broad movements to manipulate the tools should come not so much from the hands, wrists, and arms as from the shoulders, hips, and legs. Aim for a compact stance with your elbows tucked into your sides. Stand in a balanced position, with your feet placed comfortably apart and the tool handle aligned along your forearm for maximum control (see the photo at right).

It's good practice to keep your upper hand on the rest, and when working very precisely it pays to maintain contact between other parts of your anatomy and the machine as well. Lean your hip against the bed, press a leg against the stand, or lean on the headstock (see the photos below). By using the lathe to gain extra support and stability, you also establish physical points of reference between yourself and the lathe from which you can manipulate the cutting edge more precisely (see "Tool grips" on p. 72).

Develop and enjoy the control gained from this approach by moving the cutting edge with a little squeeze or push in conjunction with broader support movements from the rest of your body. As in steering a bicycle, control in

Standing with your feet apart, set the rest so that as you turn, the tool handle is tilted slightly below horizontal and tucked into your side aligned along your forearm.

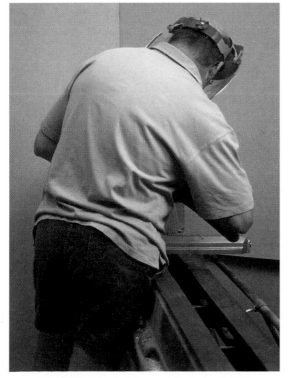

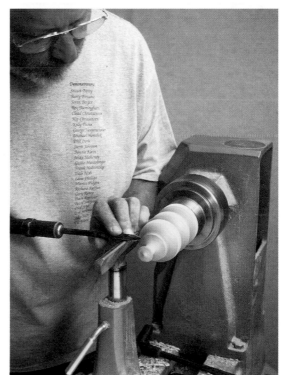

Lean on the lathe and use it for support whenever possible. It will provide more stability for the tool and a useful point of reference from which you can manipulate the cutting edge.

Here I manipulate the tool in part by shifting my weight from one foot (RIGHT) to the other (FAR RIGHT) as I straighten my right leg and bend the left very slightly.

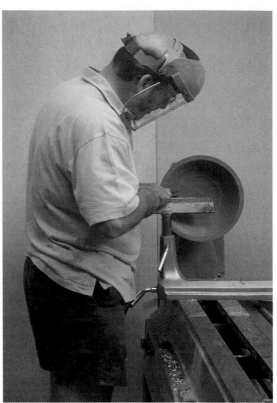

woodturning is essentially a matter of shifting weight and coordination. For example, if you want to move the tip of a tool slightly to the left, the movement should come from a nudge from your hip pushing the handle to the right, rather than simply moving the tool with an arm movement.

To move the tip to the right, draw your right elbow in close to your side, nudging the tool handle to the left. Your forearm stays close to your side and you remain compact. If you want the tool edge to drop, extend your side by stretching upward or adjusting your balance as shown in the photos above to bring the handle up (and the tip down) with the weight of your entire torso and shoulders behind the tool. If the handle must leave your side, align it along your forearm for support.

Most beginners exhibit considerable inhibition when it comes to moving their bodies with a tool handle, but it pays to overcome this self-consciousness.

TOOL GRIPS

You can grip the tool from either above or below. The former gives you less visibility but deflects shavings better than the latter, which allows you to actually watch the edge as it cuts. In either case, the idea is the same—keep the tool in contact with the rest while controlling lateral movement along it.

I am right-handed and I work right-handed: I find woodturning difficult enough without trying to be ambidextrous. Lathes are designed as right-handed machines, which is unfortunate for left-handers, who do have to come to terms with that. A very few have developed a left-handed lathe for themselves, but most learn to work right-handed, particularly around face-work and bowls. Do not swap hands if you can possibly avoid it, and keep your left (or upper) hand on the tool blade as well as in contact with the rest. Your upper hand provides all the fine control and helps deflect shavings, while your lower (right) hand has more mobility, controlling all broad movements and rotation of the tool.

I grip the handle with my lower hand near the ferrule because I find it more comfortable than at the end and because it's easier to control the tool's movement. Also, gripping the tool near the ferrule means my hand need not move quite as far as it would at the end of a long handle. For example, in the illustration on p. 70, you see that if the point of a chisel moves through an arc of ¼ in. (6mm) with the tool rest ½ in. (13mm) away, a 16-in.-(405mm) long handle will move nearly 12 in. (305mm) at its end. At the ferrule, this movement would be closer to 3 in. (75mm). I hold the handle against my side or along my forearm for additional stability whenever possible.

When a tool is to be rolled, anticipate the movement by reaching around the handle in the opposite direction (to the right if the tool will roll to the left). In this way you start a cut under some tension, like a coiled spring, then as the tool rolls into the cut, your lower hand and forearm can unwind to finish relaxed. If you start off comfortably and roll the tool, you move into an increasingly awkward position.

Don't grip the tool as though you were clutching a wire stretched across the Grand Canyon—you'll never keep it up. A light but firm grip is required, not white knuckles. You should be relaxed but ready to tighten instantly if necessary. Your grip should act as a shock absorber so that when you have a catch it will be less disastrous. Catches are the bane of any novice turner's life. A catch occurs when spinning wood bears down on an unsupported edge (a tool held loosely or at the wrong angle) or most simply when you let a tool contact the wood before the rest as shown in the illustra-

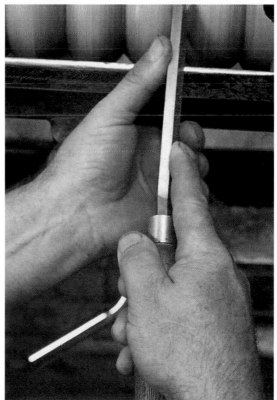

(TOP LEFT) **Whenever you are about to make a rolling cut, reach around the handle in the opposite direction so you start the cut under some tension.** (BOTTOM LEFT) **Then as the cut proceeds, you unwind to end up in a comfortable position.**

If you understand why catches occur you should be able to avoid the worst of them.

INCORRECT CUTTING

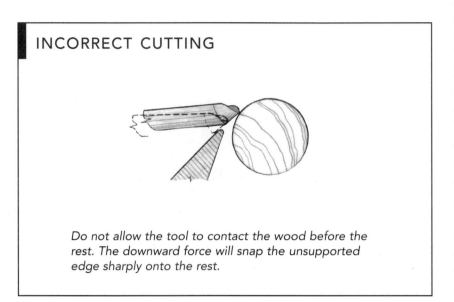

Do not allow the tool to contact the wood before the rest. The downward force will snap the unsupported edge sharply onto the rest.

tion at left. Catches happen suddenly, with a bang, and usually scar the wood.

Catches tend to make novice turners very apprehensive, even scaring some away from the craft forever, which is a pity because if you understand why catches occur you should be able to avoid the worst of them. It helps to go through them in slow motion, especially with a buddy. The best way is to rotate the lathe by hand (as I did in the top photo on p. 81), and rotate the edge into a catching situation. It should help you understand what happens, but I can guarantee it won't eliminate the catches. They never vanish entirely because there are gremlins forever lurking just over the edge of the job, waiting for an opportunity to grab the edge.

Gouges will catch when the force of the wood is against any portion of the edge not over, or very nearly over, the fulcrum, as shown in the illustration below. Skew chisels will typically catch when you try to cut using the

SUPPORTING THE POINT OF THE CUT

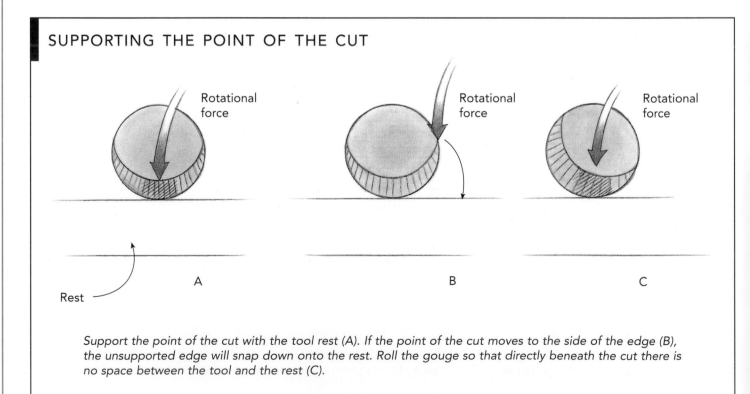

Support the point of the cut with the tool rest (A). If the point of the cut moves to the side of the edge (B), the unsupported edge will snap down onto the rest. Roll the gouge so that directly beneath the cut there is no space between the tool and the rest (C).

unsupported upper portion of the edge. Skew catches are covered in detail on pp. 109–111. When using a scraper, keep it flat on the rest: Pressure on a raised edge will snap it on to the rest (see the illustration at right).

I use four basic grips that keep the tool on the rest and enable me to control the edge as it cuts. I keep my upper (left) hand in contact with both the tool and rest at all times. This provides a point of reference from which I manipulate the tool edge precisely. Without my hand on the rest, my point of reference is the next point of contact between my body and a solid object. If you are not leaning against the lathe, this is the floor, and from there it's very difficult to move the edge exactly where you want it.

These grips and their variations should enable you to maintain control in virtually every situation you'll encounter at the lathe. To get the feel, you should try each with the lathe off. Remember the importance of stance, and let your body follow the handle as you move the tool around. Hold the tool with both hands, the upper hand on the rest near the cutting edge, the lower hand grasping the handle near the ferrule with the handle aligned along your forearm. For right-handers (as shown in the photos throughout the book), the left hand is uppermost, the right hand lower.

There are no hard and fast rules to determine which grip is used when. In the photos, I hold the tools in a variety of ways—all variations on common themes. Which grip you use depends on the cutting situation—the need to deflect shavings versus the need to see what you're doing—or just general comfort. The power you use to grip the tool is more to prevent catches than to move the tool forward.

The **hand-over grip** is the most common and comfortable method employed when the tool is moved laterally along the rest, as in roughing-down centerwork spindles (see the bottom photo on p. 76). It is a good grip for broad

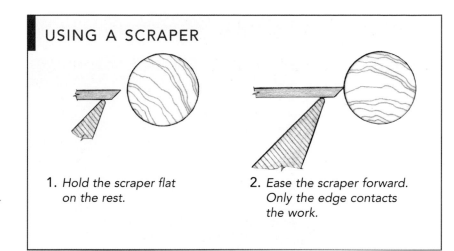

USING A SCRAPER

1. Hold the scraper flat on the rest.

2. Ease the scraper forward. Only the edge contacts the work.

movements and most roughing cuts. You can push or pull the tool along the rest, but you'll lack the precise control of the other grips because your upper hand is not stationary on the rest. The tool lies beneath your curled hand, with your palm on the rest, while your fingers can be cocked up to deflect shavings. You won't always be able to see the edge cutting, but you can watch the result of the cut on the top of the work or the opposite side if you're hollowing a bowl. (With practice, you'll be able to feel the cut without having to look at the shavings.)

The top left photo on p. 76 shows a hand-over grip with the tool cutting to the left. As I sway slightly with my body to move the handle right, the fingers of my upper hand ease the edge left. This way I get more leverage than if I merely pull the tool blade left with the fulcrum at the end of the handle. More typically, you'll want to have your thumb on the side of the blade and a couple of fingers in the air to fend off the shavings (see the photo at right on p. 76). With this grip the two lower fingers pull the tool against the thumb, which becomes a lateral fulcrum as your body moves right with the tool handle.

When you rough-out centerwork, be sure to keep your right hand near the ferrule and the handle against your forearm and side for sup-

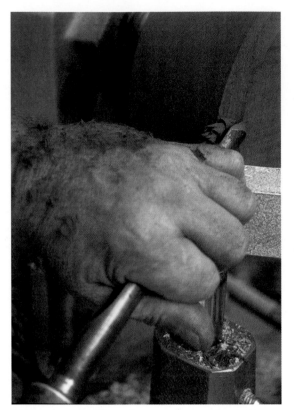

This is a normal hand-over grip cutting left.

Deflect shavings by keeping your fingers up.

A hand-over grip is ideal for roughing a spindle blank when the tool is moved flowingly from one end of the rest to the other.

port (see the photo at left). Sometimes, such as when turning beads, you may want a more secure grip. A very similar but more secure grip prevents the tool from moving sideways along the rest in either direction. I keep the lower side of my palm (at the base of the little finger) pushed firmly against the rest and bunch my fingers around the tool to keep it firm against the bottom of my little finger and thumb (see the top left photo on the facing page). By tightening and relaxing my forefinger and thumb, I can pivot the tool on the tool rest rather like I might an oar in a rowlock. I often use this grip when beginning a roughing cut, and it's excellent for fine detailing. My arm is into my side with my right hand near the ferrule rather than at the end of the handle.

A **hand-under grip** is one of my favorite grips because it enables me to see what I'm doing as I

In this very controlled hand-over grip, my hand is planted firmly on the rest to prevent lateral movement along the rest. This grip is useful when cutting beads or grooves.

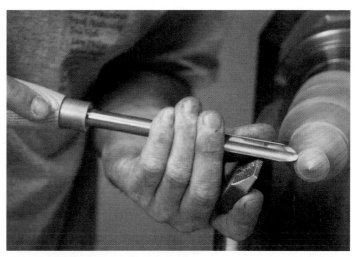

This secure hand-under grip gives very precise control of the edge for precision detailing.

pull the tool firmly down onto the rest for a high degree of fine control, typically for an initial entry cut into the wood or very fine detailing. I grip both sides of the tool from below with my thumb and outer fingers and hook my forefinger under the rest (see the top right photo). This grip allows me to move the tool in either direction along the rest under tight control, or I can relax the grip and ease the tool forward using my lower hand.

A **stop grip** is used when the tool can kick back in only one direction and all you need is a stop on one side of the tool as shown in the photo at right. If the tool happens to kick into space it's no big deal, so there's no need to prevent it doing so. As you start this cut, your right hand keeps the tool pressed against the fingers on the rest, which initially act as both stop and fulcrum for lateral movements. The fingers on top of the tool will ease it forward to cut, pushing off the other fingers that stay firmly put, using them like an athlete uses starting blocks.

You can use your thumb as a fulcrum to support the tool, leaving your fingers free to support the work. I can use my fingers to support a bowl wall (see the top left photo on p. 78) and

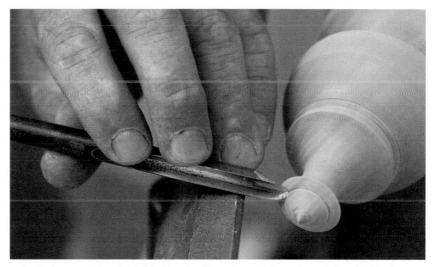

When the tool can kick back in only one direction, as when truing end grain, a stop grip is sufficient. The lower hand keeps the tool pressured against the top hand's fingers, which ease the blade into the cut.

an end-grain hollow (see the photo at right on p. 78). In each case the tool is kept firmly against my thumb by the lower (right) hand, which in turn resists that pressure. These opposing forces allow me to move the tool very precisely by increasing or decreasing the pressure on one side of the tool or the other.

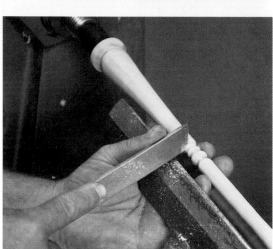

The thumb provides a fulcrum, leaving the fingers free to support the wood and dampen any vibration. Note that the thumb is against the *side* of the tool, not on top.

Much the same principle can be used to turn a small bead while supporting the cut from the far side of the spindle (see the bottom left photo above). The supporting fingers equalize the pressure exerted by the tool. If my fingers get too hot, I know I'm pushing too hard with the tool.

A tool held with one of these stop-grip variations can be eased forward under tight control over distances up to 2 in. (50mm). The fingers or thumb used as the fulcrum provide the forward power, pushing against the force exerted by the lower hand. In the top left photo above, I use my upper hand to support the wall of a thin bowl during a final shearing cut. Only a stop grip is necessary on the rest, so I can use my thumb as a moveable fulcrum for the tool. Note that my thumb is on the side of the tool, not on

top. The wall is only about ⅛ in. (3mm) thick, and the wood is green and flexible. My hand is planted firmly on the rest, and as the cut progresses my fingers can extend to remain behind the cutting edge.

My right hand keeps the tool blade pressed against my thumb, which I can use to adjust the path of the edge. The tool handle is tucked in under my forearm and against my side. The principle is similar to a thickness planer: The wood is shaved while being forced to pass between two fixed points, in this case, my fingers behind the bowl and the cutting tool in front. A smooth bowl wall is achieved by moving the gouge evenly and accurately along a predetermined parabola, with minimal tool pressure against the wood.

Remember that all of these grips should aim to prevent catches and run-backs and maintain control rather than promote forward thrust. As your skill improves, you'll develop your own variations.

A **squeeze grip** gives you very fine control over the forward movement of the edge. I find it particularly useful when using a scraper a long way over the rest when a catch would spell disaster, typically when finishing end grain deep inside a box. My left hand is anchored to the rest, gripping the tool firmly to prevent any forward motion as I try to push it forward with my right hand (see the photo at right). By relaxing my grip of the tool blade only slightly, I let the edge ease forward a tiny amount, and by tightening my grasp, I can ease it back again. It's like having the tool set in a block of thickish rubber. Also, I really hang onto the handle.

Extra support becomes more necessary as you become more adventurous and begin to turn slender pieces, and when it will not be sufficient to guide the cutting edge with one of the standard grips. When thin wood starts flexing, the cut becomes uneven, leaving spiral chatter marks. When this happens, you hear it as a high-pitched vibrating noise over normal turning sounds. If you're really overdoing it, the pitch becomes shrill, even screeching.

When the wood is vibrating so much you cannot remove the chatter marks with a steady, gentle cut, drop the lathe speed a few hundred rpm and support the job. There are all kinds of commercial gadgets to help you do this on larger spindles such as the steady shown in the center right photo on p. 32, but I use my upper hand because it's more flexible and sensitive than any mechanical steadying device and it doesn't take time to set up. Note that contact with tool, rest, and wood is maintained by the upper hand.

The tool is controlled by opposing forces. Any pressure against the wood is equalized on the other side of the spindle by my fingers, which also keep the spindle running true. My

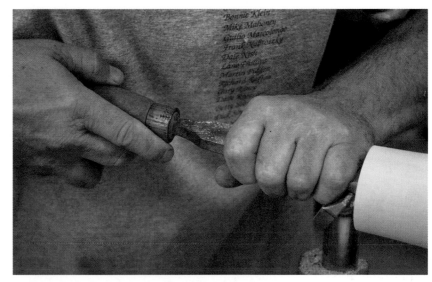

A squeeze grip gives you very fine control over the forward movement of the edge.

Extra support from the lathe, here from leaning on the headstock, always makes the job easier.

All grips should aim to prevent catches and run-backs and maintain control rather than promote forward thrust.

lower hand keeps the tool blade firmly against my thumb, which controls the rate at which the edge cuts. In addition to my fingers around the spindle, I steady myself by leaning on the headstock (see the bottom photo on p. 79).

Whether you are supporting centerwork or facework, the theory is the same: One part of your upper hand takes the bounce out of the wood while the rest of your hand maintains contact with the tool and rest. Your fingers or hand should support the wood behind the cutting area, equalizing tool pressure. (If you do have a catch, the tool will jump back away from your fingers, and you shouldn't get cut.)

If your supporting hand gets too hot, your cut is too forceful. Your hand should be warm to hot, not burning, and providing just enough pressure to keep the wood rotating centrally. Your fingers make a handy built-in thermostatic pressure gauge: If they get too hot, you know you're pushing too hard.

In each of the grips shown here, note that the thumb or fingers are pressed against the side of the tool. If they're on top of the tool, you cannot provide a fulcrum or any force to adjust the path of the edge. You'll find similar techniques constantly useful and will no doubt develop your own as the need arises.

Cutting

There is no absolutely right or wrong way to turn wood as some people contend, and there are dozens of variations of all the standard tools and ways of using them. But the bottom line is that each, apart from flat scrapers and parting tools, is designed to shear-cut—or slice—the wood. An edge set at an angle to the oncoming wood will shear-cut. The best angle is about 45°, a figure you should keep in the back of your mind whenever you turn. Regardless of which tool you're using, if you want to produce those long, curly shavings that make woodturning so appealing that you don't want to make anything else, the portion of the edge actually slicing will be at about 45° to the oncoming wood.

If the edge is vertical in the line of the oncoming wood, it will not cut, especially on centerwork where it butts into end grain (see the left shaving in the top photo on the facing page). The cleanest surfaces are cut when the fibers you are cutting are supported by other fibers (see the illustration on p. 83).

There are several basic rules and useful concepts to bear in mind as you turn. You may find it useful to refer to this list after beginning the exercises in chapters 6 and 7.

Same shaving, same effect, different tools. To shear cut, each tool has the portion of the edge cutting at about 45° to the oncoming wood. (RIGHT) The ½-in. (13mm) shallow gouge is pulled to the left. (FAR RIGHT) The ¾-in. (20mm) skew chisel is used long point down as it's pushed to the left.

STARTING A CUT

1. *The tool should contact the rest first.*

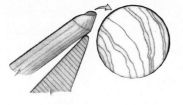

2. *Move the tool forward so the bevel shoulder rubs the wood.*

3. *With the bevel rubbing, raise the handle and bring the edge in to cut.*

Each of these shavings was produced using the edge at a different angle. The near vertical edge (left) merely pries fibers from the surface as it butts into end grain. As the edge is moved closer to 45°, the shaving becomes wider and thicker.

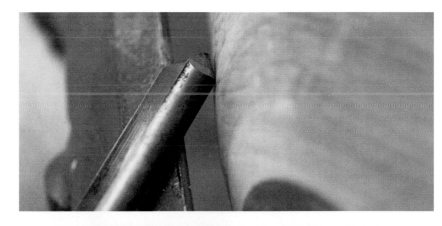

- The tool must contact the rest before the wood. When using gouges, skew chisels, and parting tools, have the bevel shoulder contact the wood before the edge (see the center and bottom photos at right). Develop a 1-2-3 approach to starting as shown in the illustration above. First, place the tool on the rest; second, bring the bevel heel to the wood; third, raise the handle to begin cutting.

- When you have to begin a cut from space, line up the bevel with the direction in which you want to cut, then pivot the edge through an arc into the wood (see the photos on the

With cutting tools (as opposed to scrapers and scraping techniques), keep the bevel rubbing the wood at all times. Always bring the bevel to ride on the wood (TOP) before pivoting the edge around to begin cutting (ABOVE).

To start a cut from space, line up the bevel with the direction in which you want to cut, then raise the handle to pivot the edge through an arc into the wood.

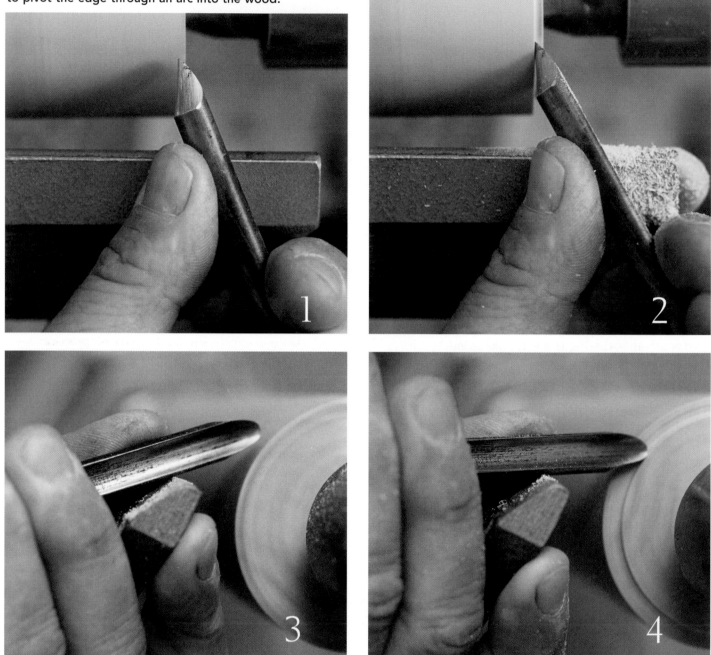

A sharp tool held in the optimum position will produce a large shaving with virtually no forward pressure against the wood.

facing page). Don't push the tool horizontally across the rest into the wood as if you're using a billiards cue. The moment the nose of the tool penetrates the wood, some bevel will rub and you will instantly have more control of the edge. The bevel and then bevel shoulder provide a secondary fulcrum against which you can pivot and roll the edge for a better shaving.

- Bevels should always rub the wood when any tool is shear cutting as shown in photo 2 on the facing page.
- Let the wood come to the tool; let the lathe do the work. Most hand-woodworking involves moving the tool to the wood, like a woodcarver using a mallet and chisel. Turners have it easy, holding an edge in the path of the oncoming wood. All we need to do is have the edge at the correct angle. The tool should move forward only when the wood in its path has been removed. In the hands of an expert, this is a rapid, flowing action. It's like an animated cartoon where slightly different static images in each frame run in quick succession to produce a single, fluid movement. A sharp tool held in the optimum position will produce a large shaving with virtually no forward pressure against the wood. If you push the tool hard into the cut, trying to take too big a shaving, you'll have a catch.
- Shear cuts are better than scraping. Wood is essentially a bundle of long fibers lying generally in the same direction. Your cleanest cut will be across the bundle (the grain) where any one fiber is supported by others. Unsupported fibers will splinter away, as anyone who has cross-sawn a board knows. Plan your cuts in such a way that there is support for the area being cut by following the directional arrows shown in the illustration above right.
- Any force exerted by the edge against the wood should be parallel to the axis, rather than against it, so the force is transferred to

CLEAN SHEARING CUTS

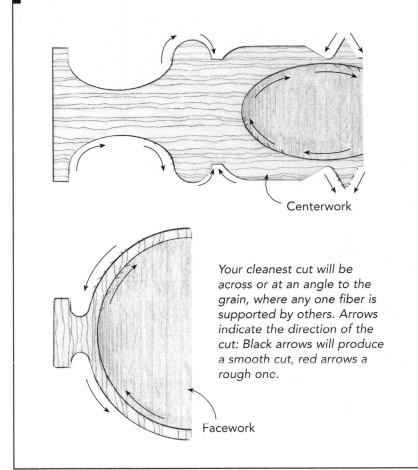

Centerwork

Your cleanest cut will be across or at an angle to the grain, where any one fiber is supported by others. Arrows indicate the direction of the cut: Black arrows will produce a smooth cut, red arrows a rough one.

Facework

the headstock or tailstock. Excessive tool pressure against the axis causes chattering, flexing, or even breaking of slender work, and it can pull facework in a chuck off-center. More importantly, tool pressure against the axis directly confronts the oncoming wood. Sadly, grain direction and the forms you want to turn tend to compromise these ideals but, as in life, it's best to avoid direct confrontations and adopt a sideways approach.

- Don't work with the tool at 90° to the surface you're cutting as shown in the photo at left on p. 84. It is very difficult to turn a curve

(ABOVE) It is very difficult to turn a flowing curve using the tool near 90° to the surface you're cutting. (TOP RIGHT) Scrapers should be skewed so they can be pulled across the surface. (BOTTOM RIGHT) Gouges should point in the direction you're cutting, so you can steer them along the line you want to cut.

accurately with the tool blade near 90° to the surface you're cutting. Scrapers should be skewed so they can be pulled across the surface as shown in the top right photo on the facing page. Gouges should point in the direction you're cutting (see the bottom right photo on the facing page), then you can steer them along the line you want to go.

- The precise height of the rest is determined by your height in relation to the lathe center height, modified by the thickness of the tool you are using. I like to use my tools with the handle dropped a few degrees below horizontal, so my lathes have centers set at about 2 in. (50mm) above my elbow.

- Peripheral speeds dwindle the nearer you get to center, so you must slow the rate at which you move the tool forward. As you cut into the center of the work, slow up and float the edge in gently. Stop at the center. If you push and overshoot, the tool will meet wood traveling upward on the other side and you'll risk a catch and tearing or pulling out fibers.

- Initial cuts should be exploratory until you determine where the wood is and the orbit of its extremities. If the tool is pushed in too fast, too much wood will contact the edge at once, making the tool clear more wood than it can cope with. That sudden force will often lead to a catch. As you cut, you want to control the leverage and path of the edge rather than force the tool forward against the work. Let the wood come to the tool. Don't try to cut too much at one go.

- If a sharp tool begins to cut less efficiently or even stops cutting altogether, adjust the tool angle or roll it to a different position where it will cut. Don't try pushing hard to find an edge. If you push hard at the wrong angle, the tool will often skate up and over the surface

with little or no effect. The tool should never shoot forward and ride on the bevel if you lose an edge; this indicates lack of control and that you're pushing too hard. The aim is to move the tool precisely and evenly along a definite path, removing all that it encounters—like spinning wood.

- Practice stopping in mid-cut by easing pressure so that the edge is barely in contact with the wood. In this position, the bevel still rubs while the edge produces light, fluffy shavings. Then proceed and stop again. Soon you should be able to withdraw the tool and return it to exactly the same position. As you do this, practice bringing the bevel shoulder in contact with the wood first and letting it rub. Next, gradually rotate and adjust the angle of the edge to pick up the cut. Move the tool into the wood slowly with precise control. Whenever you succeed in producing a good shaving and leaving a smooth surface, try to repeat the action. Do it over and over until you are confident you can make the same cut at will. Once you've done that, build on your one basic cut.

Learning what the tools can and should do isn't easy. When can a sharp tool be sharper? What is an acceptable finish from a tool? Such questions can only be answered through experience, but when difficulties arise, ask yourself:

- Does the tool need sharpening?
- Is it the wood—difficult grain or a foreign particle (silica, wire, or a nail)?
- Could the tool be used differently with better results?
- Would another tool be better?
- Is it me? In which case, keep practicing. Or go for a walk and try again later. Everyone has off days.

5 MEASURING

YOU NEED TO MEASURE all sorts of things at many stages in woodturning. The most common occasions are finding centers, marking out spindles, and gauging various diameters, depths, and wall thicknesses. Whenever possible, I prefer to rely on my eye and sense of touch. It's quick and I feel it lends spontaneity and vigor to my turnings; the work flows rather than proceeds in fits and starts. But it's a good idea to check yourself every now and then with instruments, especially in the beginning, to avoid drifting into patterns of error. Where precise measurements are essential, for example, when turning chair spindles or fitting mirrors or lids to boxes, I look for quick, simple methods that limit my margin of error.

I use an assortment of rulers and squares, inside and outside calipers, vernier calipers and dividers, plus a few small gouges and drill bits mounted in handles for establishing depths. You won't need all of these to begin with, just a couple of pairs of dividers and inside and outside calipers, vernier calipers, and some rulers—and you needn't spend a lot of money on them.

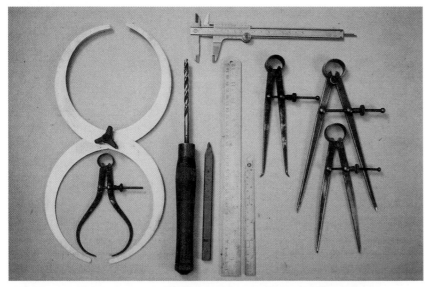

A few measuring tools are all you need to get started. Your basic kit should include (right to left): dividers, internal calipers, vernier calipers (top), rulers, pencil, depth drill, and external calipers. The double-ended calipers are useful for bowls and hollow forms.

Centering Blanks

It's important to center blanks on the lathe carefully to reduce vibration and the amount of waste wood that will be removed. Where a square section will remain, as on the ends of a spindle, an accurate center is essential or the finished piece will look unbalanced. If large turnings are mounted off-center, they may loosen fixings or

(FAR LEFT) **To locate the center of square-section stock, draw diagonal lines between opposite corners. (LEFT) If a corner is missing, draw lines parallel to and equidistant from the sides, then draw diagonals between the corners of the resulting square.**

even fly off the lathe. Your first task before mounting any object on the lathe for centerwork or facework is to find its center.

CENTERWORK

On square-section blanks, draw diagonals between opposite corners and center the piece on the lathe at the intersection of the lines, as shown in the photo above left. If the corners of a piece of wood are missing, draw lines parallel to and equidistant from the sides, as shown in the photo above right. Then draw diagonals between the corners of the resulting interior square. If the sides of an equilateral polygon are the same length, you can also draw lines between opposite corners as described for square blanks.

Once the work has been mounted between centers, the accuracy of its mounting can be checked in one of several ways. The quickest is to move the tool rest in parallel and very close to one corner of the blank and rotate the blank by hand, checking that the gap between the blank and the tool rest is the same along each corner. Another way is to move the tool rest back so that there is no danger of it touching the blank. Then start the lathe and touch a fine,

A circle marked on end grain shows how far off-center a blank is mounted.

It's important to center blanks on the lathe carefully to reduce vibration and the amount of waste wood that will be removed.

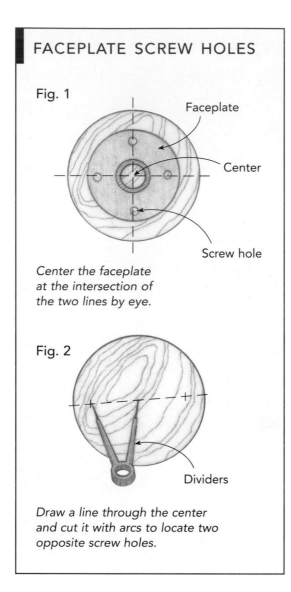

FACEPLATE SCREW HOLES

Fig. 1

Faceplate

Center

Screw hole

Center the faceplate at the intersection of the two lines by eye.

Fig. 2

Dividers

Draw a line through the center and cut it with arcs to locate two opposite screw holes.

FACEWORK

Locating the center of a blank for a screw chuck is uncomplicated if you use dividers or compasses to scribe a circle on the wood before cutting it. The center point of the divider or compass leaves a dot at center. So to mount a blank on a screw chuck, all you need is a pilot hole drilled at the center to accept the single screw.

To locate a standard faceplate accurately on a large blank, draw two lines intersecting at right angles at the center of the blank, then line them up in the screw holes, as shown in Fig. 1 in the illustration at left. (Most faceplates have four symmetrical holes.) Because my standard faceplates have hollow centers, I can see the center mark and align the faceplate pretty accurately by eye without drawing any lines.

Alternatively, scribe a circle the diameter of your faceplate when you mark out the blank. Align the faceplate within that circle and mark or drill the pilot holes with the faceplate in position.

A third way is to draw a line through the center of the blank and cut this with arcs to locate two opposite screw holes in the faceplate, as shown in Fig. 2 in the illustration at left.

With practice, your eye should develop so that you can pinpoint the center of a blank with reasonable accuracy without measuring.

hard pencil against the end grain, marking as large a circle as possible on the wood (see the bottom photo on p. 87). Stop the lathe and check how the circle is centered in the square.

If one of these checks reveals inaccurate mounting, it's simple to adjust the blank to the correct position. If you use the tool rest as a steady for your left hand, you can move the work slightly in any direction with ease while you adjust the tail-center tension with your right hand.

Marking Out Spindles

Where a square section is to remain on a spindle, it is easier to mark it out before mounting the blank on the lathe. Lay out a pattern or the spindle to be copied alongside the squared blanks. Then, using a try square, mark or scribe the crucial points on one face of the blank. I mark corners, groove centers, cove sides, and the bases of beads. When the blank is spinning on the lathe, a clear line drawn on one face will appear as a line around the spindle.

You can also lay out spindles turned to the correct diameter using a marking batten while the wood spins on the lathe, which is generally more accurate (see the center and bottom photos at right). For reference points, cut V-grooves on the batten with a pocketknife. Place the batten on the tool rest, and use a pencil or awl in the V-grooves to scribe lines on the job.

A variation of this spindle-marking technique involves a batten with nails protruding in place of the V-grooves. This method requires an accurately roughed cylinder for all the nail points to touch the surface at the same time, so it works best for short lengths of up to 12 in. (305mm). The notched batten allows more margin for error and is a less exacting approach.

Outside Diameters

Once the blank has been centered and mounted on the lathe, you are ready to begin turning. As work proceeds, you will frequently need to determine outside and inside dimensions or thickness. This can be done with calipers, dividers, rulers, and templates.

OUTSIDE CALIPERS

To establish small diameters, set the calipers to the specific diameter required and hold them around the rotating wood using your upper hand while your lower hand copes with the tool (see the top photo on p. 90). Pull the calipers gently against the cut surface until they pass over. The calipers are flexible, which allows them to pass over a diameter fractionally larger than their setting (this provides a built-in margin of error).

When you simply want to measure an outside diameter to see what you've got, rest the calipers horizontally on top of the wood while it's stationary and adjust the screw until they slip over the wood (see the center photo on p. 90).

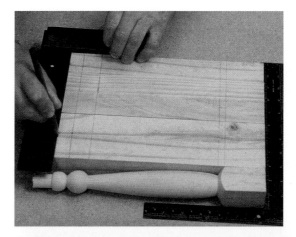

It's easier to mark out a set of spindles all at once.

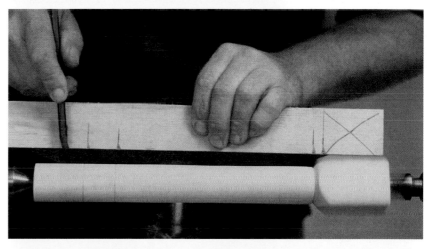

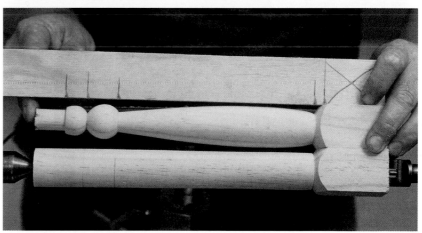

(TOP) A marking batten can be used to mark spindles on the lathe. The V-grooves at each pencil mark locate the pencil or marking awl used to mark the groove centers and bases of beads. (BOTTOM) This photo shows the relationship of the finished spindle to the batten and part-turned blank.

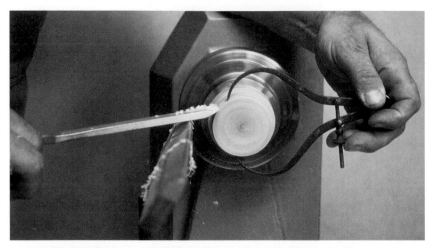

To establish a diameter, pull the calipers against the cut surface until they pass over.

To measure a diameter, rest the calipers horizontally on top of the wood and adjust the screw until they slip over.

Never push calipers directly over spinning wood. They will often catch, can break, and you might get hurt.

Because calipers are springy, never try to push them on over revolving wood (as shown in the bottom photo at left) because the arms will catch and bend and you could get hurt.

A good way to learn to use calipers properly is to rough-down hundreds of blanks to fit a chuck or to do some other repetitious job where the odd mistake doesn't matter too much.

TEMPLATES

Where absolute accuracy is essential (for example, when turning a spindle tenon to fit a drilled hole), use a template to avoid the possibility of the caliper jaws flexing or the adjustment screw coming loose. For production runs of hundreds or thousands of the same item, make a template from a hard material such as steel or very hard hardwood. Round the corners of the template jaws to lessen the likelihood of a catch as you place the template against the revolving wood (see the illustration on the facing page). For short runs, you can make a template quickly by drilling a hole the size of the desired spindle in a scrap of ⅜-in.- (10mm) thick hardwood and cutting across the diameter of the hole. Hold this template against the wood as you turn until the spindle fits the semicircle, as shown in the photos at left on the facing page.

An old production trick for cutting small centerwork to a precise diameter is to sharpen the top jaw of a wrench and round the bottom jaw. The top jaw cuts like a parting tool, while the bottom rubs until the wood fits between the two (see the photo at right on the facing page). This technique is useful for cranking out large numbers of standard-sized dowels or tenons.

VERNIER CALIPERS

Vernier calipers are very useful for measuring inside and outside diameters of small work quickly and precisely. Their inside and outside jaws lie on opposite sides of a calibrated central

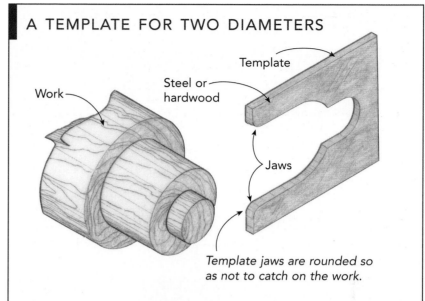

A TEMPLATE FOR TWO DIAMETERS

Template

Steel or hardwood

Work

Jaws

Template jaws are rounded so as not to catch on the work.

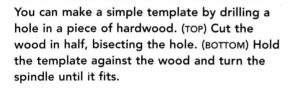

You can make a simple template by drilling a hole in a piece of hardwood. (TOP) Cut the wood in half, bisecting the hole. (BOTTOM) Hold the template against the wood and turn the spindle until it fits.

An old production trick is to sharpen the top jaw of a wrench so it cuts like a parting tool, while the rounded bottom jaw rubs until the wood fits in between.

shaft and move simultaneously. This makes vernier calipers ideal for jobs such as fitting a ferrule on a tool handle or ensuring one box will fit inside another as with the nesting boxes shown on p. 92. The inside jaws measure the inside diameter, while the outside jaws gauge the diameter of the flange that is being turned to fit it. Round over the edges of the jaws so they won't grab the spinning wood (see the right photo on p. 92).

Nesting Boxes

The smallest box was made first so that the next could be made just large enough for it to fit inside. The slightly different profiles create a more interesting group.

MATERIAL: Tasmanian blackwood

SIZE: 4 in. (100mm) diameter (largest)

Vernier calipers can be pushed over spinning wood provided the tips of the jaws are slightly rounded.

Inside Diameters

Several different kinds of calipers may be used to take inside measurements. Which tool you need is determined by the size and shape of the work and the degree of accuracy required. Turn the lathe off to measure inside diameters because the caliper points are certain to catch, spin around, and snap together, possibly with your fingers pinched between. It hurts.

The bent points on the screw-adjusted inside calipers can be inserted through a small opening to measure a wider space inside. The spring allows them to be squeezed together for withdrawal and then expanded for an exact measure of an internal diameter. I find them particularly useful for making box lids when parallel sides are essential for a good suction fit. On deeper hollows where the adjustment screw cannot fit, you can use the inside/outside calipers shown in the illustration on the facing page, but these are good only in situations where the internal diameter narrows from the opening.

CALIPERS

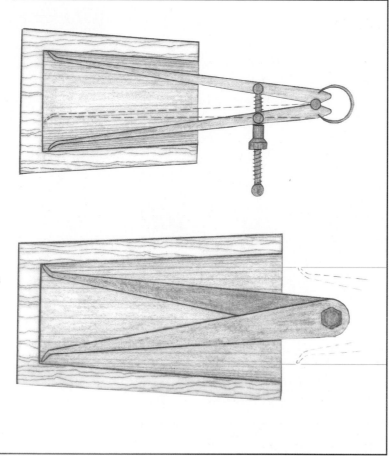

Inside Calipers

Spring-adjusted calipers will retain an internal measurement when they are withdrawn.

Inside/Outside Calipers

Inside/outside calipers are good for deeper work where the inside diameter is no larger than the rim.

Diameters on a Face

If you use the modern self-centering chucks, you will need to know how to mark a diameter on a face quickly and accurately using dividers because you will be constantly setting diameters to fit the chuck jaws.

Keep your divider points sharp by touching them up on a grinder occasionally and set them to the exact diameter required. Position the rest slightly below center height. Center the dividers by lightly touching the revolving wood with the left point so that the circle it makes lines up with the right point. In the top right photo on p. 94, the left point is too far left, placing the right point left of the line. I need to move the left point half the distance that separates the right point and the line in order to

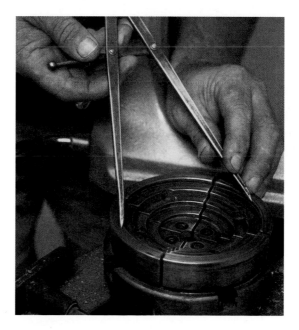

To measure a diameter, as on this step-jaw chuck, use your finger to align and hold one point firmly against the jaw while you adjust the dividers and watch the other point. It's difficult to watch both points at once.

Multitude of Bowls

Each of these little bowls has a foot that had to be measured. The fastest way is by using dividers.

MATERIALS: Gidgee,
African blackwood,
Tasmanian myrtle,
mulga, cocobolo,
Macassar ebony,
sally wattle, dead
finish, myall, yarran

SIZES: 2 in. to 6 in. (50mm
to 150mm) diameter

(TOP) To lay out a diameter, eyeball the points equally from center, then mark a line with the left point. (BOTTOM) If the line doesn't align with the right point, move the left point half the distance between the right point and that line. If the line is to the right of the right point, move the left point to the right also.

You can mark a diameter (here 200mm, or approximately 8 in.) using a pencil and ruler.

have both points equidistant from the center and in the same groove (see the center right photo on the facing page). A straight line drawn between them will pass through center.

With practice, you will be able to align the two points in a few seconds with only one or two adjustments, which makes this a valuable production technique. Be careful not to let the right-hand point touch the wood because the upward rotation of the wood on the right-hand side can grab the point and carry it around to meet the left point—you won't want your finger in the way. This is the best way to mark a chuck diameter for a bowl foot, and I have dividers permanently set for most of my chucks.

Where the diameter is greater than the maximum extension of your dividers, work from a radius instead of the diameter. Measure the diameter and halve it to get the radius. Set the dividers to the radius and place the right point at the center. (Remember that if the point makes a ring on the revolving wood, you are off-center.) Proceeding slowly, take care not to touch the work to the right of center. Once the right point is centered, bring in the left point to mark the diameter.

You can use a ruler to mark a diameter in much the same way as with the dividers. Measuring with a ruler is based on a radius laid out from the center (see the bottom photo on the facing page).

Inside Depths

It is often important to know exactly what depth a hollow is or will be. Before I hollow, I use a ¼-in. (6mm) drill bit mounted in a handle (see the illustration on p. 51) to drill a hole to establish the desired depth and then work my cuts down to that point. I have numerous marks on the drill to help me gauge the depth, so I need to keep a sharp eye on the one I'm using.

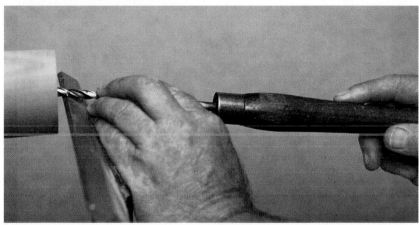

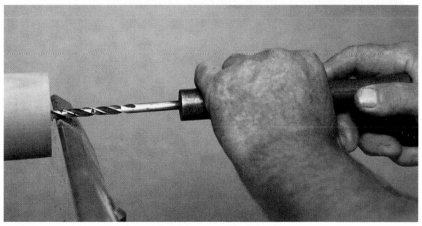

(TOP) To drill a depth hole, first cut a small V to get the drill started. (CENTER) Then rest the drill bevel on the V cut. (BOTTOM) Bring the drill parallel to the lathe axis and push into the wood.

(TOP) To mark a depth, hold the pencil at the bottom of the opening and position your thumb on the rim. (BOTTOM) Using your thumb as a stop, position the pencil outside and roll it forward to make a mark. Always mark the exact depth so you know exactly where it is.

Always mark the exact depth, then work in relation to that point.

To get the drill started accurately, I make a small V at center using either a small gouge or the long point of a skew chisel (see the top photo on p. 95). Then I present the drill bevel to the V, bring the drill blade parallel to the lathe axis, and push the tool into the wood to the desired depth (see the center and bottom photos on p. 95).

The drill doesn't have to touch the rest in this operation, but the rest is handy to get started. When the tool is centered it goes in easily, guided by the V at the first part of the hole. If the drill is not parallel to the lathe axis, it's difficult to push in and jumps about all over the place.

This action is quicker and simpler than it sounds, but if the depth is more than 1 in. (25mm), complete the cut in a series of pushes, pulling the drill out most of the way after each thrust to clear the shavings. Don't push long or hard because the end of the tool and the shavings can get hot very quickly and it's easy to burn your fingers.

There are two ways of transferring an internal depth to the outside. The quickest method is to rest a pencil at the bottom of the opening while you position your thumb at the rim (see the top photo at left). Keep your thumb rigidly in place, and lay the pencil along the outside of the work with your thumb at the top of the opening, then roll the pencil forward to mark the work as shown in the bottom photo at left. This method is especially good on small center-work and can be used with the lathe running.

The second way, which is slower but more accurate, is to stop the lathe and measure the depth with a ruler. Whichever method you use, beware of a common trap. Many people are tempted not to mark the precise depth but to add a bit, especially when making boxes or goblets, which are hollowed before the outside is shaped. This is a bad practice. If you add a bit to ensure plenty of material, you lose track of exactly where the bottom of your hole is and you have no definite point to which to relate

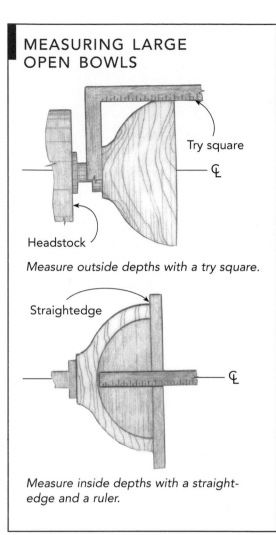

MEASURING LARGE OPEN BOWLS

Try square

C̶L̶

Headstock

Measure outside depths with a try square.

Straightedge

C̶L̶

Measure inside depths with a straight-edge and a ruler.

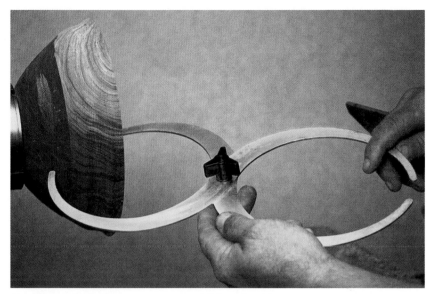

Double-ended calipers are essential for checking wall thickness accurately when the wall is thinner than the rim width.

subsequent profiling cuts. Be precise. Always mark the exact depth, then work in relation to that point.

To measure the internal depth of a large bowl, place a straightedge across the rim of the bowl and measure down from it to the bottom (see the illustration above). Then you can decide if you need to hollow further or if you're already pushing your luck by having gone deeper than intended.

Wall Thickness

Double ended calipers are the most convenient way of checking wall thickness. These tools come in a variety of shapes to enable you to get into all kinds of unlikely places. Always use these with the lathe turned off.

When I turn very thin bowls (often using green wood that is warping as I turn it), I don't have time to stop and use calipers. Instead I gauge thickness using a strong light close to the bowl wall. This works well with most pale timbers, especially if still green, but not at all with dark woods.

Shortcuts

It is possible to waste a lot of time and energy fiddling about with measuring tools. Working commercially, I save time by limiting time spent measuring, particularly once an object is on the lathe. I prefer to gauge things by eye, touch, and by relating measurements to the tools I'm using. It pays to bear this in mind, especially if you design an item for production.

Salad Set

When making a set, it helps to make each bowl in exactly the same way following the same routine. If you find a better way of doing things, don't change in the middle of the set because subsequent bowls will look slightly different. (Then it won't be a matching set.)

MATERIAL: Casuarina

SIZES: Side bowls: 8 in. by 3 in. (200mm by 75mm); main bowl: 16 in. (405mm) diameter

Some time ago, it occurred to me that the antique spindles I was copying for restoration work had certain common characteristics: Beads were the same size and spaced in multiples of tool widths. Even if this was not the intent of the old chair bodgers, it is certainly mine now. If I design a spindle with grooves and beads turned out of a square blank, I'll mark as few lines as possible on the blank. Only the square shoulders are actually laid out from a pattern. All other distances are a chisel-width, or a portion thereof, apart.

But won't the spindles vary? Yes, as will almost everything handmade, but that difference will be difficult to discern when the spindles are eventually fixed in place.

I cut my bowl blanks accurately on a bandsaw, then turn them to the largest possible diameter. This technique means there will be variations. For example, in production 6-in.-(150mm) diameter bowls might vary by as much as ⅛ in. (3mm) in diameter, but they will still be quite similar and probably blend much better with a previous batch than if I had tried to make them exactly the same. If I want to make a set of six identically shaped bowls, they'll require more precision and individual measuring.

If you need to make thousands of tenons the same size, it would make sense to use a spur drive to match the diameter of the tenon. Simply turn the wood to the diameter of the drive—without using measuring tools at all. There are hundreds of ways of saving time and effort like this, and most of them develop when boredom sets in and you're forced to do something about it.

CHAPTER

6 CENTERWORK

IN CENTERWORK, THE GRAIN of the wood is parallel to the rotational axis of the lathe. The term can be misleading, however, because centerwork jobs are not necessarily turned between two centers. While objects such as lace bobbins, rolling pins, banister spindles, and newel posts are turned between a spur drive and a tail center, items such as boxes and eggcups must be held only at the drive end so the other end can be hollowed.

The straighter the grain, the easier the wood is to work and the smoother the surface you can obtain directly from the tool. Short grain, which runs at a tangent or right angle to the axis, is difficult to cut cleanly and accurately. It is especially awkward to cut with a skew chisel, which is the main centerwork tool. Because short grain is structurally very weak, you should avoid it for long or slender work.

Consider the nature of wood: a bundle of long fibers, all running in much the same direction. The best and the cleanest cut results from slicing those fibers supported by other fibers—a technique often referred to as cutting with the grain. Cutting in the opposite direction, or against the grain, results in a torn surface because each fiber being cut is not fully supported by its neighbors. Keep the edge cutting

at around 45° to the oncoming wood for a shearing cut.

A scraping cut, with the edge parallel to the grain, will leave a torn surface, as the cutting edge levers lengths of fiber from the bundle. If you proceed gently, you might get away with a scraping cut on fine-grained hardwoods, but it is better to learn the shearing cuts. By contrast, scrapers often produce the best surface on end grain, when each fiber is well-supported by others. A delicate scrape on the end grain of many hardwoods leaves a glasslike finish.

In this chapter, I will explain the essential centerwork cuts and lead you through a series of exercises from which you can learn them. Within the chapter are three projects that give you an opportunity to put these skills to work. I encourage you to practice the exercises seriously because they will enable you to develop your technique and give you the confidence you'll need to approach the projects. Don't think of your results as successes or failures. It is experience you are after, and everything you turn will be a step in the right direction.

You will usually learn more from your failures than from your successes. You may find it useful to refer back and forth between the descriptions of tool usage to the exercises and

Tower Series

These boxes have threaded lids and small containing spaces designed to hold rings and small jewelry. They were inspired by Irish and Middle Eastern towers.

MATERIAL: Tasmanian blackwood
SIZE: 3½ in. (90mm) diameter

the project photo essays as you turn your way through this chapter. Refer to chapter 3 for further explanation of the types and shapes of tools available and how to grind their edges. If you still feel vaguely uncomfortable, review chapter 4 for a better understanding of how to approach the lathe and control leverage. But in the end, remember that there is no substitute for practice.

For these exercises you will need a 1-in. (25mm) roughing gouge, a ½-in. (13mm) shallow (spindle) gouge, and a ¾-in. (19 mm) skew chisel.

External Shaping

The cleanest cuts come from gouges and skew chisels shearing across the grain, and you can turn almost any spindle shape you want using these tools (see the illustration on the facing page). I use gouges to rough-down square sections to round and to cut coves. Otherwise, I favor a skew chisel, which gives me a superior finish faster and with less effort. The choice is a matter of personal preference—many turners use only gouges and still get satisfactory results. Parting tools, which peel the wood like a rotary veneer knife, are used at 90° to the axis to establish diameters or to cut finished work off the lathe. With a few exceptions, I feel that scraping techniques should be employed for external centerwork only when all else fails, usually on twisted grain or knots.

CHOOSING THE RIGHT GOUGES

Most shallow gouges are useful at some point in centerwork. Heavy 2-in. (50mm) gouges rough-down large square sections to round, while smaller ⅛-in. (3mm) gouges cut tiny coves and areas of twisted grain that are difficult to work with a skew chisel.

Square-ground gouges (see the illustration on p. 47) are commonly used for roughing-down—their shape allows you to use all of the edge (although not at one time)—and for fine cutting

EXTERNAL SHAPES AND TOOLS

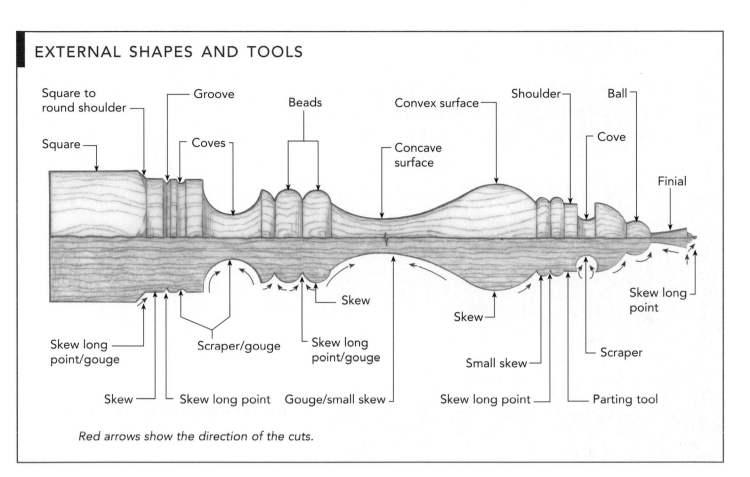

Red arrows show the direction of the cuts.

of smooth cylinders and tapers. To cut coves or beads, you'll want a long, symmetrical fingernail edge (see the bottom right photo on p. 57), with no corners to prevent you from getting into tight spots. As a guide, I suggest the following tools for roughing-down squares to round:

- For work less than 1 in. (25 mm) in diameter: ½-in. (13mm) to ¾-in. (19mm) standard gouge or skew chisel.
- For work 1 in. (25mm) to 2 in. (50mm) in diameter: 1-in. (25mm) to 1⅜-in. (35mm) standard gouge or 1-in. (25mm) to 1½-in. (38mm) skew chisel.
- For work 2 in. (50mm) to 4 in. (100mm) in diameter: 1-in. (25mm) to 1⅜-in. (35mm) gouge.
- For work above 4 in. (100mm) in diameter: 2-in. (50mm) long-and-strong gouge.

Refer to the speed chart on p. 102 for all centerwork projects.

BASIC GOUGE TECHNIQUES

When turning the cylinders, coves, and beads in the following exercises, ensure that your upper hand is always in contact with the rest. If the wood starts to chatter or flex as it becomes thinner, hold your hand behind it to equalize the pressure of the tool (see pp. 78–79). Set the rest parallel to the work and about ¼ in. (6mm) above center height. By holding the tool rigidly on the rest with your upper hand as you move it along the rest to make your cut, you can keep the cutting edge in the same plane. The rest acts as a reference point, or jig, for the tool edge.

Exercise: Make a smooth cylinder, without bumps and dips. Select a piece of wood between 8 in. (200mm) and 10 in. (255mm) long and

Centerwork Speeds for Even-Grained Blanks

DIAMETERS	LENGTHS					
	6 in. (150mm)	12 in. 305mm)	18 in. (460mm)	24 in. (610mm)	36 in. (915mm)	48 in. (1,220mm)
½ in. (13mm)	2,500	2,100	1,500	900	700	700
2 in. (50mm)	2,000	2,000	1,500	1,250	700	700
3 in. (75mm)	1,750	1,250	1,000	900	700	700
4 in. (100mm)	1,250	900	700	700	700	700
5 in. (125mm)	1,000	900	700	700	700	700
6 in. (150mm)	900	700	700	700	700	700

The figures in this chart are expressed in rpm. For safety, unevenly grained or unbalanced blanks should be started at half these speeds.

Scooping cuts using a 1-in. (25mm) deep-fluted roughing gouge reduce the square section blank to round.

Don't push the tool hard against the wood:

Let the wood come to the tool.

about 2 in. (50mm) to 3 in. (75mm) square. Ensure that the grain is straight, without knots or splits, and runs the length of the piece. Close-grained softwood or green limbwood are ideal. Mount and center the blank between a drive and tail center (see the top and center photos on p. 24), and check that it rotates without obstruction. Be sure that the tailstock is wound in tightly. Adjust the lathe speed to no more than 1,500 rpm to begin.

Start with a 1-in. (25mm) square-ground roughing gouge. The angle of the tool to the wood is dictated by a combination of personal preference, the precise shape of the gouge, and the angle of the gouge bevel. I generally use the roughing gouge almost square to the axis and angled up about 10°.

Rough-down the cylinder in two stages. First, reduce the blank to a rough cylinder, working from one end to the other in a series of short, scooping movements (numbered 1-13 in the top illustration on the facing page, then make a couple of passes the length of the job (cut 14) to refine the shape. Never start roughing cuts in the middle of a blank because you risk a whole

ROUGHING-DOWN A CENTERWORK BLANK

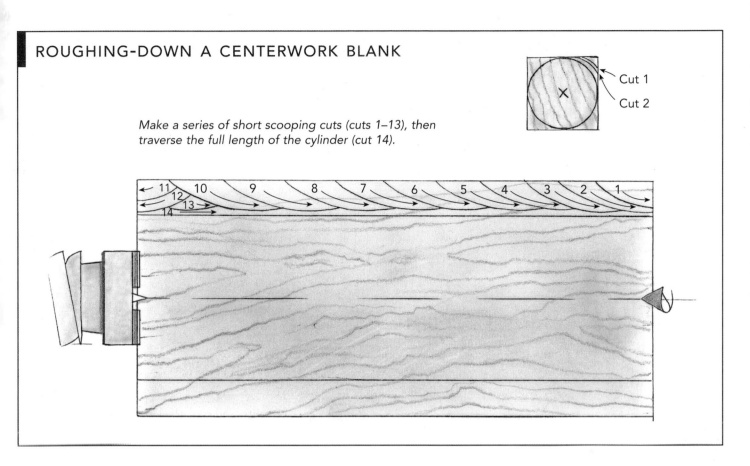

Make a series of short scooping cuts (cuts 1–13), then traverse the full length of the cylinder (cut 14).

Cut 1
Cut 2

corner splintering away or more if the grain is not absolutely straight.

In the photo on the facing page, I use a deep-fluted roughing gouge rolled slightly in the direction I'm cutting (which is to the right). This is a peeling cut, where the portion of the edge cutting lies parallel to the grain and axis. The bevel rubs the wood as the edge pivots into the cut. My upper hand pushes the tool forward into the cut, and I get the typical wide shaving.

Don't push the tool hard against the wood: Let the wood come to the tool. The bevel should rub the wood but not be forced against it. Beware of pushing the tool forward too rapidly and into the shaded area as shown in the illustration at right. Apply your power to controlling leverage. As you start to remove the corners of the blank, you develop portions of a cylinder. When there is no wood to cut, the tool

TURNING SPACE

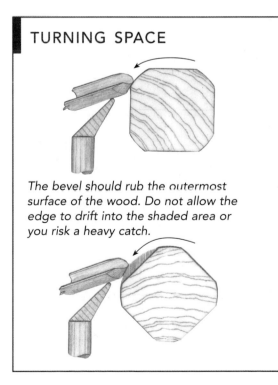

The bevel should rub the outermost surface of the wood. Do not allow the edge to drift into the shaded area or you risk a heavy catch.

A 1-in. (25mm) shallow roughing gouge is used to smooth the cylinder. I use the rest as a jig, keeping my forefinger firmly against it as my thumb pushes the tool to the right.

must be moved cautiously forward so that as the next corner comes around, the edge takes a fine shaving as the bevel rubs the cylinder surface again. When you turn a spindle with a square section left at both ends, you'll have to be able to move the tool along a definite path, turning space as well as wood. You'll develop that skill while roughing square section blanks to round.

As you make the scooping cuts, proceed down the length of the work. In the photo on p. 102, the scooping movements are made to the right, and after each one the tool moves down the rest to the left about 2 in. (50mm) to begin the next cut. The final scooping cut is made to the left, off the other end of the cylinder (see cuts 11 and 12 in the top illustration on p. 103). Try to avoid starting a cut by coming into the end of the piece from space, but rather work off the end. Because the grain runs parallel to the axis, there is a tendency for the wood to split if you cut into the end grain, and it is difficult to know exactly where the surface of the wood is in relation to the rest and the tool.

Where a cut has to be made from space into the end of a cylinder, make a trial pass just above the surface of the wood before easing the tool forward fractionally to make the cut, rather like a golfer taking a preliminary swing before hitting the ball. Try this when you feel more confident.

As the wood becomes thinner, move the rest closer to the work and drop it slightly so that the tool can still be used at the same angle. As you move the tool along the rest, keep the handle against your body with your elbows in and shift your weight from one foot to the other.

Once the blank is fairly well rounded, move the tool in long, flowing movements along the rest to true the cylinder (defined as cut 14 in the top illustration on p. 103). Beginning just inside one end of the cylinder, make two long, smoothing cuts (one in each direction), working off the ends.

Check the cylinder using a straightedge. A fairly accurate way of judging a cylinder without using measuring tools is to line up the surface with the lathe bed by eye, then check for bumps using your hand. Initially, it is more important to get smooth surfaces than a true cylinder, so if your cylinder tapers slightly from one end to the other, don't worry.

Exercise: Turn a series of identical coves using a ½-in. (13mm) shallow gouge. The gouge needs a long bevel so you don't have to swing the tool handle through too big an arc as you cut in first from one side and then the other. You should not have to change hands to turn these coves: Keep your left hand on the tool blade and the rest and your right hand on the handle near the ferrule. This exercise teaches you how to make entry cuts from space, an absolutely basic and essential skill for all woodturners.

To lay out the coves, use a pencil and a ruler to mark lines about ¾ in. (20mm) apart along the length of the smoothed cylinder. Try to keep the shoulders of the coves well defined, not rounded over.

When cutting a cove, you won't be able to rub the bevel before you start, so catches are likely if the tool is not properly presented and controlled. Use a secure grip to prevent the tool from moving on the rest, and angle the blade up about 10°. By squeezing, pushing, and pulling with the fingers and palm of the upper hand,

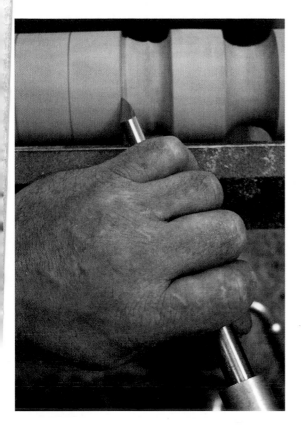

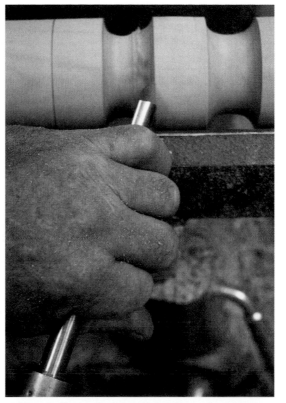

When cutting coves, the upper hand keeps the tool firmly on the rest, particularly at the start when the tool must be on its side.

(FAR LEFT) Starting a cut from the left. (LEFT) Starting a cut from the right. (BOTTOM) At the bottom of the cove, the tool gauge flute faces up.

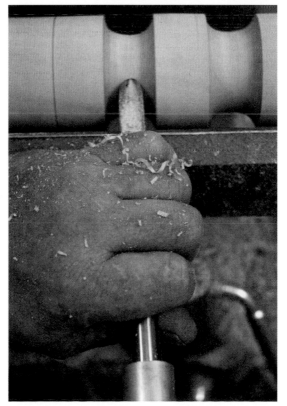

you can maintain control of the fulcrum and exert very fine control over the cutting edge.

To start the cut, the gouge must be on its side with the flute facing the center of the cove and the bevel aligned in the direction you want to cut, as shown at Fig. 1 in the illustration on p. 106 and in the photos above and at right. Raise the handle to bring the edge down into the wood, and keep the point of cut just below the center of the tool's nose. Fig. 2 in the illustration on p. 106 shows the order of cuts and how you begin at the center of the cove, then cut in from either side alternatively, widening and deepening the cove as you go. Your upper hand should barely move on the rest as the blade swings from one side to the other. Don't attempt to go down one side and back up the other in the same cut. The wood would splinter away at the top because the grain is unsupported (although you'd have a catch well before then).

CUTTING A COVE

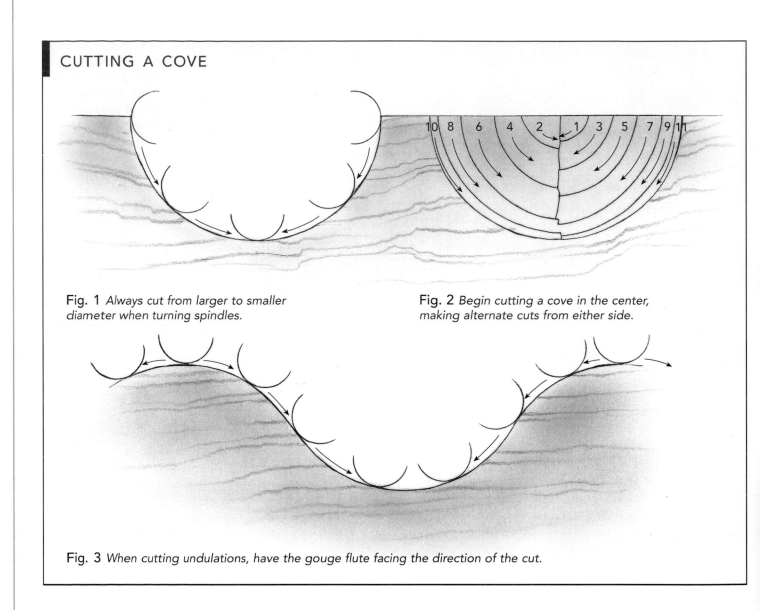

Fig. 1 *Always cut from larger to smaller diameter when turning spindles.*

Fig. 2 *Begin cutting a cove in the center, making alternate cuts from either side.*

Fig. 3 *When cutting undulations, have the gouge flute facing the direction of the cut.*

The moment the nose of the tool enters the wood the bevel begins to rub. If you fail to keep the point of cut on the lower side of the nose of the tool, it will catch because the pressure of the wood will be on an unsupported portion of the edge. As the cut progresses, ease the grip of the upper hand slightly, allowing the lower hand to roll the tool evenly until it is flute up at the bottom of the cove (see Fig. 1 in the illustration above). At the same time, push the tool across the rest into the wood, keeping the bevel rubbing on the newly cut surface.

Exercise: Undulations. Once you've achieved a cylinder with a series of coves equally spaced along its length, try rounding over the flat areas to produce an even, undulating surface. With the top of the gouge facing up, let the bevel rub the top of the cove. Then roll the tool in the direction of the cut until the edge produces a shaving, as shown in the top photos on the facing page. Again, the point of cut is just below the center of the edge.

You can use either a hand-over or hand-under grip here. Concentrate on applying your power to prevent kickbacks, and don't force the

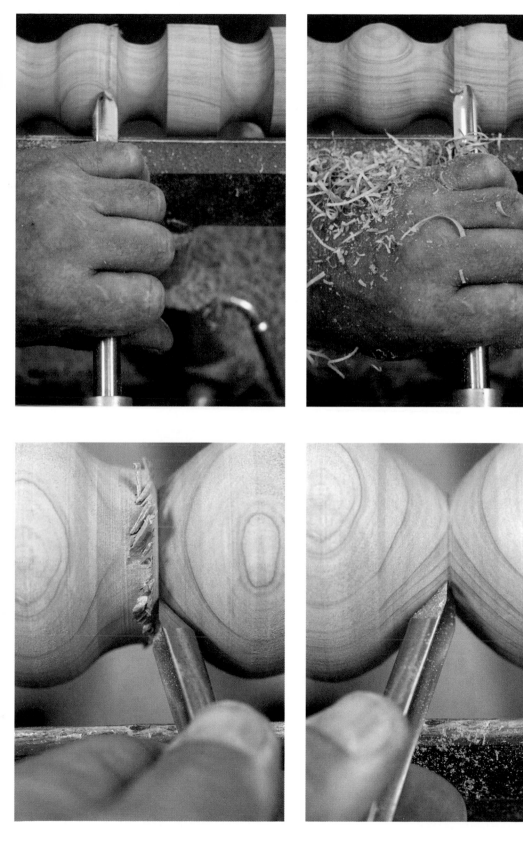

Roll the tool in the direction you're cutting, keeping the cut on the lower side of the rounded nose of the edge. Note that the upper hand barely alters position.

(FAR LEFT) To create a bead, I roll the ⅜-in. (9mm) gouge right onto its side at the end of the cut. (LEFT) The torn grain presents no problem as I cut in from the other side.

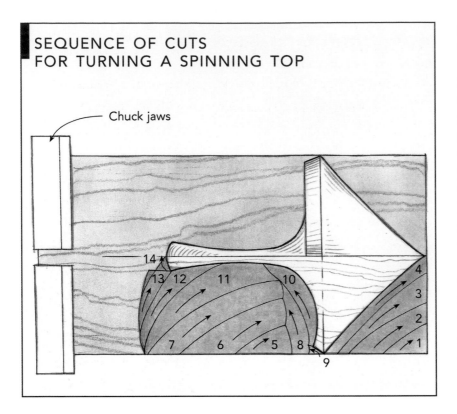

SEQUENCE OF CUTS FOR TURNING A SPINNING TOP

Chuck jaws

edge into the wood. Keep your upper hand on the rest to act as a stop that moves forward with the tool as wood is removed. As you cut down the curve, roll the gouge slightly in the direction you're cutting (so the flute faces the cove), as shown in Fig. 3 of the illustration on p. 106. At the bottom, roll it back so the flute ends up facing upward.

You can vary this procedure to make beads. Instead of rolling the tool so that it faces upward at the bottom of the cut, roll the gouge so that it completes the cut on its side. At the bottom of the curve, the point of the cut moves to the nose of the tool (see the bottom left photo on p. 107). The torn fibers are not a problem because these are removed with the next cut from the other side (see the bottom right photo on p. 107). Hold the point momentarily at the end of the cut to define the line between two beads. When you have finished a row of beads, repeat the whole cylinder-coves-beads process to create a slimmer version, and so on until the wood

snaps. You'll soon discover your limitations, which will give you something to build on.

For a more purposeful exercise, use a ⅜-in. (9mm) shallow gouge to make spinning tops out of short lengths 1½-in. (40mm) square mounted in a chuck (see the photo on p. 109 and the illustration at left). These tops are excellent for developing tool control and supporting grips, they don't waste much wood when things go wrong, and they make great little prezzies (or should I say gifts) for kids from 8 to 80 (and probably older). You know when they're well made because they spin true.

CHOOSING THE RIGHT SKEW CHISELS

The skew chisel is by far the best tool for working along the grain. It functions best on absolutely straight-grained, knot-free wood. Deft wrist movements can flick the tool from one side to another, from the long point to the short corner, shearing to a near-perfect finish. To make best use of this tool, a great deal of practice is needed, but it's all worth the effort because once mastered the skew chisel provides tremendous satisfaction.

The edge of the skew chisel is ground with a bevel on both sides and angles to a long point. All my chisels are square section with a slightly curved cutting edge. The curved edge allows me to use the chisel for a number of cuts that are nearly impossible using oval- or straight-edged chisels. More importantly, any catches are less aggressive.

I recommend using the following chisels:
- For work less than ¼ in. (6mm) in diameter: ¼-in. (6mm) to ½-in. (13mm) skew chisel.
- For work ¼ in. (6mm) to ½ in. (13mm) in diameter: ½-in. (13mm) skew chisel.
- For work ½ in. (13mm) to 2 in. (50mm) in diameter: ¾-in. (19mm) to 1-in. (25mm) skew chisel.
- For work above 2 in. (50mm) in diameter: 1-in. (25mm) to 2-in. (50mm) skew chisel.

BASIC SKEW CHISEL TECHNIQUES

Adjust the rest height so that you feel comfortable holding the tool. (With my lathe center just above elbow height, I like the handle dropped slightly below horizontal.) As the diameter of the wood reduces, you will need to lower the rest to keep the handle at about the same angle.

The tool will cut when held in a variety of positions, so your challenge lies in knowing what to strive for. The fattest shaving comes from an edge set at about 45° to the oncoming wood, while a steep edge produces the narrowest shaving (see the top photo on p. 81). When the edge is vertical, it butts right into end grain and won't cut, no matter how hard you push. End grain is tough, which is why it's used for butchers' blocks.

As with all cutting (as opposed to scraping) tools, there are two basic rules. First, keep the bevel rubbing the wood whenever possible. Second, keep your left hand in contact with the rest and tool at all times.

As the bevel rubs the wood, it acts as a jig for the next portion of the cut. If you fail to keep the bevel in contact with the wood, the edge is likely to catch or, at the very least, leave a smooth but ridged surface that is actually a very fine spiral. The bevel shoulder acts as a secondary fulcrum (besides the rest) and helps to control these kickbacks, so if the tool begins to judder, in all likelihood the bevel is not making contact with the wood.

You'll find that the skew chisel requires a lot of practice, but it is all worthwhile. In the hands of an expert, wood is removed and shaped even faster than clay on a potter's wheel. A small scoop handle, for instance, will take no more than 10 seconds to shape, while the whole external shape might take only 20 to 30 seconds. With the right straight-grained wood, the cut is clean, and different techniques flow into another as the wood curls off the tool with a rushing sound. It's a great feeling.

Spinning Tops

These tops are superb for developing your technique and general tool-handling skills using either a ⅜-in. gouge or skew chisel.

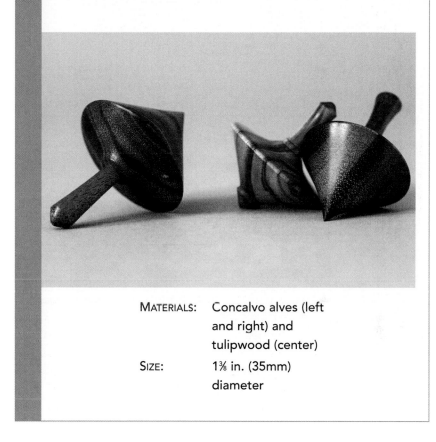

MATERIALS:	Concalvo alves (left and right) and tulipwood (center)
SIZE:	1⅜ in. (35mm) diameter

The skew chisel is by far the best tool for working along the grain.

Scoops

These utilitarian kitchen scoops paid all my basic bills in the 1970s when I made thousands of them. The bowl section is turned as a goblet, which is then cut to make the scoop. To look good, the wall needs to be of even thickness and the depth slightly more than the diameter.

MATERIALS:	Clockwise from top: English sycamore, Tasmanian blackwood, gidgee, goldiewood, radiata pine
SIZES:	¾ in. to 4 in. (20mm to 100mm) diameter

Exercise: Turning a cylinder. Begin by reducing an 8-in.- (205mm) long by 2-in.- (50mm) square blank to round, using a gouge as described on pp. 102–103. Set the rest just above center height and the speed to about 1,200 rpm. Now smooth the cylinder using the ¾-in. (19mm) skew chisel, held in a hand-over grip. You can use the skew with the long point up or down. Try both, beginning with the long point up.

When using the skew chisel, imagine a line drawn at 90° to the axis from the fulcrum through the edge (see the illustration below). If you use the lower half of the edge (to the right of the fulcral line), the downward force of the wood against the edge is easily controlled because the handle is on the other side of the fulcrum (to the left of the fulcral line), as shown in the top left photo on the facing page.

USING A SKEW CHISEL

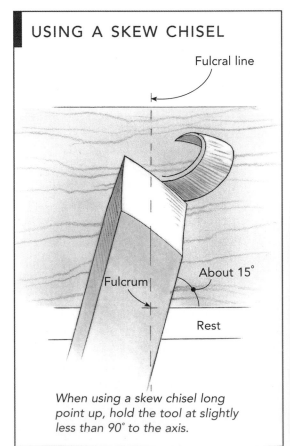

When using a skew chisel long point up, hold the tool at slightly less than 90° to the axis.

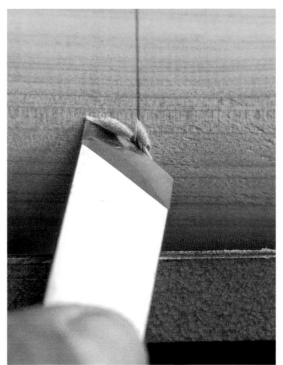

(FAR LEFT) The line indicates the position of the fulcrum. If you keep the point of the cut in the lower part of the tool and on the far side of the fulcrum from the handle, you have control of the leverage. (LEFT) If you let the point of cut drift to the upper portion of the edge on the tool handle side of the fulcrum, it will inevitably catch.

If you try to use the upper part of the edge (to the left of the fulcral line), or the long point, the tool will catch because the pressure of the wood is against an unsupported portion of the edge (see the photo above right). All catches, no matter which the tool, are a variation of this. You must always have the fulcrum beneath the point of the cut. (See also the bottom illustration on p. 74.)

When you use the skew long point up, have the blade at about 15° to the axis, as shown in the illustration on the facing page and in the photo at right. Do not place the tool flat on the rest; instead it should contact the rest only on the corner of the tool between the side and the flat. (This is an exception to the general rule that square-section tools are used flat on the rest.) The cut must be made using only the leading half of the cutting edge, ideally the portion just behind the short corner. If you use the short corner, the action is not so much a shearing as a levering-up of the wood fibers, which is rather inelegant but does leave a clean surface.

When cutting with the long point up, hold the skew at about 15° to the lathe axis and use the lower part of the edge.

To cut to the left, merely flip the tool over so the short corner is to the left. Regardless of the direction, never let the cut drift to the top of the edge near the long point because the unsupported edge will catch every time and scar the wood. If your cut leaves a ridged or slightly serrated surface without torn grain, you did not have the bevel rubbing the wood.

(TOP) **Cutting with the long point down allows you to steer the tool in the direction you're cutting. Tool chatter is reduced because pressure against the axis is minimal, and any force in the cut is absorbed by the headstock.** (BOTTOM) **If the tool is pointing in the right direction but with the long point up, it won't cut because the vertical edge butts into end grain.**

When you use the skew long point down, the tool should be pointing in the direction of the cut (see the top photo above). Have your right hand near the ferrule and the handle aligned along your forearm so the skew becomes an extension of your arm. Because the force is behind the chisel, it is easier to direct, especially along a cylinder. With the fulcrum well behind the edge, the tool is also less likely to catch than when the long point is up. As the tool cuts, any forward pressure exerted by the edge is parallel to the axis and absorbed by the drive center. If you have the tool pointing in the

right direction but are having problems cutting, the edge might be the wrong way up (long point up) as shown in the bottom photo at left, where the edge is at too steep an angle to slice the fibers.

Being right-handed, I use the skew long point down only when cutting from right to left. I find changing hands and going left to right altogether too difficult and I would not recommend it. I tend to use the skew with the long point down to rough-down most centerwork less than 2 in. (50mm) in diameter: It's an excellent thrusting cut for rapid waste removal. Take scooping cuts similar to those shown in the top illustration on p. 103, only working from left to right.

Exercise: Turn a row of grooves. Having successfully smoothed a cylinder, mark centers for the grooves 1 in. (25mm) apart. Aim to achieve a straight-sided V, about ⅜ in. (10mm) deep. A straight side will give you a goal that is easily defined and measurable.

To cut grooves, use the skew long point down so you can see what you're doing as shown in the top left photo on p. 114. Begin with the tool held at 90° to the work, and pivot the point of the skew into the center mark of the groove (see Fig. 1 in the illustration on p. 113). With the bevel aligned in the direction you're cutting, bring down the point through an arc into the wood. (Don't push it straight in as if you're using a billiards cue. The skew cuts with a softer sound and with less effort if brought through an arc.) This marks the center of the groove to which the side cuts will be made.

Next, cut from either side to the bottom of the center mark to develop the V as shown in Fig. 2 of the illustration on the facing page. (These are arcing cuts as well.) The angle of the bevel dictates the angle at which the tool lies to the wood, here about 30°. Only the bevel side and point of the tool contact the wood. Keep the edge clear, or it will catch because the pressure of the wood will be on an unsupported part of the edge.

CUTTING GROOVES

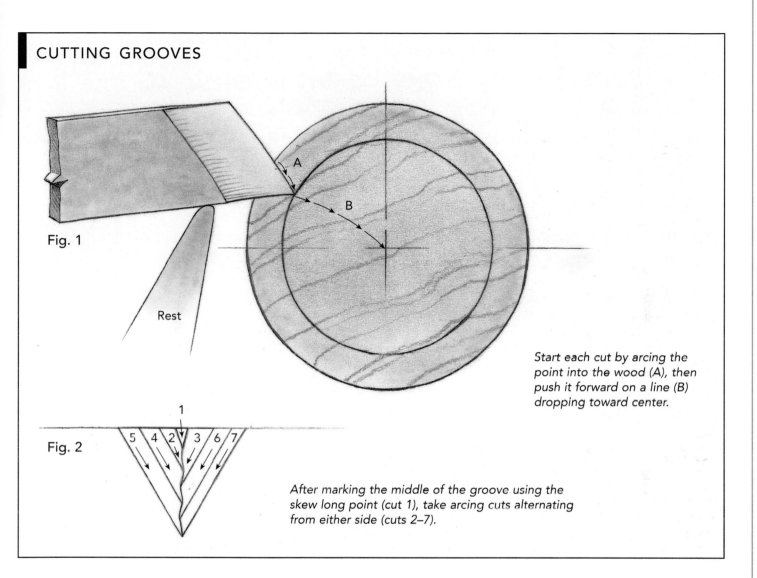

Fig. 1

Rest

A

B

Start each cut by arcing the point into the wood (A), then push it forward on a line (B) dropping toward center.

Fig. 2

1

5 4 2 3 6 7

After marking the middle of the groove using the skew long point (cut 1), take arcing cuts alternating from either side (cuts 2–7).

When cutting grooves, it is critical to keep the bevel side rubbing. If the sides of your groove are uneven or bumpy or if the tool isn't cutting properly, it is for one of two reasons. Either you are levering the point clear so it cannot cut (see the bottom left photo on p. 114), or you don't have the bevel side rubbing so the edge scores and tears the surface because it doesn't have the stabilizing contact of the bevel (see the bottom right photo on p. 114). With practice, you will sense when the bevel is rubbing and be able to align it properly each time without having to look or even think about it.

As you turn the V groove, your hands should hardly move (see the top photos on p. 115). For the entry cut, you need to pin the tool to the rest until the long point enters the wood. Then you can relax somewhat because the bevel side contacts the wood and acts as a jig for the rest of the cut.

You'll use this same technique for cutting end grain when you retain a square shoulder, except you'll also have to contend with turning space as well as wood (see the bottom left photo on p. 115 and the bottom illustration on p. 103). You need to move the edge smoothly through space regardless of what is or isn't

When cutting grooves, it is critical
to keep the bevel side rubbing.

Use the skew chisel long point down when cutting grooves.

When cutting a groove, only the bevel side and the long point of the skew chisel should contact the wood.

If you lever the long point away from the shoulder, you cannot cut anything.

If only the long point contacts the wood, you'll get a scored and torn surface.

Note that the hands barely alter position as the tool cuts one side then the other.

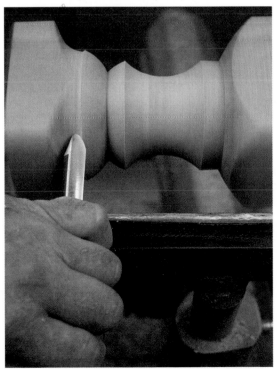

To retain a square section on a spindle, you must move the edge steadily through space regardless of what is or isn't there. (FAR LEFT) A skew long point cuts a simple square to round a shoulder. (LEFT) A ½-in. (13mm) shallow gouge cuts an ogee.

Freezing the action, we see there is little difference between the gouge-cut surface to the left and the skew-cut shoulder to the right.

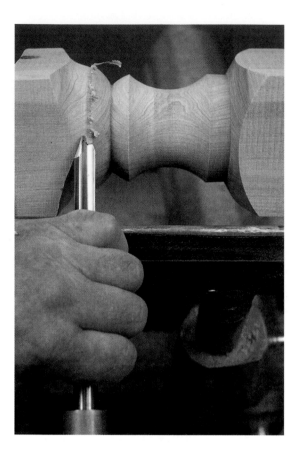

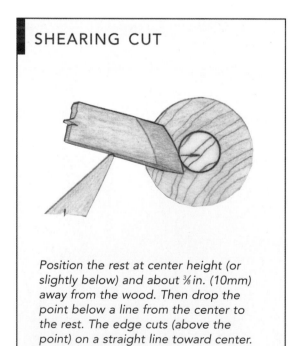

SHEARING CUT

Position the rest at center height (or slightly below) and about ⅜ in. (10mm) away from the wood. Then drop the point below a line from the center to the rest. The edge cuts (above the point) on a straight line toward center.

there. The trick is to let the wood come to the tool. Don't push the tool into the gap between the shoulders because that will break the corners. If you want a rounded shoulder, cove, or ogee as shown in the bottom right photo on p. 115, imagine you are cutting a whole bead or cove, even though you are mostly turning space. If you go steadily, the fibers should not break away on the corners.

Once you feel comfortable cutting grooves, you can learn to get an even smoother surface using the edge (rather than the long point) to turn a cone. For practice, mount a short cylindrical blank in a chuck so you can work the end grain. (You can prepare your blank between centers or in the chuck.) Making an entry cut with the edge is difficult, so take the point through an arc into the wood (as usual). Continue to raise the handle so the point of cut moves from the long point slightly up the edge, then push the tool forward. When you get this right, you'll get frilly conical petal-like shavings as shown in the top photo on p. 117. This shearing cut works well using any skew chisel on convex end grain. For flat end grain, you'll need a slightly curved skew because there's no clearance for a straight edge.

If you find yourself having difficulties with any of these techniques, forget about grooves and simply make cuts in one direction across the grain. When you achieve a satisfactory cut that feels easy and produces a good surface, repeat the action in the same place again and again. Do nothing else for 10 minutes or longer until you can do it every time.

When you've mastered one action, try it in the other direction. Then go back to the grooves. And don't be intimidated by the fact that there's a whole row to do. Just take each groove one at a time, forgetting what's to come and what's gone. Try to resist doing only a couple of grooves and instantly moving on to a bead. The best approach is to develop some expertise in one area before going on to the next.

Exercise: Turn grooves into beads using the short corner of the same skew chisel. For this exercise, first turn grooves 2 in. (50mm) apart with a center line between each. To do this, lay out the cylinder with lines 1 in. (25mm) apart, then turn grooves on every other line.

Start the cut with the tool set at about 90° to the axis and the bevel riding on what will be the top of the bead. It's very difficult to start cutting a bead with the long point down because the angle of the tool to the wood requires you to swing the handle through a wide arc, whereas using the skew long point up only involves just a roll of the wrist. Once you've positioned the tool, roll it very firmly in the direction of the cut until the short corner picks up a shaving (see the bottom left photo). Continue on to cut one side of the bead.

This technique requires the good coordination of both hands. Your lower hand rotates the

When shearing end grain, move the tool straight across the rest as you would cue a pool shot. Using the edge (rather than the long point), you should get frilly conical shavings.

(FAR LEFT) While I prefer the hand-under grip for cutting beads, a hand-over grip (LEFT) provides more support near the end of the blade when cutting left.

Spillikin Sticks

The game of spillikins, also known as pick-up sticks, is a wonderful game for kids of all ages (8 to 80+). The box is the difficult bit and should be made first so you can turn the sticks to fit. Grip the sticks at the drive end rather than mounting them between centers. The flat sections, which are cut on a sander, don't have all the beads on the same position because the sticks won't fit in the box.

MATERIAL: Cocobolo
SIZE: 7 in. (180mm) long

tool, and your upper hand moves the short corner into the wood. Your lower wrist should move in a smooth, flowing motion. The upper hand acts as a moving backstop to prevent kickback and to provide fine control while easing the tool forward with gentle pressure. The tool will move a very short distance along the rest while staying at 90° to the axis. One-half of a bead should take only a second or two. The tool should feel almost spongy on the wood, encountering little resistance and cutting cleanly.

I prefer the firm underhand grip for turning beads, but it is not that secure when cutting to the left. It offers no support behind the top of the tool, and catches are more likely. If you are having difficulties cutting to the left using the underhand grip, change to an overhand grip so your little finger is located where support for the blade is needed.

Often you'll be left with a thin frill of wood at the bottom of a bead, especially where a pair of beads meets. When removing this, it is easier to see what's happening if you turn the chisel over and use the long point as if cutting a groove. Flip the tool over and bring the bevel side in to rub the surface just cut. Use the long point to finish the bead as if you're cutting a V groove. Don't use force to remove the frill—a delicate touch is all you need.

Once you've achieved a row of beads, use the same skew chisel to reduce the spindle to a smaller cylinder. To do this, begin cutting at the top of the bead at one end of the cylinder with the long point down. Move the tool along the rest evenly, be it through space or wood. Don't allow the edge to jump forward into the spaces between the beads. This is a good opportunity to practice moving the tool evenly on a predetermined course regardless of what is or isn't there. It'll become easier as the beads are reduced in size.

When the cylinder is smooth, repeat the process, making a row of grooves first and then beads. No matter what size chisel you use, the same rules apply. The smaller the tool, the more precise your technique needs to be. I use a 5/16-in. (8mm) skew for my salt scoops, but generally you can do almost any small spindle with a 1/2-in. (13mm) tool. When each cycle is completed, do it again until the spindle breaks or, if you manage a very thin spindle, you might want to start making a set of spillikins (see the photo on the facing page). They're very good practice and make a nice heirloom. Make the box first, so you know what they'll fit into.

Once you have reduced a number of spindles to the breaking point using this cylinder-grooves-beads-cylinder process, it is sensible to move on to making something useful. I developed my skew chisel technique by making rolling pins, meat bashers, honey dippers, and knobs for window blinds or light-pull cords. These and other skill-building objects are detailed in my book *Turning Projects* (The Taunton Press, 1991). Or try the spinning tops detailed in the illustration on p. 108 and the wok stirrers shown in the photo at right.

The advantage of such objects is that they need not be identical, which is just as well when catches and general lack of tool control will probably demand an alteration to your initial concept. At first, keep your shapes simple and develop your repertoire of cuts gradually. When you make a clean cut, do the same thing again and again until you can do it every time as you want (and not as the wood or lathe dictates).

As you master each cut, go on to others. I recall that my early spindles had few rounded beads but plenty of long curves and V-shaped grooves. The rolling pins had square or conical ends that were easier to duplicate until my skill and confidence grew and I could make them rounded with buttons. Keep the lathe speed down around 1,200 rpm to start. As your confidence grows and catches become less frequent and the finish from the tool improves, raise the

Wok Stirrers

You need nonmetal spatulas for nonstick pans. Wood has to be a better choice than plastic, and hand-turned wood has to feel better than mass-produced. These stirrers are turned from wedge-shaped blanks cut to conserve material. The thin, flared blade end is held in a chuck with the fatter squared handle end supported by the tail center. This is a good skew chisel exercise. When turning the blade, there will be more air than wood, but you'll get nicely curved and radiused sides to the spatula. The fat handle fits nicely into the palm.

MATERIAL: Elm

SIZES: 8½ in. to 11 in.
(215mm to 280mm) long

VASE

For this project, you need a blank about 6 in. (150mm) long and 3 in. to 4 in. (75mm to 100mm) in diameter. The idea is to complete the lower portion of the form so it fits your chuck, then remount it for completion. One advantage of modern chucks is that you can rechuck the job and alter it if you're not satisfied with what you've made.

The chuck used here is a Vicmarc with Shark jaws. The tools are a ¾-in. (20mm) skew chisel, a ½-in. (13mm) shallow gouge, and a spear-point scraper.

1 Before truing the end grain with the gouge, make an initial cut to see how the wood will work and if the bark will stay on. This 5-in. (125mm) length of dry branchwood (mulga) has great color and contrast between the sapwood and heartwood. The end grain will be the base, so it needs to be slightly concave to sit flat.

3 Further shape the form using peeling cuts with the skew chisel.

4 Use a shearing cut to clean up the surface in preparation for the grooves.

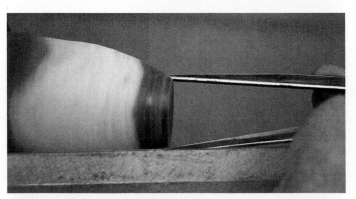

2 Because the chuck will grip on a groove, cut the curve so that the base is smaller than the gripping diameter of the chuck. The dividers burnish the wood, indicating the approximate position for the groove.

5 Cut two grooves roughly where the burnish marks are: The jaws will fit snugly over one of them. I use this technique a lot on bowls, so I am used to gauging where to put the grooves by eye. If you're not comfortable with that, you might want to measure again.

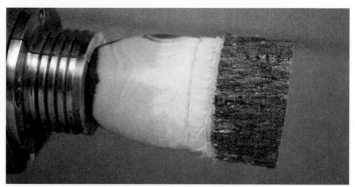

7 Rechuck the vase with the jaws fitting snugly around whichever groove fits best.

6 To complete the lower section of my vase, I detail the base by rebating the central area so the vase will sit on a rim of about ³⁄₁₆ in. (5mm). Then sand and polish the bottom half of the vase.

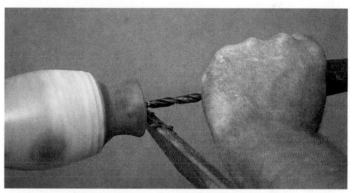

8 After some initial shaping, drill a depth hole by hand. If you want to insert a glass vase tube, just drill a hole the required size. For drills bigger than ¼ in. (6mm), mount the drill on the tail center.

9 Use the gouge to cut the inside of the rim. I prefer a simple curve here, but you can easily add some grooves using the spear-point scraper.

10 Although the gouge-cut surface is more than adequate, here I use the spear-point to shear-scrape the surface. This requires an exceedingly light touch, otherwise the vibration will leave chatter marks that might even be bad enough to be decorative. At this stage, you can hollow the form if you want. I generally make the vase with just the depth drill hole so there is plenty of weight in the base and a narrow interior space to keep the grasses I envisage in them upright.

11 Finally, complete the outside turning, then sand and polish the upper section to blend in with the lower part that was completed earlier.

If you think the form (TOP LEFT) lacks a little something, or rather has a little something too much (as I did), put it back in the chuck for modification. I thought that looked pretty good, but I still couldn't resist a further modification (BOTTOM RIGHT).

speed to as high as 1,800 rpm. When you find it reasonably easy to smooth a cylinder and to cut grooves and beads, it's time to examine several other useful functions of the skew chisel.

USING A SKEW CHISEL AS A ROTARY PEELER

By holding a skew chisel flat on the rest with the edge parallel to the axis, you can reduce a diameter drastically in an instant. This technique is especially useful when turning a goblet stem, scoop handle, or other spindle where a great deal of waste has to go quickly. It's wonderful in production.

The angle at which the cutting edge is presented to the revolving wood is crucial. Get this right and your problem may be in removing too much too quickly, with virtually no effort. Get it wrong and you lever the wood right out of a chuck just as quickly. To peel effectively, the cutting edge must be kept just below the surface of the wood. Should it drop, the action becomes a slow, heavy scrape that badly tears the grain.

As with any cutting tool, the bevel should ride the wood first. But as you bring the cutting edge down by raising the handle, you must slide the blade back across the rest slightly until the edge is just beneath the surface of the wood and producing a very fine shaving as shown in the photos above right. The moment the edge starts peeling, push the tool forward, maintaining the edge position relative to the top surface of the wood.

Deftness is required to keep the cutting edge peeling toward the center accurately. All the movement is controlled by your lower hand; your upper hand simply holds the tool on the rest. Shavings should come off the wood in a continuous paper-thin ribbon that breaks up as it leaves the tool. The surface will need to be cleaned up with a final shearing cut. This is not a technique for general use on square-section wood because the edges will splinter.

(TOP) **You can reduce a cylinder rapidly by using a rotary-peeling action. Keep the cutting edge just below the surface of the wood.** (BOTTOM) **As the edge peels, raise the handle while pushing the edge forward to maintain the relationship of the cutting edge to the wood.**

USING A SKEW CHISEL FOR PEELING AN ANGLE

This variation of the previous cut is a quick, effective way to rough-out deep V-grooves, but you will need a final shearing cut to smooth the surface. Hold the tool as if for a conventional shearing cut, with the long point leading. Raise the handle diagonally while pivoting the tool on the rest. The long point of the tool moves through an arc deep into the wood and the edge peels a thin ribbon (see the left photo on p. 124), much the same as above when the tool was held flat on the rest. Having reached the required depth, pivot the tool on its point so that the edge of the tool is moved out of the cut.

In this cut you do what you try otherwise to avoid: You cut using the point and adjacent portion of the edge, which is entirely unsupported. The wood will grab the edge given the slightest chance. You need a firm grip, and you must rotate the edge clear of disaster before the wood realizes what's happening. As with the peeling cut, deftness is required and you cannot make this cut slowly. The main power comes from the lower hand, but the upper hand adds firmness to counteract possible catches. It's a normally disastrous situation, but under control it's used to great effect.

USING A SKEW CHISEL FOR PEEL/SCRAPE CUTS

Using this cut very delicately is often the best way to deal with twisted grain on centerwork or whenever you have little margin for error and don't want to risk the grain picking-up as on a

box flange when fitting a lid. The peel/scrape is very similar to the peeling cut, only the edge is presented slightly above the center-to-rest line and below the peeling position.

You need a slight curve on the edge of the skew chisel so that you can move the point of the skew sideways into a corner without touching the surface just cut (see the photo below right). The tool must be moved in very gently to avoid tearing the grain (a vibration-free lathe is essential for such an operation). The bevel doesn't get a chance to rub and the edge strokes the surface only lightly. There should be no shavings—only fluff. Control the movement with your upper hand while your lower hand provides stability. Stand well balanced. (You might want to hold your breath for this cut as well.)

PARTING TOOL TECHNIQUES

Parting-off is the process of cutting across the grain to remove a turned piece from the lathe while it's still running. Parting tools are also used in confined spaces where a skew or a gouge

The skew chisel can be used to rotary-peel on an angle by pivoting the tool into the wood diagonally. To avoid a catch, you must be quick to rotate the edge clear at the end of the cut.

A curved edge skew is particularly useful for delicate peel/scrape cuts. Here the long point reaches into the corner without touching the rest of the surface.

cannot operate effectively or in conjunction with calipers to establish diameters in spindle work (see p 90). The tool is held at 90° to the axis so that the edge is parallel to the axis and will peel off a ribbonlike shaving in exactly the same way as a peeling skew chisel. Care must be taken not to let the edge drop too far into the wood too quickly, or it will begin scraping rather than peeling.

When parting-off small jobs, the last part has to be done with the tool held in your lower hand while your upper hand catches the piece (see the photos at right). The lathe keeps running and the work spins off into your waiting hand. Note how I keep my thumb on the rest to protect the job when it comes loose.

If a large or long job is parted-off while the lathe is still running, there is always the risk that you'll fail to catch it properly and it will bounce off the rest and be damaged. If you can stop the lathe just as you've finished cutting, this won't happen. (I can lean on the stop button or bar on my lathes, so it's possible to stop the machine at the last moment.) Try not to touch the piece until it is actually parted. The least pressure can cause the last bit of grain to spin and pull out of your finished piece.

Alternatively, you can cut in with the parting tool, leaving a slender portion between the waste and the spindle, then use a small saw to cut the work free.

While parting tools are often used to remove work from the lathe, the long point of a skew chisel leaves a cleaner surface.

When parting-off, be sure to catch the work so it is cut, rather than pulled, off the lathe.

SCRAPER TECHNIQUES

Scrapers and scraping techniques are not recommended for spindle turning or any centerwork other than end grain or hard hardwoods, where they can be used to produce complicated shapes in one pass, as on a chess piece. Scraping techniques are also generally not suitable or that efficient for roughing-down, especially on spindles. The surface obtained by using a scraper along the grain bears no comparison to what you can achieve with a good shearing cut from a gouge, let alone a skew chisel. In spindle work, scraping action tears off lengths of wood fiber, so the finish is always poor.

Scrapers can be used with better results on end grain. Many dense or oily woods, such as ebony, sandalwood, cocobolo, African blackwood, mulga, and gidgee, definitely prefer

A ½-in. (13mm) skew chisel makes an ideal scraper on box lid detail. Use only a small portion of the edge at one time. Never use it all at once.

timber—open-grained woods such as fir are almost impossible to cut cleanly on the end grain. Unseasoned wood will be easier to turn, and a small, straight branch is ideal provided it isn't split.

Be sure to always true the blank. This is a good habit to develop, and it ensures that you get rid of everything you don't want in the final object, such as saw marks from the original squared section. Even though I've been turning wood for nearly 30 years, I still take the opportunity to practice difficult cuts.

HOLLOWING END GRAIN WITH GOUGES

The best tool for hollowing end grain is a shallow ½-in. (13mm) gouge with a long bevel (about 30°) and fingernail edge. The edge should be a full curve, without any flat sections, as shown in the bottom right photo on p. 57. Adjust the rest so that the nose of the horizontal tool is at center height. You can use this tool in two ways to remove the bulk of the waste.

In the standard approach, take a series of cuts from the rim to center (cuts 1 to 5 shown in the lower half of the illustration on the facing page). Start each cut with the gouge on its side and the bevel against the end grain, then pivot the nose of the tool into the wood, rolling the tool very slightly counterclockwise for a fatter shaving as the cut proceeds.

Alternatively, there's the much faster back-hollowing technique (which I prefer), where the tool cuts on the far side of center and almost upside down—against all normal rules and expectations. I've used this method to make tens of thousands of scoops and small boxes. To shear cleanly, you need to cut from the center outward (see the illustration on p. 83).

Start the tool on its side just left of center. Instead of stopping cut 1 at center, push the tool into the center of the wood, cutting in about ⅛ in. (3mm). (Any pressure you apply here will be absorbed by the headstock.) Then

being scraped on end grain as shown in the photo above. Here, a very, very light touch can produce a glasslike surface, superior to the shearing cut of a skew chisel or gouge. But be warned that the slightest excess pressure spells disaster, with the tool often pulling lumps from the end grain.

Hollowing

You cannot hollow end grain with the work held between centers. It must be held in a chuck so the end is exposed. You can mount a drill in the tailstock and wind it into the wood to create a hollow, a method often used for boxes, scoops, eggcups, and goblets. Although this is a safe way of hollowing, it is comparatively slow. But, more important, you'll always get a poor surface (especially in the bottom) and the straight sides are uninteresting. Moreover, any spur bit will leave a mark at center. You can get a much cleaner surface much faster using gouges and scrapers.

For practice, I suggest using blanks about 6 in. (150mm) long and 2 in. (50mm) to 3 in. (75mm) square. Choose a close-grained pull your lower hand back toward your body so that the tool starts cutting on its upper left edge, moving away from center at 1 o'clock to 3 o'clock, removing wood as it revolves upward. As you pull back the handle, roll the tool slightly to the right to maintain the optimal cutting angle of 45°, remembering to keep the bevel rubbing (see the photos on p. 128). Use a hand-over grip to provide a firm backstop and fulcrum while preventing a runback. It is not possible to see what is happening most of the time while back-hollowing, especially when starting a cut at the bottom of the hole, so don't even try. You have to feel it.

The idea with the initial cut is to create a small opening, the diameter of cut 1, that will

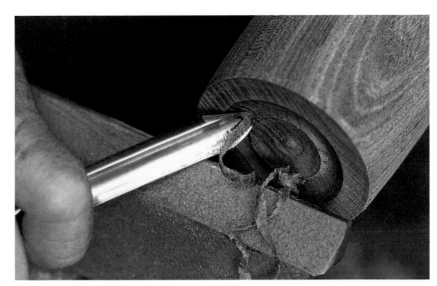

Hollowing end grain from the rim.

OPTIONS FOR HOLLOWING END GRAIN USING A ½-IN. (13MM) SHALLOW GOUGE

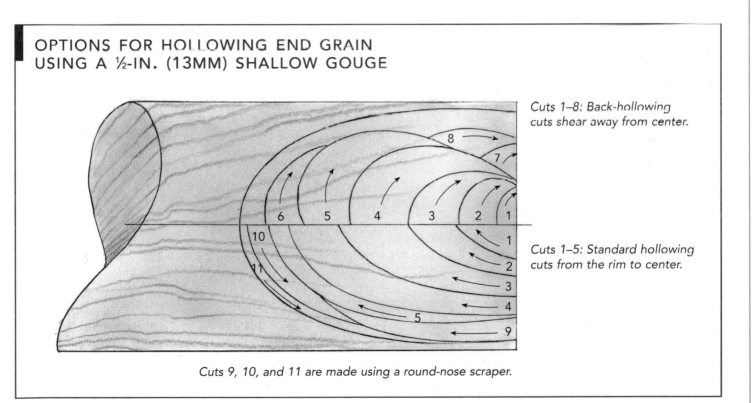

Cuts 1–8: Back-hollowing cuts shear away from center.

Cuts 1–5: Standard hollowing cuts from the rim to center.

Cuts 9, 10, and 11 are made using a round-nose scraper.

Even though I've been turning wood for nearly 30 years, I still take the opportunity to practice difficult cuts.

Start the back-hollowing near center to create a small opening.

This technique demands a fine sense of balance because the pressure put on the cutting edge must be offset precisely against the rim. Failure to do this can hook the block from the chuck, split the wood, or at least knock the block off-center. If you keep the mouth of the opening small until the internal space is hollowed, you get better leverage than if the hole were larger. It also helps you keep the tool cutting nearer to parallel to the axis, making it easier to control.

As the tool begins cutting on the far side of the hollow, it unavoidably begins to lie across the axis. If the entry hole is wide, as the edge nears the rim the tool will be cutting close to 90° to the axis, where it's very likely to catch or kick back. As you make cuts 7 and 8, the edge is likely to catch. If it does, that's probably a sign that you've gone as far as is practical with the gouge and that it's time to use the scraper.

If the rim becomes damaged and uneven, turn it true or you'll have an eccentric secondary fulcrum and cutting will be difficult. Hold the tool very firmly on the rest and gently raise the handle to pivot the edge against the rim.

From the position at the end of the cut you can perform the action in reverse (like running a video backwards), taking the edge back to the center and removing more waste as you go. The surface will not be as smooth near the bottom of the opening, where the curve sweeps back toward the center, because the tool will be cutting into end grain. But you do move a lot of wood in a hurry.

Often a central cone will develop as you hollow, and on subsequent cuts this can enlarge if you fail to locate the point of the cone accurately (which is almost unavoidable). When beginning a cut, feel for the center at the bottom of the hole, then locate the cutting edge by rolling the tool. Pull back on the handle only when you feel the edge actually cutting. Beware of rotating the tool too much and pushing the

be maintained until cuts 7 and 8 finally widen it. For the intervening cuts, you use the rim as a fulcrum and start the cuts from center (see the top photos on the facing page). Maintenance of a good fulcrum is important. In addition to the rest, you should use the rim of the opening as an additional fulcrum against which to lever the tool. Seemingly, the upward-moving wood will lift the edge, but in practice there is enough downward pressure against the blade where it contacts the rim to keep it on the rest.

Back-hollowing cuts start at center and head away at 1 o'clock to 3 o'clock.

A typical back-hollowing shaving.

tool blade clear of the rim (it should be against the rim for the entire cut).

This is not an easy technique to learn—mainly because you have to feel, rather than see, what is happening—but once mastered, this is a very rapid method of making holes. The bulk of a 2-in.- (50mm) diameter box or scoop can be removed in 3 to 4 seconds. But it is not particularly smooth, and the job is finished with scrapers.

INTERNAL SHAPING WITH SCRAPERS

Once the bulk of your hole is removed, use scrapers to finish the hollowing. I use two different scraper shapes for this process. The size used depends on the opening. Square-edge scrapers are for the sides and bottoms of cylinders (see the photo above). Scrapers ground with a long, curved left edge are for the sides and bottoms of curved hollows. To minimize vibration, I always use the biggest scrapers I can for end-grain hollowing. For practice, make two different forms: a rounded hollow and a flat-bottom cylinder, each at least 2 in. (50mm) deep. When you've turned what you consider a satisfactory hollow, break the piece in two and

A ¾-in. (20mm) square-edge scraper is used to cut a cylindrical flange in a box lid.

examine the cross section: At first it's rarely what you hope for.

For most work and woods, I find that an edge straight from a light touch on an 80-grit grinding wheel is ideal. For tough hardwoods, a honed edge is less aggressive.

Internal curved surfaces are finished using a radiused scraper (see the illustration on p. 130). Because I always work on the inboard side of the headstock, all my curved scrapers have long left-hand edges. After selecting a tool that has a

You won't obtain a good internal line jabbing at the wood with a blunt round-nose scraper.

A 1⅜-in. (35mm) round-nose scraper finishes an internal curve. Note how the thumb provides a lateral fulcrum on the side of the tool while the fingers dampen any vibration.

CURVED-EDGE SCRAPERS

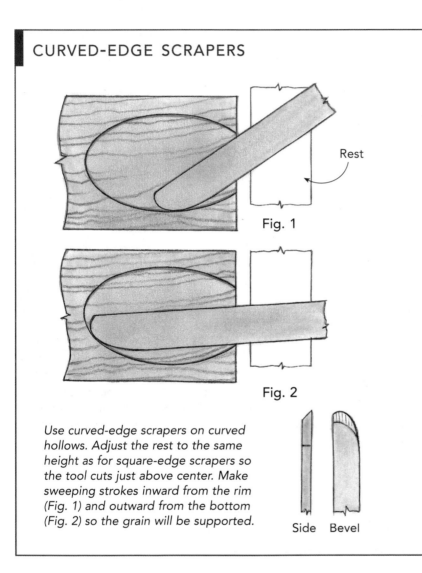

Fig. 1

Fig. 2

Use curved-edge scrapers on curved hollows. Adjust the rest to the same height as for square-edge scrapers so the tool cuts just above center. Make sweeping strokes inward from the rim (Fig. 1) and outward from the bottom (Fig. 2) so the grain will be supported.

Side   Bevel

Rest

You should get these typical shavings when hollowing end grain with a scraper.

slightly tighter radius than the curve I want to cut, I make a series of sweeping cuts, moving outward from the bottom of the hollow and inward from the rim. (In this way, the grain is supported as much as possible, as described on p. 83.) If the shape flows outward only, as in an open cup, then the cuts are made entirely from the bottom out.

Initial shaping can be forceful, but the final cuts must be light, producing only fluff. Vibration is a particular problem when cutting internal curves because tool pressure is away from center against thin and structurally weak grain. To reduce vibration, you'll need to support the work using your hand as shown in the photos above.

Cutting in from the rim, I start with the tool angled upwards as shown in the top photo at right. This has two benefits. First, there is an element of shear scraping because the edge is at an angle to the grain. The second benefit has to do with cutting a smooth curve. As the cut proceeds, I have to raise the handle to bring the edge toward center, and if I do this smoothly as I move the tool forward, I cut a smooth curve whether I want to or not. I always want to.

To cut away from center in the bottom of the hollow, start with the edge tilted down as shown in the bottom photo at right so that it cuts slightly below horizontal. Set the tool rest less than the thickness of the scraper below center height or about ⅛ in. (3mm). To cut a smooth curve across the base, all you need do is lean on the end of the handle. As the edge sweeps away from center, it automatically cuts a smooth curve as the edge moves through an arc. If you push the tool forward, you'll create a small bump, which is removed by swinging the edge through it from below as shown in the top illustration on p. 132.

Remember when scraping internal curves that flowing shapes come from flowing movements. You won't obtain a good internal line jabbing at the wood with a blunt round-nose scraper. Use a sharp tool and sweeping, light cuts, and you'll end up with a reasonably clean surface without bumps or ridges.

If you have a slightly ridged surface, a couple of swipes with coarse abrasives will smooth the surface (I use old 60-grit power-sanding discs), but they won't get rid of the bump at center.

Internal cylinders are roughed out with a gouge, then completed using a square-ground tool with a long bevel. As with all my nominally square-ground tools, the edge actually curves slightly, in this case back from the left corner. This is to avoid presenting the whole edge at once to the wood, especially 2 in. (50mm) or

The large round-nose scraper is tilted upwards to shear-cut as I begin smoothing an internal curve.

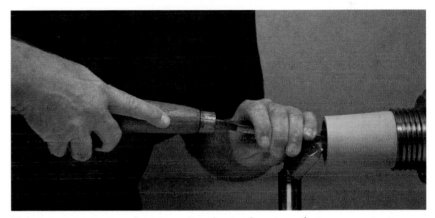

Using scrapers on end grain, raise the tool rest so that as you start a cut at center, the tool tilts down a few degrees. For a flowing internal curve, ease your elbow down on the handle and don't move the tool forward on the rest.

more away from the rest, when a heavy, damaging catch would be almost inevitable. Use about one-quarter of the cutting edge (the shaded area in the bottom illustration on p. 132).

Whenever you use a scraper to cut the long, straight wall of a deep cylinder, it is vital to set the rest high (see Fig. 3 in the bottom illustration on p. 132) so that the lower side of the tool doesn't ride against the portion just cut by the top edge. If the rest is too low and the lower side of the tool rubs (see Fig. 1 on p. 132), it

REMOVING END-GRAIN BUMPS

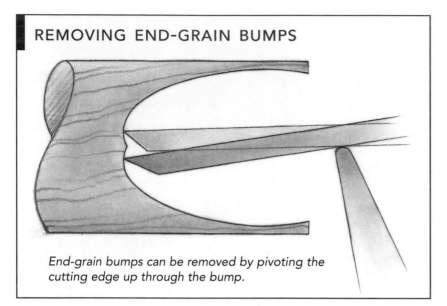

End-grain bumps can be removed by pivoting the cutting edge up through the bump.

will force the cutting edge toward the center, tapering the internal form.

Push the tool in firmly but not too fast. If you use too much pressure, the slightly brittle, hollow sound will be replaced by a vibrating, high-pitched noise, and you'll tear the end grain. It is important that your first scraping cut be accurate because the tool will be guided into the hollow by the cylindrical upper wall. (Ensure accuracy by cutting in about 1 in. [25mm] with the scraper and checking the opening with internal calipers.) You need to keep the tool horizontal in order to maintain an accurate side. If you tilt it up, your opening will be dovetailed and widen the deeper you go. If

SQUARE-EDGE SCRAPERS

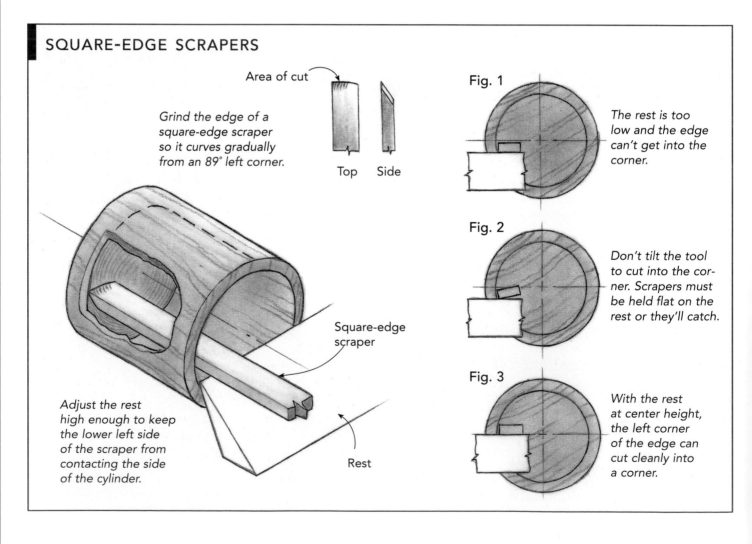

Area of cut

Grind the edge of a square-edge scraper so it curves gradually from an 89° left corner.

Top   Side

Adjust the rest high enough to keep the lower left side of the scraper from contacting the side of the cylinder.

Square-edge scraper

Rest

Fig. 1

The rest is too low and the edge can't get into the corner.

Fig. 2

Don't tilt the tool to cut into the corner. Scrapers must be held flat on the rest or they'll catch.

Fig. 3

With the rest at center height, the left corner of the edge can cut cleanly into a corner.

you tilt the edge down, the opening will narrow toward the base.

The further away from the rest you cut, the smaller the shaving should be. The leverage is tremendous, and a catch at the bottom of a deep hole is usually disastrous. (While you should escape injury, you will probably tear the end grain or split the work.) Align the tool handle along and under your forearm to counteract its tendency to catch, and keep it flat on the rest. Don't tilt the edge above horizontal on the end grain at the bottom of the hollow. As the cut nears the solid wood in the base, you'll hear the sound of the cut change, warning you that the end grain is very near. Slow the rate at which you push the tool forward to avoid the catch, which occurs when you hit end grain and are not expecting it.

If you want to go deeper than you can rough-hollow with a gouge, say, 4 in. (100mm) deep, 2 in. (50mm) diameter, first drill a hole the required depth using a drill in the tail center. Then use the ¾-in. (20mm) square-edge scraper for a series of cuts, using no more than ¼ in. (6mm) of the edge to widen the drilled hole to the required diameter.

You can do all sorts of decorative detailing on end grain using scraping techniques, typically on the inside or on top of box lids. I have a few old tools that I grind as I need them, but mostly I use a small skew to get into odd corners or along the surface as shown in the photo on p. 126. Grind or hone the under bevel of the chisel lightly to produce a small burr. Keep the skew flat on the rest with the edge at center height and the burr on the top. Use only a small portion of the edge at one time but all of the edge at some time. On a convex surface, pivot the tool on the rest so the point of cut moves along the edge. On very hard end grain, honed scrapers used very gently will give you an exceptional finish right off the tool.

Pots

The ash pots in front are among the first objects I ever turned back in 1970. Behind the horizontal scrub bark box is the bottom half of a failed spillikins box long used for pencils. The elm pot made for these pages is deeper than usual for a production item normally 4 in. (100mm) tall. That extra bit adds too much risk and takes the edge right off the profit.

MATERIALS: Horizontal scrub (with bark), voamboana (feathers), elm (chopsticks), ash (dice)

SIZES: 1¾ in. to 3⅜ in. (45mm to 85mm) diameter

PENCIL POT

Hollowing end grain is not easy, so you should try a small version of what is shown here before going on to deeper things. The further you work over the rest, the greater the difficulty, so don't be overambitious during your early attempts at hollowing end grain.

Pots provide good practice for hollowing end grain and they sell reasonably well, since people always need to contain all manner of long, thin objects. It's difficult to have too many dotted around the house, and they make great gifts. The skills you develop as you work through this exercise are essential for making boxes. You need a blank 2½ in. to 3½ in. (65mm to 90mm) in diameter and about 3 in. to 4 in. (75mm to 100mm) long.

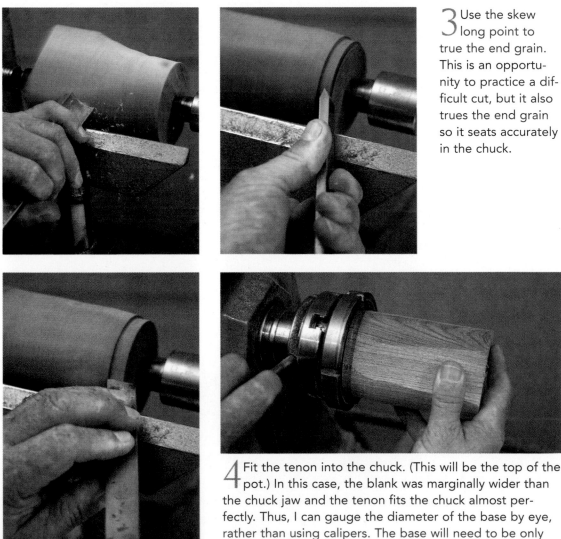

1 Mount the blank between centers, then use a roughing gouge and a ¾-in. (20mm) skew chisel to reduce the squared blank to a rough cylinder.

2 Use the skew chisel to peel a short tenon so there's a shoulder to sit against the rim of the chuck jaws. Remove just the minimum to make the tenon a true cylinder. At this stage, don't worry about removing all flat areas on the larger diameter.

3 Use the skew long point to true the end grain. This is an opportunity to practice a difficult cut, but it also trues the end grain so it seats accurately in the chuck.

4 Fit the tenon into the chuck. (This will be the top of the pot.) In this case, the blank was marginally wider than the chuck jaw and the tenon fits the chuck almost perfectly. Thus, I can gauge the diameter of the base by eye, rather than using calipers. The base will need to be only slightly narrower.

5 Use the skew chisel to true the cylinder and end grain.

6 Check that the base is slightly concave by using a straight-edge. If you want to decorate the end grain with a bead or lines, now is the time to do it.

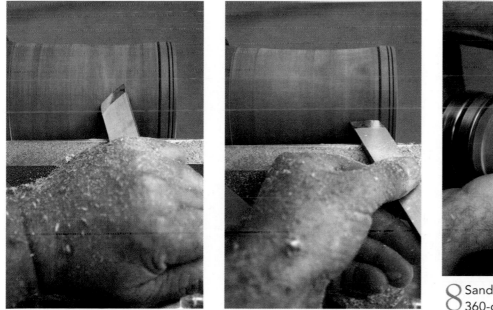

7 Turn the foot to fit the chuck and the rest of the profile as close to the chuck as you dare. (Remember that the grinder is there if you get too close.) Shear-cut when you can and use the scrape/peel technique on the uphill slope to the bead at the base.

8 Sand using 150-, 240-, and 360-grit abrasives. Finish with oil and wax before reversing the job in the chuck for hollowing.

9 With the pot now gripped around the foot, true the rim and end grain. Remove as little wood as possible around the rim. The band at the rim will be detailed later; meanwhile, it strengthens the form as hollowing proceeds.

10 Begin the hollowing process using a ½-in. (13mm) shallow gouge. Although back-hollowing is faster, conventional cuts from the rim are less risky. When you get more confident handling the square-edge scraper a long way over the rest, you'll find it is faster to drill a ½-in. (13mm) depth hole first and complete the hollow using just a scraper as a borer.

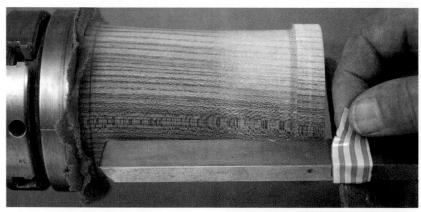

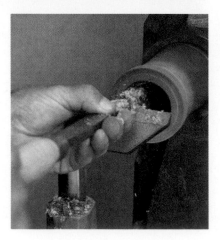

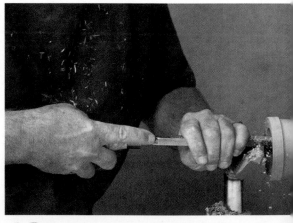

11 Complete the hollow using a ¾-in. (20mm) square-edge scraper. Even if you've drilled a depth hole, it pays to mark the depth you want on the blade of the scraper. A pencil line is okay, but plastic tape is easier to see and you can feel it under shavings. As you increase the depth, complete a series of internal bases so you get several chances to practice smoothing the end grain some distance from the rest.

12 Be very cautious easing the edge against the end grain, especially working well over the rest. Keep the tool horizontal to cut a cylinder accurately. Having smoothed a base at, say, 2 in. (50mm), push the scraper firmly into the base to bore in another ½ in. (13mm) or so, then finish another base at that level, and so on. The leverage starts getting really difficult to control at about 3 in. (75mm).

13 Using internal calipers, check the internal dimensions. Aim for a cylinder and do not be satisfied with less. A slightly dovetailed hollow is okay but not a tapered opening narrowing from the rim, which limits the number of whatever it is you hope to contain in the pot.

16 In preparation for oiling and finishing, blow out the dust using compressed air. Lovers of the old-fashioned methods can use a short length of hose and their own lungs, while those better equipped can have their compressors buzzing away, consuming the world's valuable energy.

14 This interior is slightly dovetailed. The end grain is cut cleanly and the small ridges on the sides will sand away easily using an old 60-grit sanding disc if 100-grit doesn't do the job (it did). If your fingers can't reach the bottom, use a sanding stick (see p. 186).

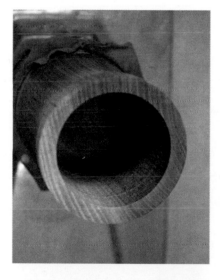

15 With the inside turned and sanded, turn the rim using a ⅜-in. (9mm) shallow gouge. Here I have the material, so I turn a couple of beads, then decide the lower would look better as a cove.

Pencil pot, elm, 4¾ in. by 3⅜ in. (120mm by 85mm).

7 FACEWORK

FACEWORK IS MOUNTED WITH the grain running at 90° to the axis on which the wood rotates. The end grain faces outwards, rather than towards the headstock and tailstock. Work is usually set this way for any job where the diameter exceeds the height, such as bowls, platters, and clocks. Generally, the work is attached to the lathe by one face, although often there is no good reason why it cannot be mounted between centers. In fact, there are several advantages to employing tail-center support with facework, as described on p. 25.

The range of tools needed for facework is greater than for centerwork because of the problems involved when cutting end grain in tight corners or some distance over the rest. I use gouges to remove the bulk of the waste with a variety of shearing and scraping techniques and finish the surface with scrapers before sanding.

When cutting end grain, always aim to cut across the fibers (across the grain), where they are supported by others, as shown in the illustration on p. 83. Cutting this way means working from a smaller to larger diameter externally and from larger to smaller diameters internally. When cutting a corner between a face and the side of a blank, always cut in from the face, as seen in the photo at left and in the illustration on the facing page. Never cut from the side to the face because the unsupported

Always cut in from a face to prevent the corners from splintering.

FACEWORK: HOW GRAIN DIRECTION AFFECTS CUTTING

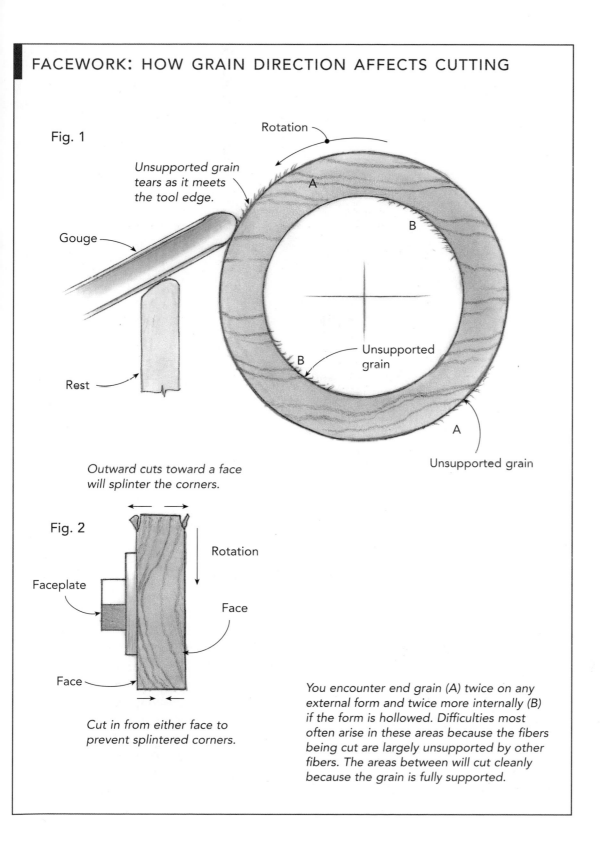

Fig. 1

Rotation

Unsupported grain tears as it meets the tool edge.

Gouge

Rest

A

B

B

Unsupported grain

A

Unsupported grain

Outward cuts toward a face will splinter the corners.

Fig. 2

Rotation

Faceplate

Face

Face

Cut in from either face to prevent splintered corners.

You encounter end grain (A) twice on any external form and twice more internally (B) if the form is hollowed. Difficulties most often arise in these areas because the fibers being cut are largely unsupported by other fibers. The areas between will cut cleanly because the grain is fully supported.

Bowls

On an outflowing form, decorative grooves near the base enable chuck jaws to grip the bowl as it's hollowed and finished.

MATERIALS:	African blackwood and cocobolo
SIZES:	About 6 in. to 8⅝ in. (150mm to 220mm) diameter

Here is a fine example of end grain torn during preliminary shaping (at A in the illustration on p. 139).

Never use a shallow gouge with the flute up for facework.

grain on the corner will splinter away. Whenever possible, the force of a cut should be parallel to the axis.

If the form you are turning has a curved profile (as in a bowl), it's not necessary to true the blank to a cylinder before developing the shape. Instead, aim to remove the bulk of the waste as quickly as possible to reduce the weight and vibration. Then if you want to increase the speed you can do so safely.

External Shaping

You can do just about all external shaping on facework with gouges, using scraping techniques as required to refine surfaces immediately before sanding. The development of power-sanding means that you can get away with a rougher surface than ever dreamed possible in the days of hand-held abrasives. Nevertheless, I suggest you aim to get the best surface possible from the tool, partly for the satisfaction of being able to do it but also because power-sanding does not enable you to get in around fine detail such as beads. They have to be cut cleanly.

In this section, I'll explain the important difference between gouges and show you how to use them. Then you'll learn about scrapers and see how scraping and shear-scraping techniques can improve just about any gouge-cut surface. At the end of the chapter is a section on turning beads, coves, and grooves to decorate the profile.

GOUGES FOR EXTERNAL FACEWORK

Gouges come as deep fluted or shallow. The deep-fluted gouges (often called bowl gouges) are strong and heavy tools designed to hollow deep bowls and cut well away from the rest. They are much more expensive than the lighter shallow gouges, which are designed primarily for centerwork detailing and function best within 1½ in. (40mm) of the rest (beyond that they tend to flex somewhat).

It is very important to appreciate the difference between the two gouges if you are to avoid horrific catches (see the illustration at right). Never use a shallow gouge with the flute up for facework. For shear cuts, make sure the flute is facing away from the surface you are cutting (see the photo on p. 138); for shear scraping, have the flute facing towards the surface you are cutting (see the illustration on p. 155).

I have found most of my gouges to be useful and effective for external shaping, with the exception of the shallow tools wider than 1 in. (25mm). I grind my gouges to a long fingernail shape, as described on p. 57.

I have four gouges in almost constant use: ⅜-in. (9mm) and ½-in. (13mm) deep-fluted

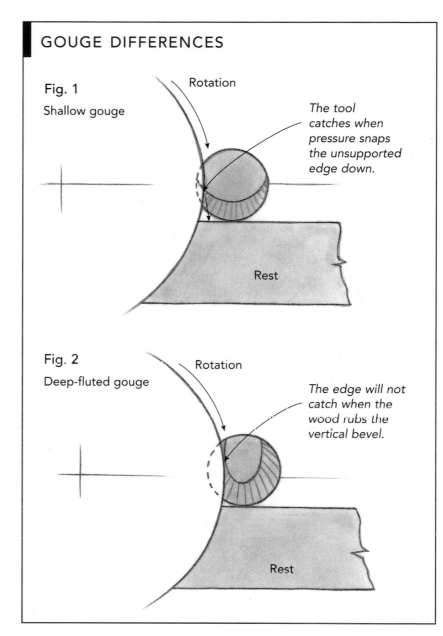

GOUGE DIFFERENCES

Fig. 1
Shallow gouge

Rotation

The tool catches when pressure snaps the unsupported edge down.

Rest

Fig. 2
Deep-fluted gouge

Rotation

The edge will not catch when the wood rubs the vertical bevel.

Rest

gouges and two shallow gouges in the same sizes. These gouges are all you need for the normal run of facework and the exercises in this chapter. The fingernail edge can be used for shearing cuts, or you can use each tool on its side for scraping cuts. I tend to use shallow gouges for external shaping because they are much less expensive than deep-fluted tools. There is no point in wasting expensive steel when working close to the rest if there is a

Facework Speeds			
DIAMETERS	**LENGTHS**		
	2 in. (50mm)	3 in. (75mm)	4 in. (100mm)
8 in. (205mm)	1,250	1,250	1,000
10 in. (255mm)	1,250	1,000	900
12 in. (305mm)	1,250	1,000	900
14 in. (355mm)	1,000	900	850
16 in. (405mm)	750	650	600
18 in. (460mm)	650	500	400

The figures in this chart are expressed in rpm. For safety, unevenly grained or unbalanced blanks should be started at half these speeds.

Remember to choose a wood that is easy to work. Unseasoned wood is by far the easiest. Hardwood such as cherry, ash, and walnut should present fewer problems than softwood, particularly on end grain. Set the speed of the lathe no higher than 850 rpm. Although blanks of this size can be rotated safely at 1,250 rpm, speed is not necessary at this stage, and the slower speed will demand correct use of the tool and give you a better view of what is happening. Also, the inevitable catches, when they occur, will be less frightening at this speed. Refer to the speed chart at left for guidance in tackling blanks of different sizes.

The best way to learn how to use the gouges is by turning a series of curves and cones similar to lines A–G in the illustration on the facing page. Begin by truing the face of the blank (A), then turn a smooth convex curve (B). You will gain experience on all the basic cuts. You can then use them to reduce the form to a straight line (C), followed by a shallow concave curve (D), and so on until the block is turned away. It pays to waste several blocks practicing curves before proceeding to turn a cylinder, which is more difficult (particularly coping with the end grain).

Stop the lathe frequently to examine the surface and the quality of your cut. Listen to the sounds as you cut and relate them to the quality of the surface. You'll find that the most effective cut can vary from blank to blank, sometimes even when the blanks are from the same plank if the grain is particularly wild.

Often during the shearing cuts the tool will start chattering at about one-third of the way around the curve. When this happens, start the cut again where the surface runs true, keeping the tool firmly on the rest as you take the edge through the bumps and across the dips for a smooth surface.

Exercise: Line A. Truing a face. This is the easiest place to begin because there is no end grain to contend with. You are confronted by the full length of the fibers running at 90° to

cheaper option. As deep-fluted gouges become too short for hollowing, I use them for external finishing cuts but hardly ever for roughing cuts because the flute tends to jam with shavings. With shallow gouges, this is not a problem because the more open flute allows the shavings to get away faster.

BASIC GOUGE TECHNIQUES

Gouge techniques are similar for cutting both internal and external surfaces, but there are fewer problems with the latter, mainly because the wood is easier to reach and the edge of the tool can be supported close to the point of cut. It's best to learn what gouges can do on external surfaces before attempting to hollow a bowl or cut at any great distance from the rest, where the leverage will be much more difficult to control.

Start by mounting an 8-in.- (200mm) to 10-in.- (250mm) diameter by 3-in.- (75mm) to 4-in.- (100mm) thick blank on a center-screw or standard faceplate (see pp. 28–30). Do not mount the block between centers while you are learning how to use the gouges because you will restrict yourself and limit the use of the tool.

the axis. As you cut, these fibers will be lifted off the surface. Consequently, it's difficult to achieve an absolutely smooth surface when truing a face because the fibers lie at the wrong angle for a shearing cut, but you learn a very useful basic technique.

To achieve a flat face, adjust the rest parallel to the eventual finished surface so that the tool can be held in a constant position relative to the rest. Use a gouge on its side, making a series of squeezing cuts from the rim towards center. You can use either a deep-fluted or shallow

GOUGE EXERCISES

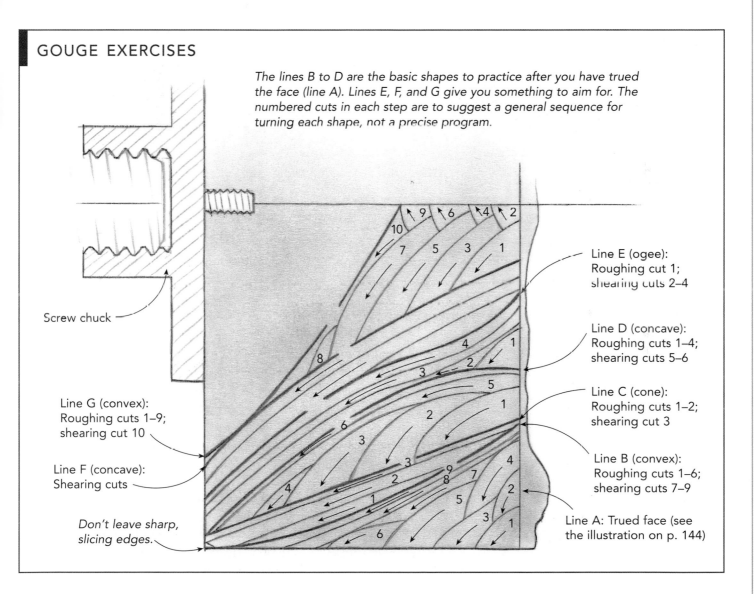

The lines B to D are the basic shapes to practice after you have trued the face (line A). Lines E, F, and G give you something to aim for. The numbered cuts in each step are to suggest a general sequence for turning each shape, not a precise program.

Screw chuck

Line G (convex):
Roughing cuts 1–9;
shearing cut 10

Line F (concave):
Shearing cuts

Don't leave sharp,
slicing edges.

Line E (ogee):
Roughing cut 1;
shearing cuts 2–4

Line D (concave):
Roughing cuts 1–4;
shearing cuts 5–6

Line C (cone):
Roughing cuts 1–2;
shearing cut 3

Line B (convex):
Roughing cuts 1–6;
shearing cuts 7–9

Line A: Trued face (see
the illustration on p. 144)

Listen to the sounds as you cut
and relate them to the quality of the surface.

TRUING THE FACE

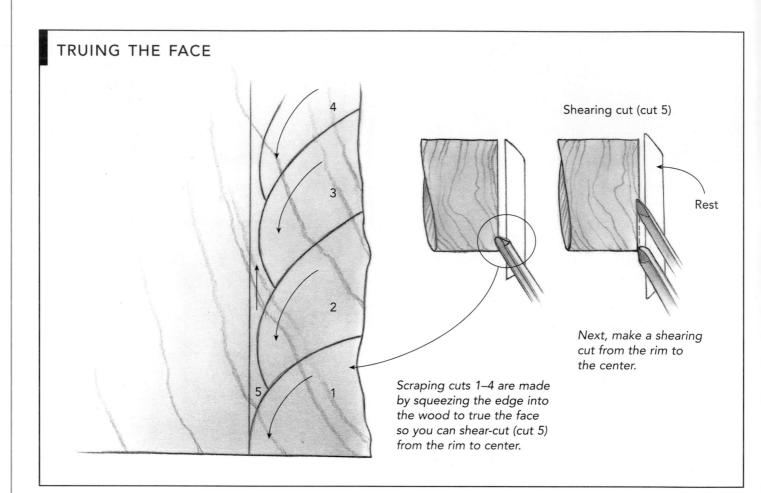

4

3

2

5   1

Shearing cut (cut 5)

Rest

Next, make a shearing cut from the rim to the center.

Scraping cuts 1–4 are made by squeezing the edge into the wood to true the face so you can shear-cut (cut 5) from the rim to center.

gouge, but the latter allows you to see what is happening. If the blank is not too off-center, I'll make only a couple of squeeze cuts to true the rim (cuts 1–4 in the illustration above), then roll the tool over for a shear cut (cut 5) back to center.

Although cuts 1–4 are shearing cuts, the bevel doesn't rub the wood. Have the gouge rolled over at least 45° with the flute facing the blank. Never use the tool flute up: It will catch every time as the wood bears down on the tool's unsupported left edge (see Fig. 1 in the illustration on p. 141 and the bottom illustration on p. 74). The effect is the same as if you stepped on the gunwale of an empty dinghy. Both the dinghy and the gouge will roll with disastrous consequences. When the tool is rolled towards the wood, the edge is supported close to the

point of cut and you'll be able to cut without fear of catching.

At the start of each cut, plant the heel of your left hand firmly on the rest with your fingers extended. Then bring the edge into the wood by squeezing the blade into your palm, which stays planted on the rest (see the top photo on the facing page). The idea is that the edge can go only so far because the heel of your hand acts as a stop. The tool pivots from where the handle rests against your hip (as shown in Fig. 2 in the illustration on p. 70). You will know when the rim is flat because the knocking or tick-tick sounds stop, indicating the surface is smooth.

Once the rim is flat, you can make a shearing cut from the rim in to center (cut 5). For a shearing cut, position the top of the gouge fac-

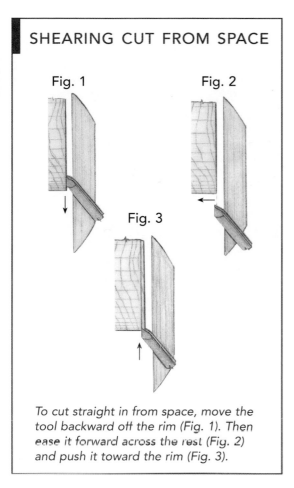

SHEARING CUT FROM SPACE

Fig. 1

Fig. 2

Fig. 3

To cut straight in from space, move the tool backward off the rim (Fig. 1). Then ease it forward across the rest (Fig. 2) and push it toward the rim (Fig. 3).

(TOP) **To true a face, first use a squeeze cut with the flute facing toward the face. (BOTTOM) Then roll the tool over so the bevel rubs for a shear cut into center.**

ing away from the blank with the flute at about 45° as shown in the bottom photo at right. Beginning at the rim, bring the bevel shoulder in to rub before pivoting the edge forward to start a shearing cut to the center using the nose of the tool.

When you gain some confidence, you can attempt to cut into the rim from space. To begin the cut this way, tee it up like a golf shot as shown in the illustration above. Hold the tool right on its side, with the bevel rubbing, and move it backward off the rim, away from the direction it will cut. Then ease the tool slightly forward across the rest before pushing it in to the rim, keeping the edge moving at 90° to the axis. To prevent kickback, the motion towards center must be firm and the point of cut must be on the lower side of the nose of the edge.

Exercise: Line B. Cutting a convex curve. To turn the curve at line B in the illustration on p. 143, use roughing cuts (cuts 1–6) to establish the overall form, then shearing cuts (cuts 7–9) to smooth it.

Roughing cuts remove wood very efficiently and are ideal for the early stages of rough-turning an external shape or profile. The finished surface will not be particularly smooth because the tool lies nearly 90° to the wood sur-

ROUGHING CUTS

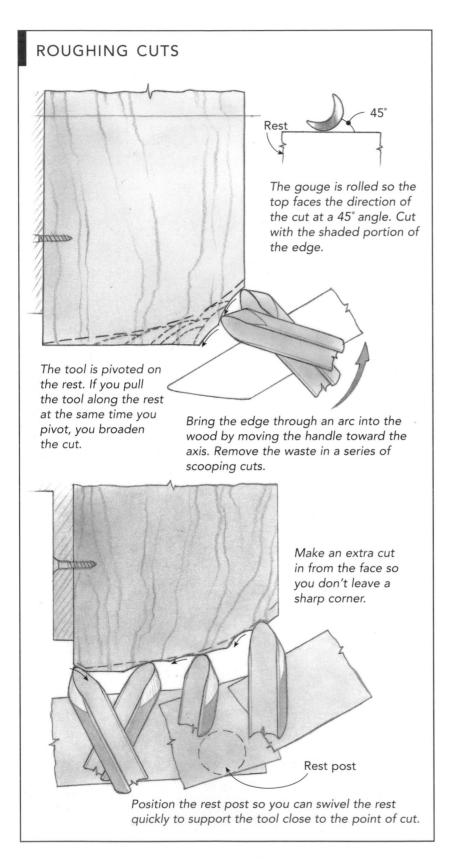

The gouge is rolled so the top faces the direction of the cut at a 45° angle. Cut with the shaded portion of the edge.

The tool is pivoted on the rest. If you pull the tool along the rest at the same time you pivot, you broaden the cut.

Bring the edge through an arc into the wood by moving the handle toward the axis. Remove the waste in a series of scooping cuts.

Make an extra cut in from the face so you don't leave a sharp corner.

Position the rest post so you can swivel the rest quickly to support the tool close to the point of cut.

In the early stage of truing a bowl blank, the edge swings through an arc. Here the shallow gouge pivots on my thumb as my fingers pull the blade to the left. Out of sight, my hip eases the handle to the right.

face, but there should be a minimum of torn end grain (see the photo above).

Shallow gouges are generally better than deep-fluted gouges for roughing cuts because the upper edge of the deep-fluted gouges can get in the way and limit the size of the shaving. Whichever gouge you use, you need rounded wings on the edge, or a sort of stubby fingernail shape. This cut employs a relatively safe arcing and pulling action, always made from the smaller to larger diameter so that in the horizontal plane every fiber you cut is supported by another.

Start with the gouge on the rest tilted up slightly and rolled over about 45° so the flute faces away from the wood. Your upper hand must maintain firm contact with the rest, with your fingers gripping over and around the tool.

Your lower hand rotates the tool to control the angle of the cut. Move the edge into the cut partly by squeezing the tool with your upper hand but mostly by easing the handle towards the lathe. Use your body rather than just your arm to move the handle. You'll have more control with less effort as you swing the edge through an arc in towards the wood, as shown in the illustration on the facing page.

After the initial cut, swing the tool back to its original angle as your upper hand pulls it about 1 in. (25mm) along the rest to begin a similar cut farther down the curve. Keep your elbows tucked in and the tool handle aligned against your body or along your forearm (preferably both as shown in the photo at right). You must ensure a balanced stance so that you can place your weight behind the tool as you pivot back and forth with the handle. A common fault that leads to a hefty catch is holding the tool flat with the flute up—it should be on its side.

As you reduce the bulk of the corner in a series of arcing cuts, you'll need to adjust the rest several times so you are not working too far over the rest. (Position the tool rest banjo so you can simply swivel the tee rest to make your initial adjustments without having to move the entire assembly.) As each cut becomes longer, you can pull the tool along the rest with your upper hand while swinging the handle around.

When the tool is cutting well, it feels almost spongy. If you think the shaving could be larger, don't exert more force but instead adjust the cutting angle by rotating the tool slightly with your lower hand. Remember not to cut off the side of the blank into space, which will splinter the corner, but cut in from the face, as shown in the illustration on the facing page. Because the bevel doesn't rub in this cut, you should achieve a clean but ridged surface. This can now be smoothed using the same tool from a different direction.

To shear-cut a curve, you can use either a shallow or deep-fluted gouge. Each tool is presented to the wood in a different way, but in

When the tool is cutting well
it feels almost spongy.

Gain maximum support for the tool by keeping the handle against your body. Use your little finger to deflect shavings.

As the blank is trued, you can pull the edge around the curve for an efficient roughing cut, which prepares the surface for the shearing cuts. Here I use a deep-fluted gouge.

The tool is easier to steer when it's pointing in the direction you're cutting. Note that this shallow gouge is rolled over about 45°.

When shear-cutting with a shallow gouge, the gouge is used nearly on its side.

(RIGHT) A deep-fluted gouge can be used almost on its side for a heavy shear cut, or it can be used flute up (FAR RIGHT) for a finer shear cut (often called a back-cut).

each case the bevel rubs the wood, and the portion of each edge doing the cutting is at the same 45° to the oncoming wood. The gouge points in the direction you're cutting. The shallow gouge is used rolled over about 45°, with the flute facing away from the wood (see the top photos on the facing page). The deep-fluted gouge is also used this way for a heavy cut (see the bottom left photo on the facing page), but for a finer cut it's used flute up (see the bottom right photo on the facing page and the illustration at right).

The shearing cuts are thrusting cuts, with the tool pointing in the direction you're cutting. As I grasp the tool near the ferrule with the handle tucked along my forearm and into my side, I think of it being like a medieval lance. The key to cutting a flowing curve is to move smoothly as you manipulate the tool. You know where you are going to start, you know roughly the route you're taking, and you know where you would like to finish. All you have to do is take the tool evenly along that path.

When cutting around a long curve, be prepared to move your body quite a distance as you move with the tool handle. It's always a good feeling to cut a curve in one pass, but to achieve it your feet will have to be well apart so you can transfer your weight from one foot to the other as you follow the tool. If your starting position is leaning across the lathe bed, you can get a good start levering your body clear of the lathe bed. If the point of cut gets to be more than 1 in. (25mm) from the rest, consider stopping and adjusting both the rest and your stance to reduce the leverage, then carry on.

Of course it's not always as easy as that, and things go wrong. First, you can set off in the wrong direction. If you are cutting on a line that takes you out into space, just follow that line until the edge ceases to cut (see A in the illustration on p. 150). Then start again a little farther back at a slightly steeper angle. Don't suddenly alter the trajectory during your cut

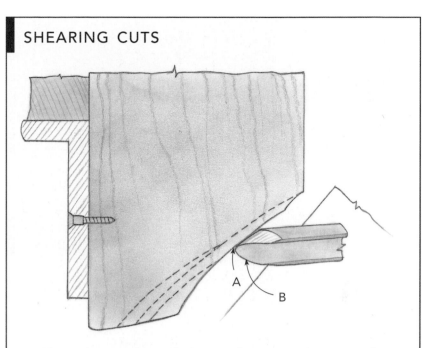

SHEARING CUTS

The tool cut combines shearing and scraping. The center of the edge (A) shears, while the lower portion of the edge (B) removes the bulk with a scraping action.

To make a back-cut with this ⅜-in. (9mm) deep-fluted gouge, I have the tool pointing in the direction I'm cutting with the handle dropped slightly below horizontal. Note how I keep the handle against my forearm so the tool becomes an extension of my arm.

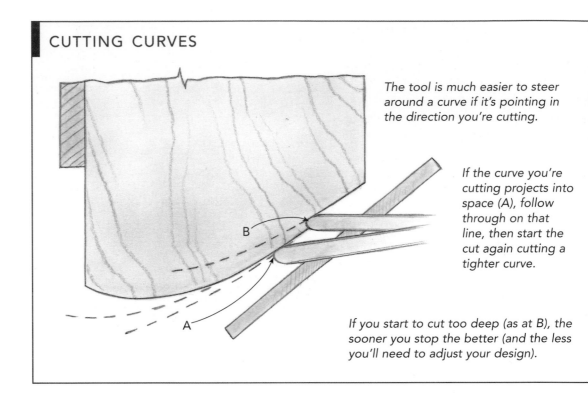

CUTTING CURVES

The tool is much easier to steer around a curve if it's pointing in the direction you're cutting.

If the curve you're cutting projects into space (A), follow through on that line, then start the cut again cutting a tighter curve.

If you start to cut too deep (as at B), the sooner you stop the better (and the less you'll need to adjust your design).

because you'll create a rounded corner and your curve will cease to be a curve. If you set off trying to take too deep a cut (as in B in the illustration above), the sooner you realize it the better, otherwise you'll end up with a completely different or much smaller form.

The most difficult part of this cut is the start, when the bevel doesn't have a surface to rub on. Keep the rest close to the work to reduce the leverage. To make the initial cut from space, start with the gouge on its side and the bevel lined up in the direction you want to cut, just as you did cutting a groove on a spindle. Then pivot the edge through an arc into the wood or ease it straight in using a very firm grip. The edge can be supported effectively on as little as ⅛ in. (3mm) of bevel/wood contact, so once the bevel is rubbing, you have a secondary fulcrum that gives you very fine control over the edge. You use the smooth surface you've cut to jig the edge for the next part of the cut.

To continue the cut around the curve, keep the shallow gouge at much the same angle but rolled slightly into the wood for a marginally wider shaving. For a heavy cut, you can keep the deep-fluted gouge on its side (its starting position) or roll it so the flute is up and the shaving comes off the steep wing of the tool for what is often called a back-cut, as shown in the bottom right photo on p. 148. The steep bevel on the side of the tool should support the cut, but be warned that the tool will catch if you roll it too far. You'll know when you are making a back-cut correctly because the shavings will rise straight out of the flute, hit you in the face, and bounce back to mound up on the tool. If you haven't been wearing a face shield, you soon will.

The bevel should rub against the newly cut surface at all times. If it doesn't and only the edge is in contact with the wood, it is virtually impossible to cut a smooth surface. The angle and movement of the tool is always controlled by the lower hand while the upper hand keeps the tool on the rest, makes sure the bevel rubs, and deflects shavings.

By using the cuts described above to turn the curve, you will experience most of what gouges have to offer. Different-sized gouges will do the same thing only on a larger or smaller scale. You will see huge bowl-roughing gouges in catalogs, and although the prospect of even bigger and fatter shavings is appealing, the fact is that most professional turners find ½-in. (13mm) gouges to be the most efficient. The bigger gouges might take a wider shaving, but there seems to be a law of diminishing returns in inverse proportion to the size of the tool. You generally get there quicker with the smaller tools.

When you've achieved a nice smoothly cut form at line B (see the illustration on p. 143), go on to turn lines C, D, E, F, G, and H using the same techniques. Then go through all the cuts again, varying the lines of the curves. I realize it will be difficult to resist the temptation to proceed straight to hollowing, but I urge you to reduce several blocks to shavings in order to practice the cuts.

If you want to shear-cut a dramatic pedestal concave form, you will need a steep bevel so the tool handle is in a more convenient position and the fulcrum is nearer the point of cut.

With practice you will start to combine the different techniques, probably being barely aware of the fact. Particularly in the roughing-down stages, I find I move the tool in one fluid motion, alternating from one technique to another, cutting all the while. Pay attention to and learn the sounds of your cutting. If the pitch changes, stop and find out why. Don't forget to turn away the sharp edge that can easily develop on the top rim of the blank or indeed on any acute angle.

ROUNDED PROFILES AND ENCLOSED FORMS

Although I try to discourage the practice, novice turners (myself included all those years ago) are drawn to enclosed forms like moths to

This is what you get when you back-cut correctly: shavings everywhere and you can't see what you're doing! What a small price to pay.

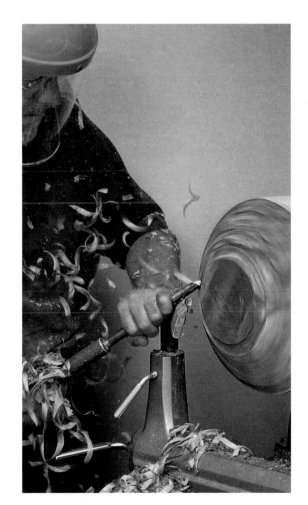

Medium-sized gouges are the most efficient for rapid removal of waste. Here I use a ⁹⁄₁₆-in. (15mm) gouge to shape a large bowl profile.

Calabash Bowls

Turned green with rounded bases, these pieces are intended to wobble slightly but not roll over. The walnut-like surface results from the wood structure collapsing as it dries.

MATERIAL:	Eucalypt burl
SIZE:	About 8⅝ in. (220mm) diameter

When cutting from left to right (here truing up an off-center bowl), I use an underhand grip and move the edge onto the cut with my thumb.

a flame. And like moths, they are in for a bad experience, only not usually so terminal. Things go easily enough on the outside forms—the profiles. But you encounter the real problems when hollowing because the grain beneath the rim is virtually unsupported and you have to cut right into the end of it (see area B in Fig. 1 in the illustration on p. 139). The smaller the diameter the worse the problem.

To shear-cut the top of a rounded profile, the same rules apply as for all facework, so you cut from smaller to larger diameter. This can be tricky on the headstock side of the blank unless your gouge has a steep bevel to keep the handle from knocking against the headstock. I continue to hold the handle with my right hand in an underhand grip, pushing the tool forward with my thumb (see the photo above). Left-handers should have no problems with this one! Here you are practicing the cuts, but in reality it is easier to leave the finishing cuts until the form is remounted for hollowing.

No matter how good your gouge technique, the surface will, at best, be a very fine and barely discernible spiral, a finer version of an old vinyl recording. And in addition, you will inevitably get some end-grain tearout. All this can be power-sanded smooth in a few seconds (see pp. 186–189), but it's more satisfying and useful, particularly around beads or other detailing, to be able to refine the surface using scrapers and scraping techniques.

To shear-scrape, the tool rides on its lower side so the blade lies at about 45° to the oncoming wood. The upper (left) hand gently pulls the edge in to stroke the surface. Use the lower portion of the edge.

SCRAPERS FOR EXTERNAL FACEWORK

I regard scrapers primarily as tools for fine finishing, especially on external forms. To use them effectively requires a smooth, flowing, and very delicate touch that removes only fluff and small curly shavings. Most scrapers are intended to be used flat on the rest with the edge at 90° to the oncoming wood, but manufacturers now make shear-scraping tools designed to be tilted so the edge lies nearer 45° to the passing wood (see the photo above and Fig. 2 in the illustration at right).

Shear scrapers come left-hand, right-hand, and spear-point. I have left-hand and spear-point scrapers in almost constant use. Shear scrapers have a rounded side so the tool moves smoothly along all but the roughest rests. But, as on rounded skew chisels (see the top photo on p. 50), you need to grind a flat on the end of the side to create a really sharp corner.

SCRAPING FACEWORK

Fig. 1: Scrapers Used Flat on a Facework Profile

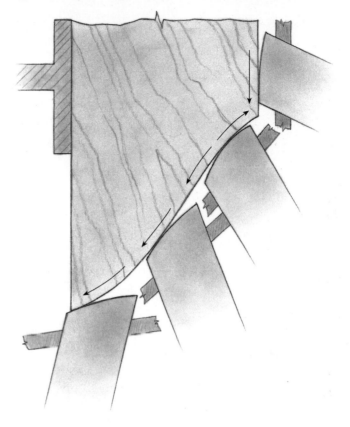

Fig. 2: Shear Scraping (End View)

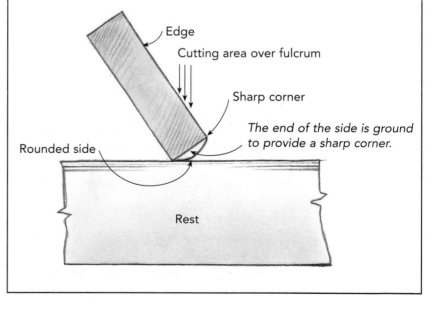

Edge

Cutting area over fulcrum

Sharp corner

The end of the side is ground to provide a sharp corner.

Rounded side

Rest

For a usable sharp corner on a shear scraper, grind a flat on the end of the curved side.

Shear-scraping with a spear-point scraper.

My scrapers are mostly radiused and skewed. Over the years, I have amassed a number of scrapers of various lengths, but I use only the older short ones for profile work close to the rest so as not to fritter away valuable steel needlessly, which is what I would be doing by using longer tools. It's handy to have a range of odd bits of steel so you can make up scrapers as needed for such tasks as making a recess for an expanding chuck, a common way of gripping a bowl for hollowing (see the top right photo on p. 173).

BASIC SCRAPING TECHNIQUES

When using scrapers, work from smaller to larger diameters as usual. Most scrapers are meant to be used with the tool flat on the rest because if you raise one side even slightly the tool will catch. I keep the tool working at about 30° to the surface I'm scraping for maximum control, squeezing the tool in the direction I want to go.

On convex surfaces, I mostly use the skewed, slightly radiused tool shown in the illustration on p. 153, which allows me to finish slightly concave surfaces but is not too rounded for convex curves. Scrapers used flat are good for ensuring flowing curves, but the surface they leave rarely equals that shear-cut by a gouge. To improve a gouge-cut surface, you shear-scrape.

SHEAR-SCRAPING TECHNIQUES

To shear-scrape, tilt the edge upward and pitch the top face of the scraper slightly toward the surface being cut, as shown in the photos above

and on p. 153. The edge is presented at about 45° (there's that figure again) to the oncoming wood. Use the lower part of the edge because theoretically any pressure on the unsupported upper section will cause a catch (although in reality there is so little pressure against the edge that this is rarely a problem). The aim is to stroke the surface with much the same pressure you use rubbing your hands under a hot-air dryer. Notice how firm a grip I have of the tool, with the handle against my side.

On broad curves or flat profiles, you can use any scraper on its side, but in places where the top edge might catch it's safer to use a spear-point. Spear-point scrapers are rounded on both sides so they slide more readily along the rest in either direction. They are available commercially, but it's easy to make your own using an old 1-in. (25mm) by ¼-in. (6mm) skew chisel or scraper.

FINISH SCRAPING CUTS

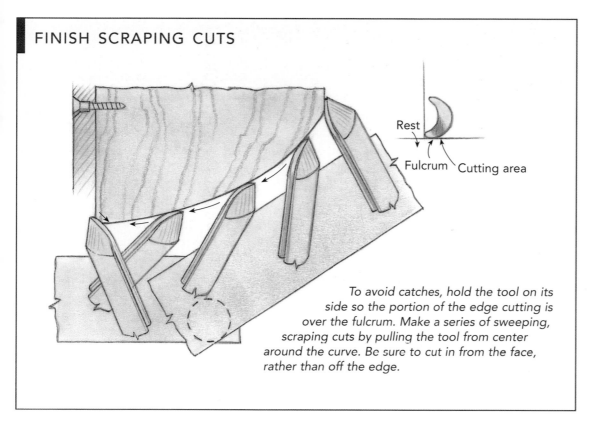

Rest

Fulcrum Cutting area

To avoid catches, hold the tool on its side so the portion of the edge cutting is over the fulcrum. Make a series of sweeping, scraping cuts by pulling the tool from center around the curve. Be sure to cut in from the face, rather than off the edge.

For years I used my shallow gouge rolled over on its side for shear scraping (see the illustration above). I hadn't analyzed what I was doing, but I knew it worked, despite being told by several self-anointed woodturning gurus that real turners don't do such things. The portion of the edge cutting is at around 45° to the oncoming wood, which is stroked in a series of sweeping passes. Proper square-section scrapers do a better job, but this is a useful technique if you already have the gouge in your hand and just need a quick shear scrape to soften a rim or remove a bump.

CUTTING A SHOULDER

When turning bowls, you often need to cut a foot or tenon so that the bowl can be gripped by a chuck. And on clock rims and traditional chopping boards, shoulders are a common design feature.

You can shear-scrape right into a corner using a spear-point scraper. With the tool tilted towards the wood, the right-side edge is clear of the bowl foot and unlikely to catch.

When cutting these short, cylindrical sections lying parallel to the axis, I use a ⅜-in. (9mm) shallow gouge with a long fingernail grind that can reach into a corner, unlike a deep-fluted tool. As always, start the cut with the tool right over on its side, with the top facing away from the wood and the bevel lined up in the direction you want to cut. Then pivot the edge through an arc into the wood, making the

initial cut using the point and the area just below it (see the photos on p. 82).

Shoulders stand proud of another surface, like a foot on a bowl or a bead. A well-defined corner between the two generally looks better than a sort-of-vaguely-rounded-sort-of-a-corner. As you cut into the corner, roll the gouge on its side and hold it briefly so the nose of the tool slices through the fibers but doesn't remove a shaving (see the photos at left). Often you have to cut against the grain to get into the corner. Just go steadily and roll the tool on its side to get into the corner without catching.

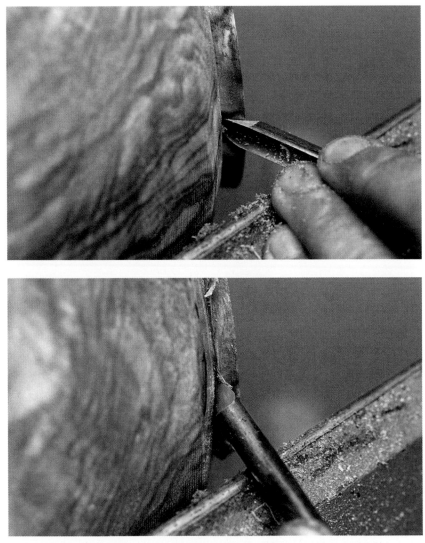

A foot is turned with a ⅜-in. (9mm) shallow gouge. At the end of each cut, ensure you have the gouge on its side to prevent the edge from catching.

Hollowing

Once you have reduced a few blocks to shavings and feel comfortable turning outside curves, it is time to try hollowing. Start with an open-shaped bowl about 8 in. (200mm) to 10 in. (250mm) in diameter and 4 in. (100mm) deep. Avoid curved-over rims for now, which present all sorts of control and cutting problems. Do not be deceived by the simplicity of the form. It is very difficult to produce a really good-looking, flowing line. The inside curve is as important as the outside one, and how the two relate to each other is just as critical if you are to create a truly satisfying object.

These days it is common practice to save the center of a bowl to create smaller bowls, rather than lose it all to shavings (see pp. 196–198 about nesting bowls). Although wasteful, it pays to go through the complete hollowing process—just don't use your best wood when practicing.

GOUGES FOR HOLLOWING FACEWORK

You'll soon discover that as the diameter and depth increase, so do the problems of controlling leverage. Because there is more weight in the wood, the catches will be heavier, and you'll need more weight over a longer tool handle. On external shapes, you mostly arrange the rest close to the work, so there's little leverage to cope with after the blank has been trued. Inside shapes are a different story. The tool will often be cutting 5 in. (125mm) or more away from the fulcrum. You need tools with long handles and you have to proceed with a good deal of caution.

When hollowing, I use a long bevel gouge as far as possible around the curve, which means until the bevel ceases to rub or the leverage becomes too much to control. Then I transfer to a heavier gouge with a steeper bevel or use a scraper. The advantage of the steeper bevel on a gouge is that bevel contact can be maintained from rim to center and you can shear-cut all the way, even across the bottom of a deep bowl.

When roughing a bowl using a deep-fluted gouge, these are the shavings you're after.

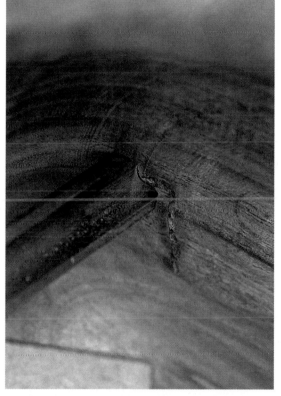

To shear-cut across the bottom of a deep form, you need a steep bevel on the nose and right wing of your gouge.

The inside curve is as important as the outside one,
and how the two relate to each other is just as critical
if you are to create a truly satisfying object.

Many turners have gouges with near-vertical bevels for this, but I tend not to use them because of the problems involved in cutting a precise line using a tool held at a right angle to the surface. I prefer a heavy scraper.

BASIC GOUGE TECHNIQUES

When hollowing, my basic rule is to direct any force in the cut towards the drive shaft and within the circumference of the area supported by the chuck. I never work from the center back up a curve to the rim because there are too many problems in controlling the tool, and besides, the cut is against the grain.

The main concern with hollowing is how to remove waste material as quickly and efficiently as possible, while still leaving a relatively smooth surface. In these days of nesting bowls, the process is much faster than formerly, with the added bonus that the former wasted shavings are now bowls or blanks for something smaller.

With a solid blank, drill a depth hole in the center first (see p. 95). Not only will this give you one less thing to worry about (you won't need to stop frequently to measure depth) but also by removing the center you can be much freer in using the tool at the end of a cut (you don't have to work accurately into center because it isn't there). Try to keep the cut moving as close to parallel to the axis as possible so that any force is directed towards the drive shaft.

When your cut is within the diameter of the fixing, you can use a certain amount of forward pressure. However, if the pressure is too great and you have a catch, the wood is likely to be pulled out of the chuck or come loose on the faceplate screws. Only practice and experience can tell you what the limitations are. Wood insecurely mounted will rattle as you cut. As always, if something sounds unusual, stop and find out why.

I rough-out bowls using gouges, then finish the form with scrapers. By far the best way of learning how to use a gouge is to rough-turn a large quantity of bowls for seasoning. When I started turning, I used a ¼-in. (6mm) deep-fluted gouge because it required me to make more cuts to hollow the small bowls I was making than a larger tool would have. The greater number of cuts provided more practice on each bowl. Try to make each cut as clean as possible, using every opportunity to improve your technique.

Because the cuts are made towards the drive shaft, it is difficult to use the tool without having the bevel rub. Deep-fluted bowl gouges are better than shallow gouges for hollowing because they are stronger and have an edge designed to cut a heavy shaving. The clean cut comes from the nose of the tool shearing at about 45°, while the right wing of the edge removes the bulk of the shaving with a scraping action. It's like a plough shear breaking ground.

Make the bowl in two stages. First, attach your blank to a screw chuck or faceplate by

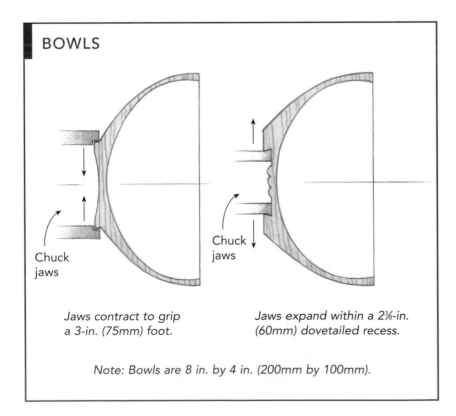

BOWLS

Jaws contract to grip a 3-in. (75mm) foot.

Jaws expand within a 2⅜-in. (60mm) dovetailed recess.

Chuck jaws

Chuck jaws

Note: Bowls are 8 in. by 4 in. (200mm by 100mm).

HOLLOWING

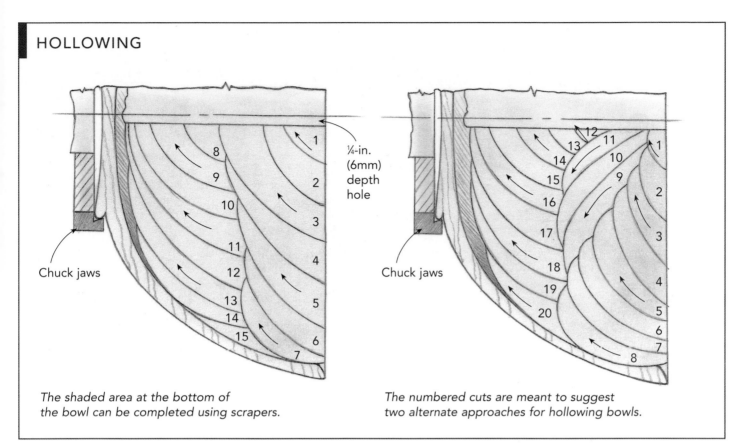

¼-in. (6mm) depth hole

Chuck jaws

The shaded area at the bottom of the bowl can be completed using scrapers.

The numbered cuts are meant to suggest two alternate approaches for hollowing bowls.

what will be the top surface of the bowl and turn an external shape similar to one shown in the illustration on the facing page. Which design you make for the foot will depend on the chuck available. The contracting grip with the bigger jaws will provide the better grip. Next, reverse the half-finished bowl so that it is held by its base in a chuck or on a faceplate and hollow the inside. Make the walls of your first few bowls about ⅜ in. (10mm) thick.

Adjust the rest across the face that will be hollowed so that the nose of the gouge is at center. Before any hollowing, true the face as you did the profile base (see the photos on p. 145) and drill the depth hole.

The gouges are used for hollowing just as they were for the profile cuts, only now the angle of the bevel becomes more relevant. The longer the bevel, the more convenient the angle of the handle for the higher part of the bowl wall.

Making the entry cut presents two problems. First, as usual, there is no surface for the bevel to rub. Second, there's a danger of a catch, which can severely damage the rim of your bowl (see the illustration above).

To begin the cut cleanly without a catch, use a secure stop-grip, with the gouge held on its side with its flute facing center (away from the surface you're about to cut), as shown in the top and center photos at left on p. 160. Line up the bevel in the direction of the cut, and tilt the edge of the tool up 15° to 20° so that you can bring it down through an arc into the wood. Once you have cut in about ⅛ in. (3mm) and the bevel is rubbing, roll the tool slightly counterclockwise, so the cutting portion of the edge is around 45° to the oncoming wood, creating a fatter shaving. Aim for a single, fluid movement. When you feel more confident, try keeping the tool horizontal and easing it forward

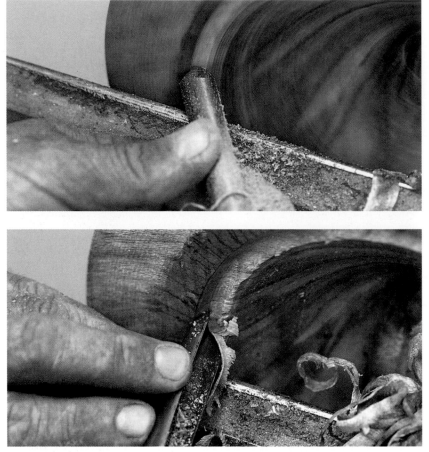

(TOP) For the entry cut, have the tool on its side with the bevel aligned in the direction you want to cut. (BOTTOM) Then roll the tool slightly counterclockwise to pick up a better shaving.

If you have trouble with the tool kicking back while making an entry cut, use a skew chisel flat on the rest to cut a small shoulder against which to rub the gouge bevel.

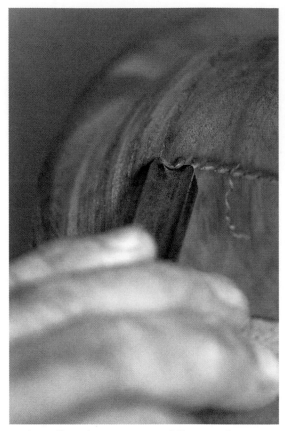

A deep-fluted gouge is used flute up for a back-cut—the finest finishing cut. Note how the rounded wing of the tool keeps clear of the wood and the possibility of a catch.

firmly until the bevel can rub but always with the tool on its side until you get a shaving.

If you have trouble with the tool kicking back during an entry cut, make a groove against which you can rest the gouge bevel. Use the long point of a skew chisel to make the groove (see the photo at left). Keep the tool flat on the rest and ease the point gently but firmly ⅛ in. (3mm) into the wood. For a finer cut, bring the tool flute up for a back-cut after you start the tool on its side (see the photo above right).

When I cut away from the center (cuts 9-11 in the righthand illustration on p. 159), as shown in the top left photo on the facing page, my fingers will be over the tool while my hand provides a firm backstop and fulcrum to control

An alternative way of hollowing is to work away from center. Hold the tool firmly on the rest to prevent chatter, and make the cuts as close to parallel to the axis as possible to keep any pressure directed into the chuck.

Starting a cut on an enclosed form is exactly the same technique as for open forms, but you need a longer left-side bevel on the gouge. Started on its side, this tool has been rolled counterclockwise for a larger shaving. On small enclosed forms, be particularly aware of how close the left wing of the edge is to catching and be cautious of bringing the flute too upright.

the chatter. When working from the rim into the center, as shown in the photo at right, the forward motion of the tool opposes the centrifugal force. All you need to do is provide a stop on the rest, which in turn allows you to provide support for the thin wall with your upper hand.

The most effective roughing-out cut is made with the lower edge of the gouge. The tool will cut when it is rolled at almost any angle, from a fine shaving back-cut, where the possibility of a catch is omnipresent, to a heavy scrape as the tool is rolled on its side. As you move it forward, rotate it slightly to find the biggest shaving with the least effort.

As your skills develop, you'll be micro-adjusting the edge all the time just in case

As a bowl wall becomes thinner, you will need to support the flexing wall by using your fingers to equalize the pressure of the tool. If your fingers become too hot, you are being too forceful in the cut.

there's a slightly better shaving to be had. Again, don't push if the tool is not cutting but adjust the angle or regrind or both. If the tool is cutting well, force won't be needed to move it forward. Your attention should be directed towards moving the edge in the direction you want without its wavering and providing maximum support for the tool using your body and weight. I can usually cut the first 2 in. (50mm) cleanly enough to sand, but further along there are often small ridges or undulations from tool chatter, best eliminated with a scraper.

As the depth of your hollow increases, the gouge will be cutting farther away from the rest. You'll need to get more weight over the tool handle to maintain control. In these situations, long-and-strong tools are essential because their bulk of metal will keep flexing to a minimum. Ideally you have these mounted in weighted handles (see pp. 51–52). The curved rests sold for internal shaping are mostly flat-topped and are more suitable for flat-section scrapers than gouges. I've never found them very satisfactory for use with gouges, so I don't have any.

SCRAPERS FOR HOLLOWING FACEWORK

Mostly I keep scrapers for finishing since gouges are much faster and safer to use when roughing the form. I have many scrapers of various lengths and never use a long blade if I have a shorter one to do the job. There's no point in wasting good steel when I don't have to. I find heavy scrapers much easier to control, particularly across the bottom of a curve into center. Used delicately, they will leave an excellent surface.

The scraper I use in any given situation will have a radius slightly tighter than the curve I want to cut, as shown in the photo above right. Those scrapers shown in the illustration on the facing page are the shapes I use for almost all my bowls more than 5 in. (125mm) in diameter. The bowl scrapers (A and B) are ideal for inter-

When I sweep my 1⅜-in. (35mm) radiused scraper toward center, I can use about half the edge at one time. This slightly radiused edge is much better than a round-nose scraper for obtaining flowing curves.

nal surfaces. I use all of the edge at some time during the cut but no more than ½ in. (13mm) of the edge at one time. When cutting a curve, you can relate it easily to a wide scraper edge and produce a flowing curve with relative ease. It is very difficult to sweep a narrow or domed tool evenly enough to cut a smooth curve. The shear scrapers (C and D) are used on profiles and around details such as beads and feet.

I use asymmetrical and skewed edges so I have the handle at an angle to the wood surface rather than at 90° to it (see the illustration on the facing page). All the bevels are about 45° with a small burr on the edge. As with the other tools (only more so), don't use forward

SCRAPING A BOWL

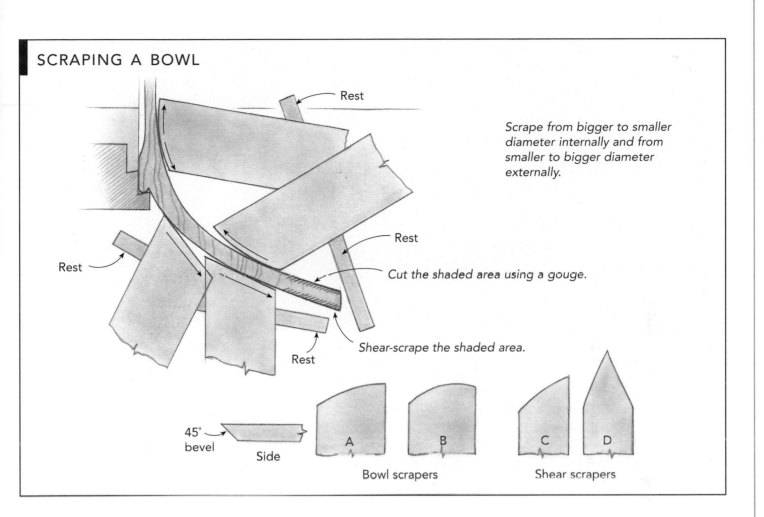

Rest

Scrape from bigger to smaller diameter internally and from smaller to bigger diameter externally.

Rest

Cut the shaded area using a gouge.

Rest

Shear-scrape the shaded area.

Rest

45° bevel

Side

A B

Bowl scrapers

C D

Shear scrapers

The scraper I use in any given situation will have a radius slightly tighter than the curve I want to cut.

pressure if the scraper is not cutting. Go back to the grinder.

When there is only a small opening through which to hollow, narrow round-nose square section scrapers (¼ in. [6mm] to ½ in. [13mm]) are typically best. A square-edge scraper with a sharp corner is very effective, but the surface it leaves is poor, so it should be used for roughing only.

BASIC SCRAPING TECHNIQUES

The golden rule when using square-section scrapers is to keep them flat on the rest. There is a tendency to lift one side, which then gets caught by the wood, bangs down, and usually scars the surface you're trying to smooth. It is good practice to keep pressure on top of the tool to ensure it stays flat on the rest at all times. Always position scrapers so that in the event of a catch the edge swings into space.

Always position scrapers so that in the event of a catch the edge swings into space.

Don't use a scraper near the rim of a bowl unless you absolutely have to. If scraping is the only solution, don't place the tool flat on the rest, but shear-scrape using a round-nose scraper. Have the lathe running slowly and support the wall with your hand.

Mostly you'll have the tool pitched down a few degrees. For external surfaces, the rest should be set slightly below center, while for internal scraping, it should be set at center.

I don't use scrapers to rough-out hollows if I can avoid it. But sometimes they're the best tool to use for heavy internal cuts made far away from the rest where gouges cannot operate at their best. For this purpose, I use ⅜-in.- (10mm) thick and 1⅜-in.- (35mm) wide scrapers. You need this width for weight and strength, but if you present such a wide edge, or even a ⅝-in.- (15mm) wide edge to the wood at once, the catch will be larger than you can control. Never use more than a small portion (about ½ in. [13mm]) of the edge at one time.

Scrapers must be moved into the wood gently because the bevel can't rub. The normal technique of lowering the tool through an arc

and rubbing the bevel to begin a cut, which applies to all gouges and chisels, is reversed for scrapers. With a scraper, you swing it into the cut from below by leaning on the handle. Having your elbow on the handle helps control the sudden increase in pressure as wood and tool meet.

You can use scrapers to even out gouge-cut curves that don't flow well. Hold the tool firmly and keep the handle against your side or forearm and move your body with it. The upper hand ensures that the flat section remains fully on the rest and provides the fine adjustments for the cut. Move the tool cautiously so that the wood brushes past, barely touching the edge. Any real pressure will lead to a catch or a possible tick-tick sound, which indicates torn grain (usually pulled from end grain). If the job is thin and vibrates, it needs support and an even lighter cut.

The biggest problem with scraping techniques is that often, especially on internal shapes, the point of cut will be well away from the fulcrum—perhaps as far as 8 in. (200mm). The greater the distance, the greater the leverage there is to control. Most of my scrapers have handles between 14 in. (355mm) and 18 in. (460mm) long, which I align under my forearm for greater support and control. The farther from the rest you cut, the more cautious you must be in moving the edge and the less of it should contact the wood.

Aside from controlling the leverage, you will have to keep the edge moving to produce flowing curves. On a regular curve, you'll be able to swing the edge through an arc by pivoting the tool on the rest, but this rarely happens because it's more common to encounter a parabolic curve. The tool will have to move along and across the rest at the same time that it sweeps around the curve. You'll need to develop good coordination for such complex movements. As you swing the tool (using the lower hand), the upper hand provides a moveable stop, firmly maintaining the path of the edge to remove the ridges.

I try never to use scrapers near the rim of a thin bowl (a wall less than 15% of the bowl diameter) because thinner wood is likely to flex and, consequently, chatter marks or catches are inevitable. When I absolutely have to use a scraper, I lower the lathe speed to 400 rpm to 600 rpm on a 10-in.- (250mm) diameter bowl. I shear-scrape using a round-nose tool, taking care to fully support the bowl wall.

I learned to use scrapers by making hundreds of breadboards, platters, and shallow dishes, and you might try the same (only maybe not quite so many). I suggest 1¼-in. (32mm) by 12-in. (305mm) blanks for breadboards, 1⅛-in. (28mm) by 10-in. (255mm) blanks for platters, and 2-in. (50mm) by 10-in. (255mm) blanks for dishes. Blanks of these sizes will present fewer cutting problems than larger ones, when weight and peripheral speed combine against you. Blanks can be flattened and sanded on one side, which will be the base, and then mounted on a screw chuck and turned completely without being transferred to another fixing.

CYLINDERS AND DEEP HOLLOWS

The inside of a deep form is always difficult to finish. The usual problems with the end grain extend the length of the wall, particularly with cylinders, and the base is a long way from the rest. Flat bottoms in forms such as bottle coasters are best finished using scrapers after the bulk of the waste is removed with a gouge.

If a long-beveled gouge will reach, a shear cut will produce the cleanest surface (see Fig. 1 in the illustration at right), but for accuracy I prefer to use the sharp left corner of a 1-in. (25mm) long-and-strong square-edge scraper. Actually, the edge is ground with a slight curve making the left corner about 88° (Fig. 2). For a really sharp corner, you should hone the three surfaces that make it: the bevel, side, and top. As when hollowing end grain, the trick to cutting a cylinder is to keep the blade horizontal and parallel to the axis.

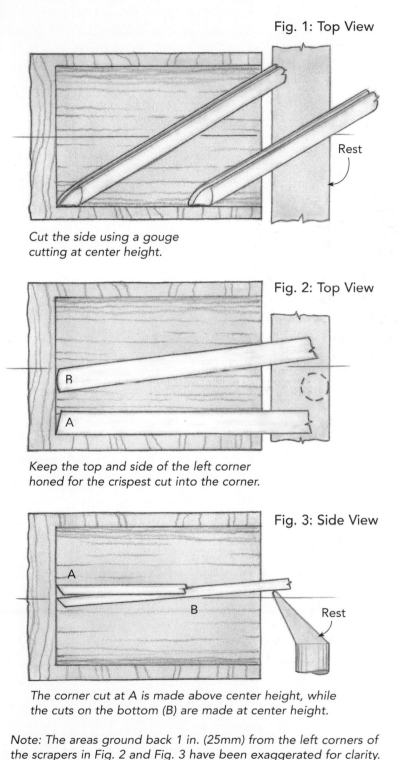

CUTTING INTERNAL CYLINDERS

Fig. 1: Top View

Rest

Cut the side using a gouge cutting at center height.

Fig. 2: Top View

Keep the top and side of the left corner honed for the crispest cut into the corner.

Fig. 3: Side View

Rest

The corner cut at A is made above center height, while the cuts on the bottom (B) are made at center height.

Note: The areas ground back 1 in. (25mm) from the left corners of the scrapers in Fig. 2 and Fig. 3 have been exaggerated for clarity.

Turn the base flat in a series of steps working from the bottom of the depth hole out, then move the edge across the surface in one sweep to eliminate any small ridges. You can decorate an internal base by easing either corner of the scraper into the base to create beads or use a spear-point scraper very gently for grooves. (For more on decoration, see the facing page.)

Pushing Your Limits

Once you've made several 8-in. (200mm) to 10-in. (250mm) open-shaped bowls with a ½-in.- (13mm) thick wall and you feel ready for a greater challenge, try a thinner version of the same form. This version demands a more precise and controlled use of the same techniques and, if you are successful, will show what you

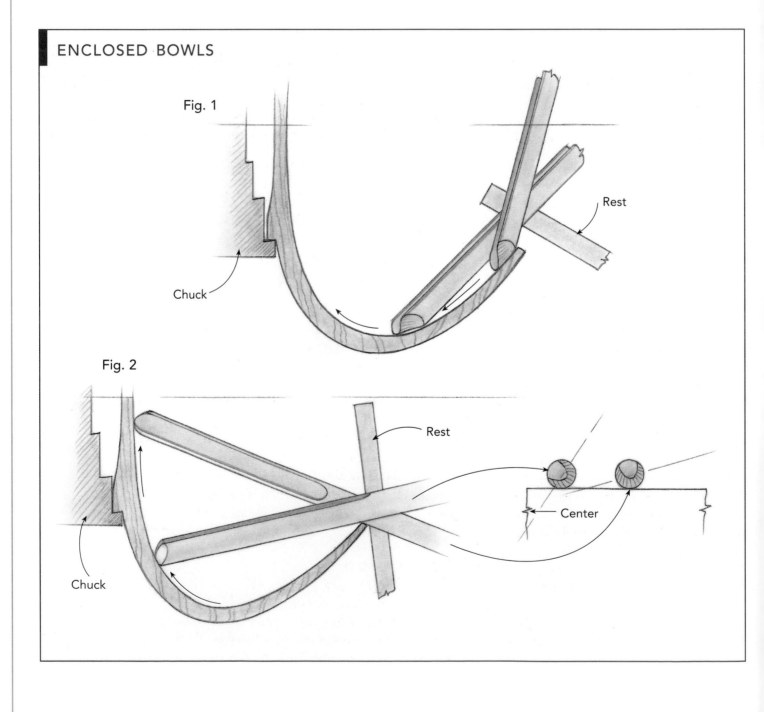

ENCLOSED BOWLS

Fig. 1

Chuck

Rest

Fig. 2

Rest

Chuck

Center

can achieve. I can cajole most students into producing an ultra-thin bowl, and I do so as a
confidence-builder. After that, a thicker (and
usually more practical) wall will be easy to
achieve. I see no point in making ultra-thin
bowls simply because they present technical
problems: There should be reasons other than
pure exhibitionism. Do one or two to boost
your confidence and then return to reality.

As a bowl wall becomes thinner, you will
encounter problems with chatter. Too much
tool pressure against the wood causes it to flex
and vibrate, developing characteristic parallel-
angled ridges (this effect can be controlled for
surface decoration when you get the hang of it).
You'll hear chatter long before you see it. If you
cut too forcefully, the pitch will rise to a shrill
screech. The thinner the wall, the worse the
noise. Eliminate this by equalizing the tool
pressure, holding your fingers around the rim
to support the wood, as in the photos at right
on p. 161.

When you feel comfortable turning an open,
outwards-flowing bowl shape, move on to one
with upper walls that curve inward to form a
narrower opening. The standard tools are more
awkward to handle on this sort of shape
because of the restricted angle of approach.
(Short-bed lathes, with the tailstock removed,
are designed for this kind of job, enabling you
to move freely around the face, working from
any angle.)

The angle of the bevel becomes more critical
and it will need to be longer the more you
undercut the rim. I use a narrow ¼-in. (6mm)
gouge, ground with a very long left bevel. Get
the rest as near as possible to 90° to the direction of the cut (see Fig. 1 in the illustration on
the facing page). In order to shear-cut around
the curve, you need a steeper bevel, preferably
on a heavier tool with a longer handle.

If your turning interests lie chiefly in bowls,
hollow forms, and vessels, while you practice
the cuts you have the opportunity to develop
your feel for form and wall thickness. It is only

It pays to cut bowls in half occasionally—even very good ones—so you
can see and analyze the cross section. The curves in these bowls flow
well and each is well balanced with the weight evenly distributed, which
is why they felt good in my hand.

natural that you'll want to keep at least a couple
of early bowls, but to really develop your skills
in this direction you should cut a few practice
bowls in half so you can see if you actually
turned what you think you turned (see the
photo above). It is often a sobering experience!

Plane or sand the cross section smooth and
trace the outline on paper if it helps. You'll see
clearly how your lines flow (or don't flow), how
inside and outside curves relate, and where
more wood could have been left or removed to
improve the balance and tactile quality of the
whole. Even now, I still cut bowls in half from
time to time. Bowls of marginal quality serve
you far better cut and learned from than being
placed on public display to damage your reputa-
tion. I look at bowl design in depth in my book
Turned Bowl Design (The Taunton Press, 1987).

Decoration

There will be occasions when you feel some
decorative grooves, coves, or beads are required.
Fortunately, most decoration is applied to external shapes that are easy to get at. When you
need to cut a groove or bead into an internal

Cutting Boards

I mount these in extra-large jaws initially so I don't mess up the surface with screw holes. For a one-sided board, turn a recess as shown in the bottom right photo on p. 33. Alternatively, finish one side with a vertical lip or thick side that can be gripped by the same jaws. Then you can reverse the job in the chuck and complete the other side with no obvious fixing points. You end up with a double-sided cutting board that any cook will find very handy.

MATERIAL: Tasmanian blackwood
SIZE: 14 in. (355mm) diameter

curve, you'll probably have to grind a special tool. I keep all my old skew chisels, parting tools, and scrapers for this purpose.

Grooves and coves on a profile are simple to turn because they are cut into a finished sur-face. Beads are different. Beads look best when seemingly applied to a finished surface. The form on which they sit should flow beneath them unless the bead is used at a point where the profile changes direction dramatically. If the basic form looks as though it should flow beneath a bead or other raised area but doesn't, the whole thing will look uncomfortable. In commercial terms, grooves and coves can be used to good effect in breaking the surface visually and are easier to cut than beads.

GROOVES AND COVES
Grooves are most easily made by placing a spear-point scraper flat on the rest and easing it straight into the wood, but the finished surface will rarely be equal to one that is shear-cut. You need to move the spear-point into the wood very gently to produce tiny feathery shavings. Any hint of real pressure against the wood will cause the tool to flex, tearing the groove sides. To create inset beads as shown in the bottom photo on the facing page, make a series of grooves then tilt the tool on edge and round the shoulders using a shear scraper.

To cut coves into a curve or cylinder, use a ⅜-in.-(10mm) long fingernail gouge in the same manner as for a centerwork cove (see pp. 104–108). Cutting coves into a flat face, such as a breadboard or clock face, is the same as making an entry cut when hollowing a bowl (see the top left photo on p. 160). For each cut, you need to pin the tool firmly to the rest to prevent it kicking sideways. The main problem is keep-ing the coves visually crisp with well-defined angles on the cove rims, so when sanding, finish the cove first, then sand the flat surface.

BEADS
Cutting beads into the side of a bowl profile is good fun and not half as difficult as it looks at first glance. You just need to go very gently and rhythmically. Once you get the hang of it, the chief danger is that you want to enjoy your new skill and cover everything with beads. My favorite tool for the job is a ⅜-in. (9mm) shallow gouge with a long bevel and fingernail edge. The

edge shear-cuts as it pivots out of the wood, then goes against the grain as it cuts in. I always use a freshly ground tool to ensure the best edge when turning beads.

The trick to cutting beads is to pivot the edge in and out of the wood. Keep the tool pinned firmly on the rest as you cut each bead so it's like an oar in a rowlock. Don't move the tool forward or sideways while you are actually cutting a bead. Cut the bead, then move the tool a bead-width along the rest by pivoting it on the nose of the edge.

As you cut a bead, the end of the handle performs a little counterclockwise circle. So if you are cutting a line of beads, the rhythm for the end of the handle becomes: circle (while cutting the bead), sideways swing (pivot the tool along the rest), circle (another bead), swing, circle, swing, and so on. Beware of rolling the gouge too much, especially on the inward cut, because contrary to most expectations, this creates a step rather than the anticipated round. To cut larger or wider beads, you merely rotate the handle through a bigger circle.

This technique usually enables me to cut even really difficult grain cleanly, such as the Tasmanian blackwood shown in the top photo above right. On many woods, I don't bother to spoil the surface by using abrasives.

On top-quality close-grained woods, you can use a spear-point scraper to create beads, making V-grooves then rounding the corners to a series of facets that can be sanded smooth. However, the quality of the surface is rarely equal to a shear-cut one. You apply the same technique for turning beads sitting proud of a curved profile: roughing them out square while the surrounding surface is finished, as shown in the top photos on p. 171.

Beads on a flat face, such as a bowl base, clock face, or breadboard, require a slightly different approach because of the grain alignment. Cut to each side from the top of the roughed bead (working from smaller to larger diameter for the shear cut).

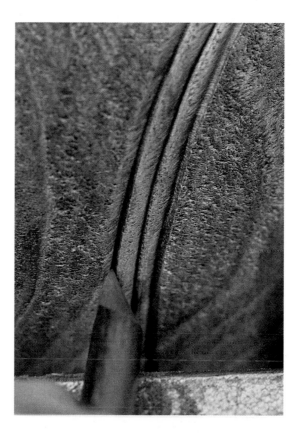

A small gouge cuts so cleanly that even on this difficult Tasmanian black-wood, the beads require only minimal sanding.

Beads can be turned using a spear-point scraper, but typically (as seen to the right) beads shear-cut with a gouge will be cleaner.

CUTTING BEADS

Cutting beads into the side of a bowl profile is not half as difficult as it looks at first glance. You just need to go very gently and rhythmically. Use a ⅜-in. (9mm) shallow gouge.

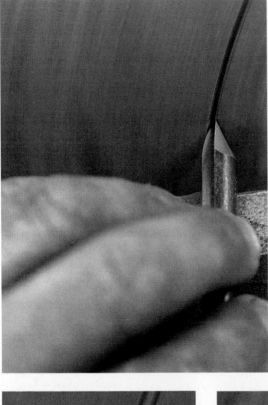

1 Pivot the tool into the wood, with the flute facing the direction of the cut.

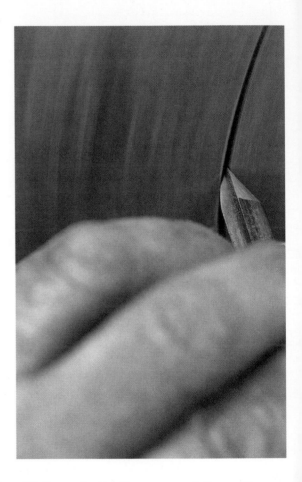

2 Drop the handle as you roll the tool slightly clockwise to cut the right side of the bead.

3 (FAR LEFT) To cut the left side of the bead, pivot the edge back into the wood, keeping the gouge at the same angle for the top section of the curve. (LEFT) Then gradually roll it on its side so it doesn't catch at the end of the cut.

To cut beads inset into a flat face, start the gouge on its side with the bevel rubbing and pivot the edge into the wood using as little pressure as possible. This gives you a groove with a cleanly cut left side and torn end grain on the right (see the photos below left).

To clean up the right side, take an arcing cut from the right, ensuring that the tool ends up on its side at the end of the cut. Hold the nose of the tool a second to detail the angle between the two half-beads. Then begin the next cut with the bevel riding the right shoulder of the groove you've just cut, and pivot the edge into the wood again to create an inset bead. Next, clean up the right side, and so on. Make sure the gouge always finishes on its side so you get good definition at the base of the bead and lessen the risk of a catch.

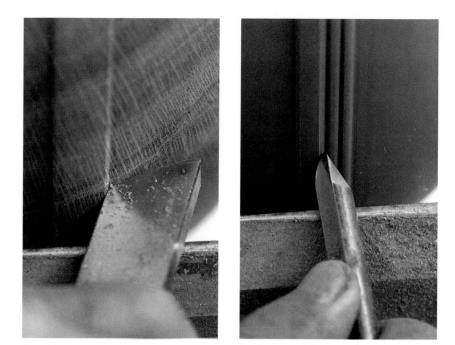

(LEFT) Beads sitting on a curve are blocked out, (RIGHT) then cut using a ⅜-in. (9mm) shallow gouge.

(TOP) To cut a groove into a face, start the tool on its side, then pivot it into the wood. (BOTTOM) Pivot the edge in from the right to clean up the right shoulder.

These beads turned in green camphor laurel are ready for sanding, starting with 150 grit. (LEFT) The ridges on the larger beads on a bowl profile will sand away without difficulties. (RIGHT) On the underside of the same bowl, three grooves make two beads to decorate the base. The wood is soft enough that abrasives will easily smooth the somewhat rugged surface.

TURNING A BOWL

It is good practice to rough-turn your bowl blanks whether the wood is seasoned or not because even dry wood can warp somewhat when the stresses alter as the center is removed. In this project, you'll see how to complete a rough-turned bowl using a step-jaw chuck. The idea is to finish the outside, then rechuck the bowl for hollowing and finishing. When you take the bowl from the chuck after hollowing, it's finished.

1 Grip the rough-turned bowl by the foot and turn a square or slightly dovetailed shoulder for the chuck jaws to expand into. Gauge this by eye, cutting the groove slightly wider than the jaws.

2 Remount the bowl over the chuck jaws, which expand into the shoulder you've just turned. The aim in the first two steps is to mount the bowl so the whole of the profile is exposed without the tail center getting in the way.

3 Use a sweeping roughing cut to true the surface.

4 Don't forget to cut in from the rim and remove any razor edge.

5 True the base, making it slightly concave so it sits flat on a rim.

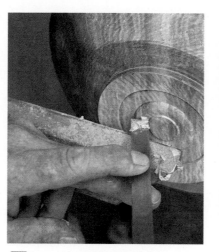

6 Use a ½-in. (13mm) square-edge scraper to turn a rebate. Here I use small jaws expanding into the rebate to hold the bowl for hollowing. If you have larger jaws, a better and more secure option is to turn a foot that can be gripped.

7 I use the corners of the scraper to decorate the center of the base.

8 You can grind a special skewed scraper to cut the dovetail for the chuck jaws, but here I use a ½-in. (13mm) skew chisel flat on the rest as a scraper. The depth of the rebate needs to be about ⅛ in. (4mm). If you make it too deep, you commit yourself to a thick base for the bowl, which doesn't do much for the bowl's tactile qualities.

9 A shear cut refines the curve. I have the gouge pointing in the direction I'm cutting so I can steer it easily around the corner.

10 Use a shear scraper to refine the surface prior to sanding. Just below the rim, I ease the corner into the wood to create a small bead.

11 To detail the underside of a bead at the rim, use the long point of the shear scraper.

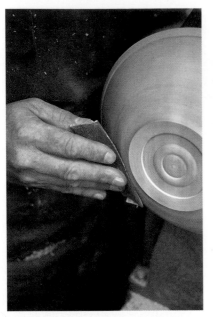

12 Sand, working through 100-, 150-, 240-, and 360-grit abrasives.

13 Oil the sanded surface with the lathe off so all the pores get filled.

14 With the lathe running, hold a block of beeswax against the wood and melt a layer onto the surface. Friction provides the heat, so you need a bit of pressure.

15 Finally, use a soft cloth bunched in your hands (never wrapped around your fingers) to melt the wax into the wood. You need a fair amount of pressure to melt the wax, so try to direct it toward the chuck rather than directly against the axis. The whole process takes a few seconds and the job's done.

16 (LEFT) Remount the bowl for hollowing by expanding the step jaws into the rebate. (ABOVE) This is a key chuck, so I can hold the bowl in the jaws with my right hand while I use the left to adjust the jaws.

20 Next, use the same scraper more delicately so it barely brushes the wood as you blend the gouge-cut surface into the scraped curve that sweeps into the base.

17 Before anything else, true the rim. It can be difficult to do later, so develop the habit of truing any job the moment you rechuck it.

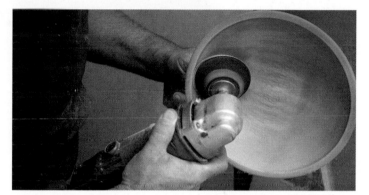

18 Shear-cut the inner curve as far as possible with the gouge bevel rubbing.

21 Complete the internal form by power-sanding. Small ridges vanish with 120 grit, but any dips remain untouched and obvious. Large dips can be removed by sanding the ridges on either side with 60 grit but, unless the bowl wall is thin and vibration is a problem, it's generally better to try to turn a smoother curve.

19 Using a heavy scraper, remove the waste towards the center of the bowl where the area is fully supported by the chuck.

The finished bowl. Forest she-oak. 8 in. by 3 in. (200mm by 75mm).

LIDDED BOX

This project not only shows you how useful chucks can be but also provides good scraping practice. The base, a sort of squarish bowl, is made first, then the lid is made to fit the base. The amount of rechucking and the attention to detail make this an interesting project with a useful end product. You can play around with the basic process and come up with your own variations. When making the lid, you can take the lid in and out of the chuck as many times as you like to see how it fits and looks on the base.

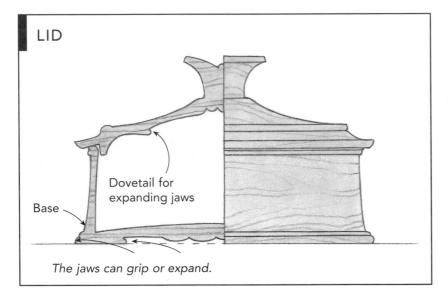

LID

Dovetail for expanding jaws

Base

The jaws can grip or expand.

1 Cut the base and lid from the same block. (Shown here is bone-dry sally wattle.)

2 Grip the base section by what will be the top and true the face. Mark out the diameter of the base, which will be gripped by the chuck. If you have only small chuck jaws, use them to expand into a shallow rebate within the base as on the bowl (see the photos for step 16 on p. 174).

3 Rough-out the base profile, ensuring that there are no flat sections left from the bandsaw.

4 Turn the bottom and decorate as desired. Here I ease the left corner of a shear scraper to create a recessed dome for the bottom.

5 Turn a bead on the rim of the base, which will disguise any possible chuck marks. At this stage, the lower part of the base is sanded, waxed, and polished, then remounted for hollowing.

6 Use a cloth to protect the finished surface from the chuck jaws as you true the rim of the base section in preparation for the completion of the profile and hollowing.

7 Complete the profile, leaving a bead at the rim. This can be removed later if it doesn't seem appropriate.

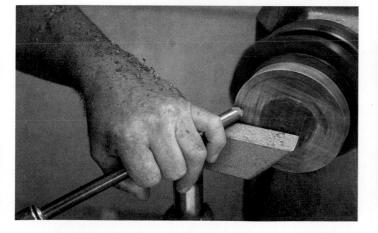

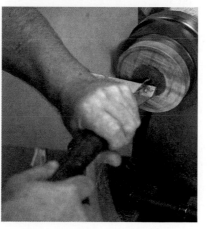

8 (FAR LEFT) True the face, (LEFT) then drill a depth hole in the base.

9 Begin hollowing with a ⅜-in. (9mm) deep-fluted gouge.

10 Complete the hollowing with a ¾-in. (20mm) square-edge scraper.

11 Sand and finish the base. If you follow exactly the same procedure, you should have no problem blending in the portion completed in step 5.

13 Remount the lid with smaller-diameter jaws gripping the roughed knob so the inside can be completed. True the rim.

12 Grip the lid by the base and rough-out a knob that fits 2-in. (50mm) jaws.

14 (ABOVE) Mark the internal diameter of the base, and (RIGHT) turn a short tenon on that diameter to fit the base.

15 Test-fit the base to the lid.

16 (LEFT) Turn the inside of the lid. Having removed the bulk with a small bowl gouge, I refine the surface with a 1⅜-in. (35mm) scraper. (RIGHT) Then I use a skew chisel on its side to make a small dovetail for the chuck to expand into.

17 Cut small beads to decorate the inside.

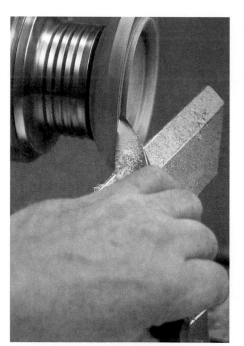

18 Shear-scrape the flange, undercutting it slightly so it'll sit well on the base rim. The less you sand here, the better the fit. Sand and finish the inside of the lid.

19 Assess how the lid looks on the base. At this stage, it is physically and visually far too heavy.

20 Remount the lid over the expanding jaws. Rough-out the form using a ½-in. (13mm) shallow gouge. From this stage on, you can pop the lid in and out of the chuck as often as you like to see how it looks on the base and to check its thickness.

21 Refine and detail the top of the lid using scrapers. Here I use a shear scraper flat and ease the left corner into the blank near the rim to create a small bead.

22 Shear-scrape the cove on the rim with a 1-in. (25mm) round-nose scraper tilted on its side.

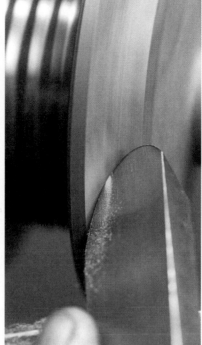

23 Finally, shear-scrape the curved underside of the knob with a ⅜-in. (9mm) shallow gouge. The convex edge allows me to turn a slightly concave stem to the knob.

The finished box. If I don't like the lid, I can pop it back on the chuck and refine it further.

8 FINISHING

WE ARE SURROUNDED BY examples of what use can do for a surface. Consider wooden handrails on an old staircase, the handle of a well-used garden, workshop, or building tool, or the arms and seat of an old and favored chair. All have been polished by sweaty palms and grubby hands to produce a wondrous patina, a surface that begs for a caress of the hand. Unfortunately, it comes with age and handling, not from a tin to be applied with a brush.

Wood benefits from being polished regularly, be it through sweaty palms or wax polishes. It's the surface I aspire to for all my bowls and boxes, but it requires input, first from me and then, more importantly, from the custodians of my work. You may call them owners if you like, but since I make bowls and boxes to last generations, I regard owners as temporary guardians.

If you are looking forward to a chapter packed with information on polishing compounds, chemical formulas, and sealers, you will be disappointed. I belong to the school that believes if you want a plastic-looking bowl, you should buy a molded one. Don't splash polyurethane over a piece of wood that has done no harm to anyone. I don't even like hard-wax finishes. Synthetic finishes might do wonderful things for wood as it leaves the workshop, but it will still look the same years later. Nothing gets through the surface, so the wood fails to develop character and will never have the patina of a well-used piece left natural.

I am inclined to leave the surface of a piece unsanded and even unfinished—directly as it comes from the tool—because I know that the wood will look so good in seasoned old age. But customers, presumably attracted by (or conditioned to expect) the polished surface of high-gloss polyurethane, are not generally so keen. So I have reached a happy compromise by employing an oil-and-wax finish that enhances, but does not obscure, the sensual quality of the wood. This compromise allows the custodian of a piece the option of either oiling or polishing depending on how it is used or kept.

Abrasives

Although an oil-and-wax finish can be applied to any surface, it is general practice to smooth the work with abrasives first. Abrasives are graded by number, according to the size of the cutting agent and its density on the backing paper or cloth. The abrasives I use normally range from 60 grit (coarse) to 400 grit (fine). They are hand-held against the revolving wood or stuck to a pad for power-sanding. It is possible to do the most amazing things with coarser grits, which sometimes seem to cut as fast as chisels, although they leave a torn and scratched surface. Before you start, be sure to arrange your dust-collection duct as close to the area being sanded as possible.

HAND-SANDING

The hand-held grits I use most are 100, 150, 240, and 400 grit. I normally start with 100 grit, but it will not always cope with difficult end grain on facework. For those occasions, I use old, partly worn, cloth-backed sanding discs.

A cardinal rule of sanding is that you proceed to a finer grade of abrasive only when all marks from previous coarser papers have been removed. You should see an even scoring pattern with no obvious deeper scratching before moving on. Move the paper evenly and slowly across the face or along the axis of the work in a final sweep before moving on to the next grade of paper. Jabbing and dabbing will increase scratching.

I always use as much pressure as possible, although if you press too hard or too long in one place, the friction will produce heat cracks in almost any wood. Often it is better to sand at a lower speed than you use for turning, especially with larger facework, where peripheral speeds can be high. If the speed is too high, the sandpaper can skate over the surface rather than cut. If I'm working on a variable-speed lathe, I'll drop the speed 10% to 15%. But it is too time-consuming to adjust the belt manually on a standard lathe, so in that case I wind up sanding at the same speed I use for turning.

Frequently, I will wipe on oil after an initial sanding with 80-grit paper to raise the grain. The paper clogs rapidly but the muck can

usually be removed by slapping the paper against the lathe bed. The oil also helps keep the dust down.

I use silicon-carbide cloth-backed abrasives, which can be purchased by the roll or in shorter lengths. I find these cut better and longer than any paper-backed abrasives, which I've never found to perform well in the extremes of humidity. They become floppy in the damp weather and too brittle in the dry. You need lightweight backing material that remains flexible in all conditions. Thick abrasive backings tend to produce stiff corners and edges, which increase the likelihood of scratches, especially on concave surfaces.

I cut abrasives in pieces about 4½ in. (110mm) by 6 in. (150mm) and fold each one in thirds so that one cutting surface is not in contact with another. Each piece also forms its own pad and is easier to hold. Paper folded over only once has a habit of unfolding and deteriorating more rapidly. Never wrap abrasive around your fingers. Hold the folded sheet between your fingers and thumb, and press it against the revolving wood.

Beware of letting your hand drift to the far side of the work when sanding a flat face or internally (see A in the illustration below). The upward rotation of the wood can grab the paper and carry your hand up to the top of the work's

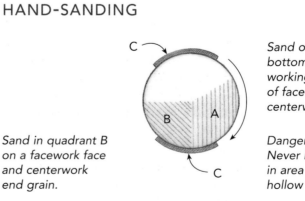

HAND-SANDING

Sand in quadrant B on a facework face and centerwork end grain.

Sand on top or bottom (C) when working the outside of facework or centerwork.

Danger area: Never hand-sand in area A on flat or hollow forms.

Ash Bowl

The wood was turned unseasoned with a rounded base to accommodate the warping, then sand-blasted. Sand-blasting removes softer material while retaining every turned detail and scratch. You need to sand the surface just as assiduously in preparation for sand-blasting as for polishing.

MATERIAL: Ash
SIZE: 14½ in. by 4¾ in.
(370mm by 120mm)

Never wrap abrasive around your fingers.

Sand in the lower-left quadrant of the work when sanding end grain or a face.

orbit. From there, your hand can shoot forward, back to the far side to meet the upward swing of the wood. Your fingers would be hit end-on and bent back. The result is as if you had taken a dive onto your extended fingertips. All this occurs in a fraction of a second. I have broken three knuckles this way on two separate occasions and know others who have done the same.

For safety, keep sanding pressure toward you when working on the inside and on top when working on the outside of facework. If the work is thin, provide support with your free hand as you would when turning delicate work (see the top photos on the facing page). Centerwork is generally sanded on the top or bottom of the work (see C in the illustration on p. 183) or in the lower-left quadrant (B) for end grain. Be careful not to allow the sandpaper to wrap around a spindle. To avoid this, hold the sheet of paper by both ends around the bottom of the work and apply pressure by lifting up (see the bottom photo on the facing page). The important thing is to prevent the ends of the paper from overlapping around the wood.

When sanding a fragile bowl, don't wrap abrasives around your fingers. Support the work with your free hand to equalize the pressure of the sanding.

It's very easy as you sand to lose your original turned form, making the definite indefinite and insipid. Beware of rounding edges that would be better left crisp, as on a bowl or platter rim. Avoid rounding edges by sanding one surface first and then the other—never sand both together. But, for safety, remember to soften the resultant sharp edge with a quick touch of fine abrasive. Crisp does not mean razor sharp.

Often when you finish sanding and run your hand back and forth across the wood surface, the end grain will feel slightly rough. This occurs because the lathe rotates in one direction and the fibers have been bent the opposite way. I typically hand-sand this with the lathe at rest, but a reversing switch on the lathe makes the job easier. If you can run your lathe in the opposite direction, you can cut back all those lifted fibers easily. The sanding sequence might then

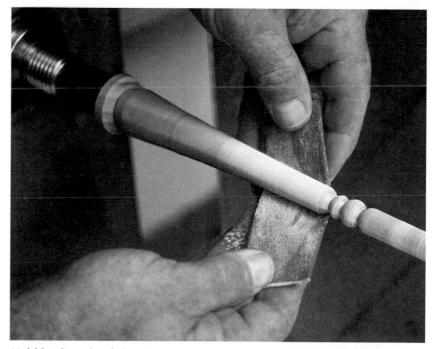

Hold both ends of the abrasive when sanding a spindle. By working from below, you can see what you're doing.

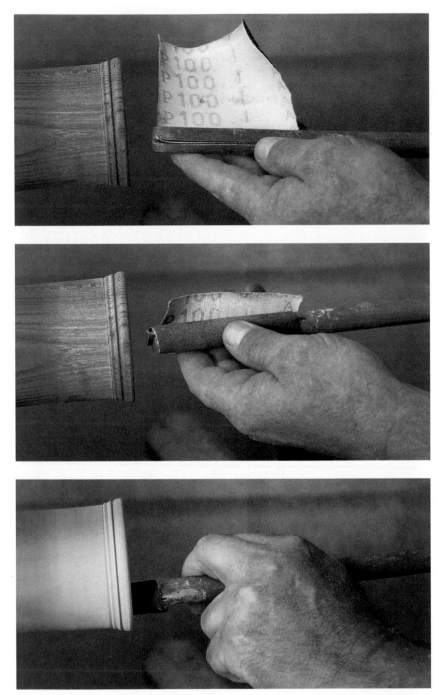

To sand inside a deep cylinder where it's difficult to reach, wrap abrasives around a stick. (TOP AND CENTER) Cut a slot in the end to secure the left side of the abrasive (when face down). (BOTTOM) Note how I hook my fingers over the stick to keep it pressured against the wood and to prevent the wood from grabbing it and rattling it about. If the stick gets loose, hit the off button immediately, otherwise you could split a fragile piece.

run 80 grit forward/reverse, 100 grit reverse/forward, 180 grit forward/reverse. To finish, always polish with the lathe in forward so it's running in the correct direction for the next job.

When running a lathe in reverse, problems can arise if you are using a chuck or faceplate. Unless screwed on firmly, they'll unscrew when the lathe is reversed. I help to start the lathe in reverse rotation by spinning the handwheel (on the outboard shaft) as I switch on the machine. Some manufacturers provide a lock for chucks, or you could drill and insert a locking screw through the threads of the fixing and the drive shaft.

For those awkward little hollows and miniatures where a finger won't fit, a surgical clamp comes in handy for gripping small bits of abrasive or polishing rag.

To sand inside a deep cylinder where it's difficult to reach with your fingers, wrap abrasives around a stick. Cut a slot in the end to secure the left side of the abrasive (when face down), as shown in the top and center photos at left. In the bottom photo at left, note how I hook my fingers over the stick to keep it pressured against the wood and prevent the wood from grabbing it and rattling it about. If the stick gets loose, hit the off button immediately, otherwise you could split a fragile piece.

POWER-SANDING

Although I enjoy the contact and control of hand-held abrasives against the wood, in most situations—with the exception of beads, coves, corners, and other fine details—power-sanding is a vastly speedier option. On the inside of a bowl, it's a powerful shaping tool, especially on bowls less than 8-in. (200mm) in diameter.

For power-sanding, an abrasive disc is attached to a spongy rubber backing pad mounted in an electric hand drill. The best tool for the job is an angle drill, which is easier to control than a standard drill because the body lies parallel to the surface being sanded. This provides better leverage than the conventional drill body, which lies at 90° to the work surface and is more likely to kick sideways. Better still is a pneumatic angle sander, but you need a big compressor to run it.

Both abrasive and pad must be flexible to avoid deep scoring, especially in the tight curves of concave shapes. Most brands of abrasive discs are backed with hook-and-loop tape, so these can be peeled on and off with ease. If you use adhesive-backed discs as I do, you have to keep the adhesive free of dust at all times. I store the discs not in use on top of the lathe where I can clear the metal surface of dust with my palm before attaching the disc.

Because the disc on the drill revolves at the same time that the wood is rotating, the position in which the disc is held against the wood will vary the cutting power and the quality of the finished surface. The wood normally revolves in only one direction—counterclockwise on the inboard side. Most drills revolve in a clockwise direction, but you can use any portion of the disc for sanding.

If you use the top or bottom, the grit will cut across the path of the rotating grain (as shown at B and D in the illustration at right, leaving swirling score marks. Hand-held abrasives always leave concentric score marks, and you get the same marks power-sanding when the disc rotates on the same path as the wood (see A or C in the illustration at right). However, the side traveling against the wood's rotation (C) cuts much more aggressively than the one traveling with it (A).

Present one side of the revolving disc to the work at or slightly below center height. Keep the disc moving across the surface to prevent heat buildup or excessive sanding in one spot. This gives a good finish with less obvious swirling sanding marks. When sanding the inside of facework, apply pressure with the bottom of the disc in the lower-left quadrant of the work or with the top of the disc in the lower-right quadrant.

An angle drill is easier to handle than a conventional drill and you can use it one-handed. Use the trailing edge of the sanding disc to avoid a catch.

POWER-SANDING

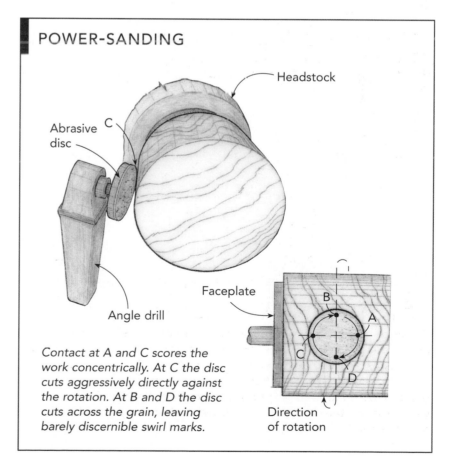

Headstock

Abrasive disc

Angle drill

Faceplate

Direction of rotation

Contact at A and C scores the work concentrically. At C the disc cuts aggressively directly against the rotation. At B and D the disc cuts across the grain, leaving barely discernible swirl marks.

Wavy Bowl

This bowl was turned green. Had it been small enough to fit in my oven it would have been microwaved. Instead it was left to change shape and dry and stabilize over seven months. The base was flattened on a sander.

MATERIAL:	Jarrah burl
SIZE:	22¾ in. (580mm) diameter

The major advantage of power tools, apart from speed, is that a particularly difficult area can receive special attention with much less effort than by hand. With the really rough or torn surfaces associated with spalted woods, a coarse abrasive disc—say 60 grit—is probably the only efficient way to obtain a clean surface.

To sand a free-form rim, as shown in the photos on p. 8 and p. 23, switch off the lathe and swing the wood on the lathe back and forth through an arc using one hand while the other hand holds the drill firmly in a fixed position. This is a relatively easy task with an angled rather than a conventional drill. The aim is to keep the tool steady as the wood swings through an arc, so that the leading edges of an uneven rim are not cut back faster than the remainder, a common feature of oversanding. This prevents the edges from being sanded unevenly.

In the mid-'90s, Australian Kevin Davidson developed the Rotary Sander, which looks like a cordless angle drill but in fact has no motor. Tested and promoted by his friend and well-known woodturner Vic Wood, the 3-in. (75mm) Rotary Sander has been copied by other manufacturers and several versions have found their way into woodturning catalogs. The original is still by far the best. The Rotary Sander works by freewheeling against the work as the lathe runs, removing clouds of dust and leaving few if any swirl marks (see the top photo on the facing page). It is not quite as efficient for removing material across center where the wood is moving more slowly, so I use power-sanding for coarser grits and keep the Rotary Sander for 180 grit and finer.

Often a surface will be marred by some defect such as a split knot. To fix a defect, fill the gap with fine dust, then add a few drops of thin cyanoacrylate adhesive (also known as Super Glue). The glue percolates the dust and sets in a few seconds. The mixture can then be worked as wood, which indeed it is. Darker dust looks best in knots, so I keep a stock of dark shavings from gidgee and African blackwood that I pulverize in an old kitchen blender.

Deciding upon an acceptable finish for a given situation can be a dilemma because there is no single, ideal finish for every turning. Spindles for a rush-seated chair, for example, might be incompatible with the rustic seat if they are sanded at all. Yet a miniature ebony box might be underfinished with a 400-grit surface when much finer grit would lend the wood a superior, glowing quality.

If I am copying spindles for the antique trade, I rarely use abrasives and, on occasion, I have even used a blunt tool carelessly to match the original most closely. I've also done batches of chair spindles for cabinetmakers (who varnish the end product), which need sanding only to 150 grit to provide a key for the final finish. In such cases, I will stop the lathe and give the spindle a final rub along its length so that the scratch marks will align with the grain.

Most of my bowls are finished with 400 grit, which I feel is sufficient and suitable for their functional nature. If they're too finely sanded, people won't use them for fear of ruining the surface, which defeats their intended purpose. Only the smaller, finer, or less functional decorative pieces get a finer sanding.

Occasionally, I'll sand a bowl particularly forcefully with 60 grit to remove some of the softer grain and create an undulating surface. The result is almost the same as the wear of the decades and produces a worn quality that might be hard to identify but registers in the subconscious in the same way as a well-worn handrail or a friendly tool handle.

Oil-and-Wax Finishes

Just about everything I make is meant to be used, and all the bowls have a little label saying so. They are designed to be washed with the dishes, although probably not in the dishwasher. Or they can be oiled or polished along with the furniture. Most of my work gets the same treatment, be it stair rail, rolling pin, salad bowl, decorative bowl, or door handle. It is sanded or not, as befits its purpose, and then oiled, currently with mineral oil. A coat of beeswax is applied on top to mix in with the oil and to keep the oil in the wood during its shelf life in a gallery or store. A waxed surface is

The Rotary Sander is similar to an angle drill. Powered by the rotating wood, the tool produces the finest sanded surface.

Fill gaps and defects with fine dust before adding a few drops of thin cyanoacrylate adhesive (Super Glue) to set it in place.

Bowls

I finish burls with holes and gaps with a liberal coating of oil off the lathe. I allow this to dry for a day before wiping it clean and lightly buffing the surface. Don't apply wax, especially when the lathe is running, because it builds up in the holes and is difficult to remove. And it looks terrible.

MATERIAL:	River red gum
SIZES:	10 in. to 18½ in. (255mm to 470mm) diameter

easier to maintain than an oiled surface, which often attracts dust.

To oil your work, apply the oil liberally with a soft cloth to the spinning wood. If it fails to penetrate the grain thoroughly, as often happens with open-grained woods such as ash and oak, stop the lathe and rub it in. Next, press a lump of beeswax firmly against the revolving wood so that it melts on with the friction, leaving a thin and visible layer on the surface.

With the work still spinning, apply a rag firmly enough to melt the wax so that it either mixes with the oil in the wood or stays in the cloth. In time, the rag will become so impregnated with oil and wax that its application alone will be sufficient. I find the best rags come from old, soft, cotton shirts or underwear. If the work is delicate, absorb the pressure of the wax and rag in much the same way that you support thin work while turning or sanding. And remember never to wrap a finishing rag around your fingers in case the lathe catches it.

You can use any wax, provided it is soft and pale and opaque. Beeswax works well, as does paraffin wax. A plain paraffin candle is ideal; it even has a convenient length of string down the middle to keep it from crumbling to pieces. I use soft waxes because they provide a good base for later care and whatever finish is ultimately employed. A small container might be used to hold anything from stamps to curry paste, so the stamp box gets furniture polish while the curry box gets washed periodically and reoiled. Food bowls for salads, rice, or breakfast cereals need frequent washing and no oiling. These can be hand-washed (not by machine) in hot water, exactly as any other kitchen or table item. The intense and prolonged heat of a dishwasher could split or warp the wood.

Soft wax will wash right off and the wood can be reoiled. But hard waxes, such as carnauba, create problems. Hard wax is fine if the wood will always be polished—though it gives too high and hard a gloss for my taste—but it doesn't like water. Water or dampness can spot the surface, which will then have to be sanded off and rewaxed, a capability most people don't have. So I shall stay with my humble technique and leave the custodians of my bowls to decide on their future character.

I know of two collections of my work that have found very different end uses, each calling for different treatment. One set of 6-in. (150mm) English sycamore porridge bowls is in heavy daily use, washed often and never oiled. Once white, they are now a lustrous gold on the outside and a pale cream within. The action of the spoon moving around the contents in the bowl has sanded better than any man-made abrasive could possibly manage and the surface is utterly smooth. The larger salad and serving bowls in the same collection are well on their way to acquiring the same handsome finish and quality.

The second group of bowls belongs to a collector of treen. The dozens of pieces are wiped lovingly with a wax-impregnated cloth every week. It is interesting to note that most have toned down to a dark gold/burnt umber or deep rose, with the grain becoming less obtrusive. In pieces more than 100 years old, the types of wood are mostly difficult to discern.

Most wood, regardless of how it's treated, will eventually become dark and either reddish-brown, if polished, or gray, if left unfinished. Keep this in mind when you are busily bringing out the grain. It's a great aid at the point of sale but in the end you'll leave posterity with the shape to look at and the balance to feel, not the flashy finish.

Sanding and finishing are two of the most subjective and controversial aspects of wood-turning. In general, it is better to learn to use your tools well, get a clean cut with a chisel, gouge, or scraper, and keep the use of abrasives to a minimum. Whatever your inclination, I suggest you experiment to produce varied surfaces rather than the uniform, flat, plastic coating that smacks of technical, rather than aesthetic, achievement. Perfection can be boring.

Bowls and Scoops

While the bowls get my standard oil-and-wax finish on the lathe, I oil the scoops off the lathe after the bowl has been cut and sanded so dust doesn't collect in the bead detail.

MATERIAL: Gidgee

SIZE: About 5 in. (130mm) diameter

AFTERWORD

As you will discover, it is fairly easy to achieve a bowl that functions as a bowl, a box with a lid that fits more or less satisfactorily, or a spindle covered with beads, grooves, and coves. What's not so easy is to produce a really beautiful, well-balanced bowl that is a joy to hold as well as to look at, or a box with just the right degree of suction in the fit of the lid, or a slender, elegant spindle with a few beads in just the right places.

Many amateur turners will be tempted to try to earn a livelihood from the craft, spurred on by the odd sale and encouraging remarks from friends and relations. If you are one, consider the problems. Over the years, I have helped a number of would-be professionals, many of whom are now well established and widely known internationally, but it has been a struggle for them as it was for me. The problem is not in producing a salable object. For no matter how hideous or impractical a piece might be, someone somewhere will buy it. Sales are no guide to quality. But if your work is to sell readily, it must be very well marketed or produced at the right price in a competitive market. The latter requires speed and speed requires practice.

Old World apprentices spent five to seven years at their trade before they were regarded as fully competent and could produce their masterpieces. In today's ever faster world of instant everything, this is an awesome thought, but I think that the old-timers were right. It was at least five years before I developed real speed in my turning and another year or so before I had the fluent technique to convert my ideas readily into woodturnings.

I provided my own apprenticeship by making lots of small, repetitious shapes: scoops, bowls, honey dippers, meat bashers, and so on. I still produce many items by the hundreds and, unlike many of today's craftspeople, I do not regard them as a necessary evil. They provide the vital practice that keeps my technique sharp; I need them as a musician needs scales.

Once you've acquired the speed and skills, your problem becomes how to sell everything that you can make in a normal working day. If you want to make large, decorative salad bowls, that's fine, but where do you sell 10 to 15 of them a day? Or 30 to 40 plates? Many aspiring turners have started out without considering this important aspect.

If you do take the plunge, I hope you enjoy it as much as I have. And just remember as you churn out the goods, there is absolutely no reason why the speed required for production should in any way compromise the quality.

As your skill develops, beware of complacency. Aim to get things right the first time. Don't poke or jab at the wood. Any shape poked at and messed about looks it. When you achieve flowing movements and sounds, flowing forms will follow.

Never be afraid to risk ruining a job with a final cut. It is all too easy to find turnery where a shape just misses because the maker has settled for a surface that is more or less okay, but where one or two more cuts would have made all the difference. Too many people say "that'll do" and either don't care about achieving quality or don't want to risk an hour's work in looking for it. But it is worth pushing yourself to develop your skill so that if you want to try something technically outrageous, you can tackle it with some prospect of success.

I can recall a 4-in. (100mm) by 10-in. (255mm) burr elm bowl I had turned with a ¼-in.- (6mm) thick wall that, upon inspection, I found to be less than ⅛ in. (3mm) thick near the base. (The bowl had holes in its side so it was easy to check the wall's thickness.) I held my breath and turned the whole wall down to match the thinner section. It was cut in one minute and not bludgeoned into submission with 20-grit abrasive in 10. That venture was successful. Other, smaller bowls have shattered with the final cut, but it is always worth the risk.

Decide what you want to make and go for it, and don't be satisfied with less. You will always know when you could have done better, even if others don't. Learn to be hypercritical and enjoy the long-term results. I find I am rarely satisfied with yesterday's masterpiece because it becomes today's run-of-the-mill. The better you get, the smaller your steps forward will be, but progress is always possible. And rest assured, you will never reach perfection—but you might have glimpses of it.

APPENDIX A:
TROUBLESHOOTING

PROBLEM/SYMPTOM	TOOL	REMEDY
Tool chatter/chattermarks	Chisels/gouges	Ensure the bevel rubs. Try a lighter, firmer cut. Grind the tool.
	Scrapers	Keep the tool flat on the rest. Try a lighter, firmer cut.
	All tools	Check fixing. Try a lower speed. Move the rest closer to the work. Tighten the rest. Hold the tool firmly. Try a stronger, heavier tool. Cut over the rest support post. Provide extra support for thin work. Cut from a different angle.
Catches/torn or lifted grain	Chisels/gouges	Ensure the bevel rubs. Adjust the point of cut on the tool edge.
	Scrapers	Keep the tool flat on the rest. Angle the tool so the edge cuts below horizontal externally. Angle the tool so the edge cuts slightly below horizontal and at center height on the bottom of a hollow.
	All tools	Move the rest closer to the point of cut. Provide a solid fulcrum and prevent lateral movement. Cut from a different direction. Try a firmer and gentler cut. Adjust the cutting angle. Try a different tool. Try shear scraping. Finish with a power-sander (when all else fails).
Tool won't cut	All tools	Check the edge for sharpness. Adjust the cutting angle.
Vibration/tick-tick sound	All tools	Check for splits, torn grain, loose knots, and the wood hitting the rest or lathe bed. True the surface. Check for exposed fixing screws.
Vibration/high-pitched sound	All tools	Provide extra support for thin work. Try a lighter cut with less pressure against the work.
Vibration/rattles and other sounds	All tools	Check the lathe mountings, the bearings, and the fixing. Tighten the tailstock and the rest. Center the work. Try a lower speed.
Abrasive scratch marks		Try a coarser grit. Try a power-sander.

APPENDIX B:
SELECTING AND SEASONING WOOD

Timbers are broadly classified into hardwoods (deciduous) and softwoods (coniferous), although you'll find plenty of soft hardwoods and hard softwoods. In general, softwoods grow more rapidly, developing wider growth rings and, therefore, more open grain. This tends to make the end grain difficult to work, so softwoods are more suitable for centerwork, such as banister spindles, where the end grain is typically hidden away. Hardwoods generally grow more slowly and have a tighter grain. They are suitable for both facework and centerwork.

A real advantage of working wood is that it is commercially available almost everywhere in the world in either logs or cut into squared sections. If the wood is green (freshly felled), it will contain a great deal of moisture and will need to be seasoned (dried out). As moisture leaves the wood, a board or log will hardly shrink in length, but it will shrink considerably in its width, causing splits and checks. (Because checking occurs most dramatically at the ends of the wood, they are often coated with wax or paint to slow the drying process.)

DRYING THE WOOD

Wood can be air-dried naturally, allowing about one year for every 1 in. (25mm) of wood thickness. Or wood can be kiln-dried, often with the aid of chemicals that also help to preserve it. I prefer air-dried to kiln-dried timber because it turns better and there is no risk of inhaling unknown substances that might have been used in the kiln-drying process.

You can turn wood either green or seasoned, but it becomes tougher and more difficult to work as it dries. Before the machine age when all wood was worked by hand, as much work as possible was done while the wood was green and at its easiest to work. When you turn green wood, you can expect it to change shape as it dries, so you'll have to make allowances for the movement.

The ends of boards sawn from green logs should be sealed to help prevent splits. Boards should be separated by sticks for six months while the surfaces dry. After that they can be close-stacked to save space until seasoned. These she-oak boards were sold by weight, which is written on the end grain.

I am primarily a bowl turner and I have neither the space nor capital to invest in sufficient seasoning and seasoned stocks of bowl material. Also I don't have the energy to turn so much seasoned wood: It's often hard work. I purchase most of my wood green and transform it into part-turned bowls as soon as possible, before the material starts to split.

After a few weeks of drying in a loose pile, I keep my roughed bowls in open boxes until I need them. Every few months, I transfer them to another box so I can see how they are drying, check for insect attack, and shift the bottom of the pile to the top.

Some of the warping takes place because stresses change as the form is hollowed, so on the odd occasion when I work dry wood, I part-turn that as well and allow it to stabilize for a few days before the final turning.

Roughed bowls need a wall thickness about one-tenth of the bowl's diameter. Therefore, a 10-in.- (255mm) diameter bowl has a wall 1 in. (25mm) thick. The wall should be much the same thickness from the rim to the base to allow for even drying. After dating them with the month and year so I know when they were roughed, I leave the bowls in a loose pile out of direct sunlight where air can circulate freely around them for a few weeks until the surface dries. Then I toss them into boxes until the seasoning process is complete. Every few months, I transfer the bowls to another box, partly to check how they're drying and partly to check for insect attack, borers, termites, and such, but also to get the bottom ones to the top.

Since the late 1970s, many woodturners have been experimenting with the microwave oven as a means of seasoning timber. While I have flirted with attempts to speed the sea-

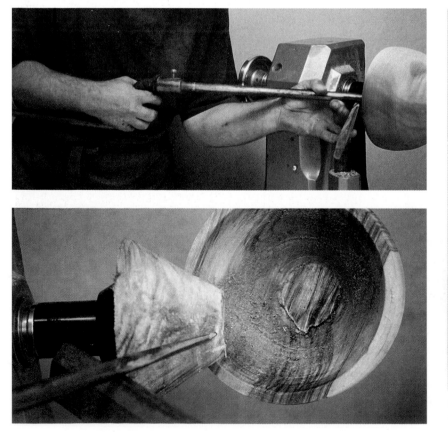

A Stewart System Slicer is used to save the inside of a bowl.

soning of roughed-out bowls, I have not found microwave seasoning worthwhile commercially and cannot recommend it to anyone as a standard practice. Most microwaves do not seem to penetrate more than 1 in. (25mm) of wood satisfactorily. So, while you can undoubtedly dry wood thinner than this, the process is time-consuming, often requiring each piece to have several short periods in and out of the oven. However, I do use the microwave oven to dry out my more delicate green-turned wavy bowls (see the photo on p. 18).

Professionals can maintain a stock of roughed bowls for standard production runs. Amateurs, especially when starting out, might practice their gouge technique while roughing-out bowls and then return later to finish them when their skills have developed and they can proceed with a greater likelihood of success. In schools, students can rough standard-shaped bowls to go in a general stockpile and take others to finish that have already dried.

GETTING THE MOST FROM YOUR WOOD

To extract as much value as possible from increasingly expensive raw material, it is now common practice to save the inside of open bowls. There are several bowl-saving systems available commercially and, although expensive, you soon recoup the initial outlay when you can sell the innermost bowl to cover the cost of the whole blank. While most systems are set up to hollow from the right (tailstock) side when the bowl is held by its foot, I prefer to work from the left (headstock) side with the blank mounted on a screw chuck (see the bottom photos on the facing page). That way I can peel off the bowls without stopping the lathe for more than a few seconds.

For woods with tough end grain, I find the narrow carbide-tipped Stewart System Slicer (seen in the bottom photos on the facing page) to be the most efficient tool. On easier woods such as unseasoned burl, I use a McNaughton System curved slicer as shown in the photo at right. The curved slicers (see the illustration at left on p. 198) are a joy to use on easily worked wood, and the various systems come with instructions.

However, a straight slicer is the simplest tool to use because it sits on a normal rest cutting at center height. In the illustration at right on p. 198, note that cuts are directed toward the center of the base and that several cuts are needed to widen the opening to accommodate the slicer blade as the cut deepens. As the cut nears the base, the bowl

being peeled away starts to wobble somewhat and can be easily levered free as the wood splits along the grain. Stop the lathe to lever the bowl free. The disadvantage of the straight slicer is that the first bowl needs remounting so the wall can be turned to an even thickness (indicated by the dotted line) for seasoning.

THE RIGHT WOOD FOR THE JOB

When you begin turning, you'll want a supply of inexpensive material and plenty of it (so you won't feel guilty or inhibited about wasting it, which at first you must). But the kind of wood you look for also will depend on what you intend to

The McNaughton System uses a vertical gate and antikickback arm to counteract the leverage exerted against the curved blades.

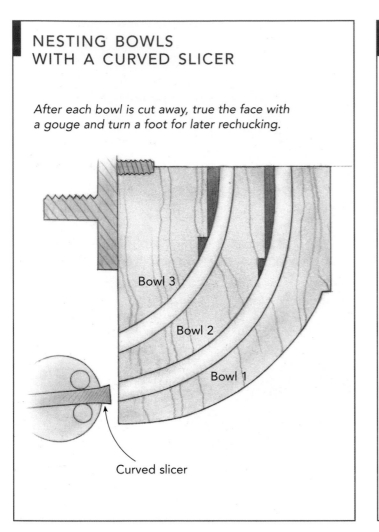

NESTING BOWLS WITH A CURVED SLICER

After each bowl is cut away, true the face with a gouge and turn a foot for later rechucking.

Bowl 3

Bowl 2

Bowl 1

Curved slicer

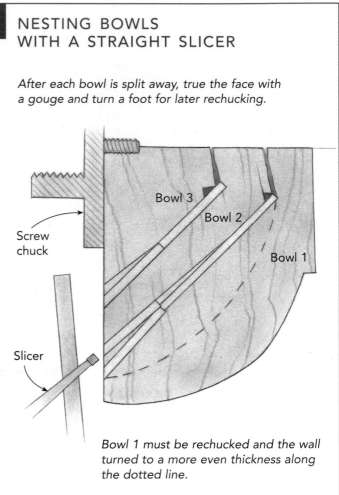

NESTING BOWLS WITH A STRAIGHT SLICER

After each bowl is split away, true the face with a gouge and turn a foot for later rechucking.

Screw chuck

Bowl 3

Bowl 2

Bowl 1

Slicer

Bowl 1 must be rechucked and the wall turned to a more even thickness along the dotted line.

make and whether it's centerwork or facework. For example, the best wood for wavy bowls is an even-grained piece of timber where the growth rings are symmetrical around the pith. An outward-flowing ogee shape will produce an undulating rim; a parabolic curve will become oval.

To practice the centerwork exercises (see chapter 6), you'll need lengths 2 in. (50mm) to 3 in. (75mm) in diameter with straight grain running the length of the blank and no knots. Try to get your wood green; it is not too soon to turn it within an hour of its being felled, although you'll be sprayed with moisture as you cut. (You can get so hooked on producing long shavings that you'll forget about making anything else.)

When you're ready to move on to projects instead of exercises, you'll want to work with seasoned wood. Centerwork turnings, such as small boxes, bowls or lidded containers, egg

cups, candle holders, door knobs, spindles, and rolling pins, will require short lengths of seasoned wood with the grain running the length of the blank. You need dry timber so that the wood moves as little as possible in the finished piece.

You can cut facework blanks out of sawn boards or round logs. For flatware such as plates, clock faces, and breadboards, you'll need seasoned wood to avoid warping. Unless you have space to season boards, you'll need to buy wood that has been seasoned already. Short planks, less than 6 ft. (1.8m) long, called shorts, are often available and are usually less expensive than longer boards. Examine the wood for end splits and surface checks before you buy it.

For large-dimension facework such as bowls, obtaining material can be a problem (amazing though it may seem, considering the number of trees felled). Suitable material is

GETTING STOCK FROM LOGS

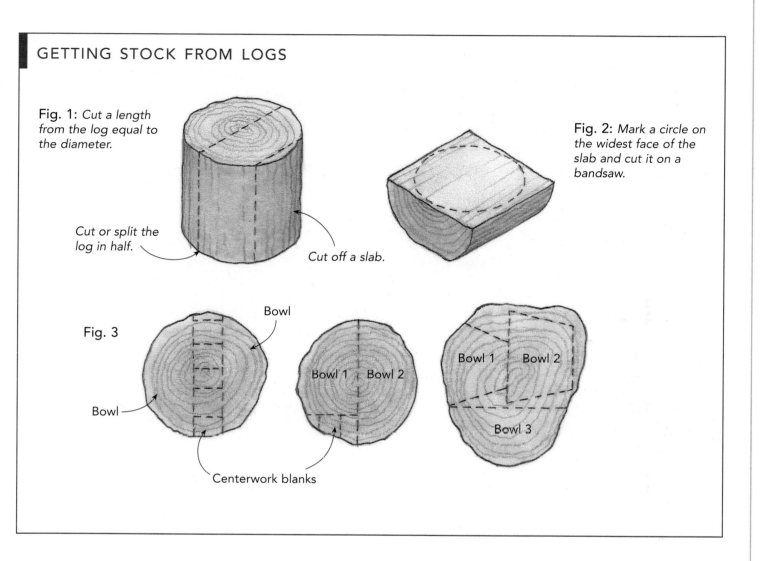

Fig. 1: *Cut a length from the log equal to the diameter.*

Cut or split the log in half.

Cut off a slab.

Fig. 2: *Mark a circle on the widest face of the slab and cut it on a bandsaw.*

Fig. 3

Bowl

Bowl

Centerwork blanks

Bowl 1 | Bowl 2

Bowl 1 | Bowl 2

Bowl 3

---

very scarce in most sawmills and lumberyards. In my experience, seasoned wood in excess of 8 in. (205mm) wide by 2 in. (50mm) thick is rare, as are boards more than 12 in. (305mm) wide. Requests for anything in excess of 8 in. (205mm) wide by 3 in. (75mm) thick will be greeted by stares of blank amazement. And if it's available, it almost certainly won't be dry—despite what you might be told. Dry to a sawmiller tends to be around 20% moisture content, while 12% to 14% (approximating the humidity of most home interiors) is nearer the mark.

Because the wood for deep bowls takes so long to season and is easier to turn while green, turners usually rough-turn bowls from unseasoned timber and true them up after they have dried and warped. The bowls in this book were mostly rough-turned and set aside to be air-dried for many months (or years) before being finished.

Although it's convenient to be able to cut bowl blanks from a plank, planks provide less of an opportunity to manipulate grain patterns and are more expensive than logs. I cut most of my bowl blanks straight from the log these days, following the process shown in the illustration above. Cut a length from the log equal to its diameter, stand the section on the end grain, and cut it down the center or along a split. Although I use a chainsaw for this, a log splitter will do fine if you have the skill to use it.

A half-log can go between centers or on a screw chuck or faceplate if you true up the flat side. Fig. 3 in the illustration above indicates several variations that will provide blanks of different shapes. This is the most basic way to get timber, and all you need is a predatory eye. You can get blanks for bowls from a log as small as 7 in. (180mm) to 8 in. (205mm) in diameter. If you wait for whole logs to air-dry, they will often split badly, leaving you with little usable material. I generally cut logs as soon as possible and rough them out into bowl or spindle blanks.

As a beginner, your requirements are basic. All you need is close-grained wood that is easy to work. (Pretty patterns in the wood are wasted at this stage, and highly figured grain may present more of a problem than it's worth.) Many ornamental and fruit trees are ideal, such as apple, pear, cherry, maple, privet, and laburnum. But at first, you might as well try every variety of wood you can get—there's no substitute for first-hand experience, and you'll soon learn what to avoid or look for. As your skills develop, you'll want more interesting material, so color and grain patterns will become more relevant.

WHERE TO FIND THE WOOD

Wood is commercially available from sawmills, timber merchants, lumberyards, and do-it-yourself stores. The last two sources will be more expensive than the first two, who are, metaphorically speaking, nearer the standing tree. If you live near a sawmill that will give you permission, hunt around its scrap pile and you're likely to find all you need. Merchants, too, will probably have scrap piles or an odds-and-ends section.

Both sources should be able to offer expert advice on what wood is suitable for a job, which woods work easily, and which do not. They should also be able to tell you if the wood is seasoned and what its moisture content is by measuring it on the spot with a meter. (Whether they will bother to or not is a different matter—many large mills and yards do not like small orders.)

There are a number of companies that cater to the needs of the amateur and artist-craftsman, stocking a wide range of woods such as ebony, cocobolo, African blackwood, mulga, and gidgee in addition to all the standard cabinet woods.

Many of these woods grow in arid or tropical areas, but they are exported to broader markets around the world.

There is a great deal of wood just lying around that can provide suitable material, especially for practice. Demolished buildings can yield vast quantities, although nails can be a problem and must be carefully removed. Urban trees that need pruning are another good source. Keep your eye on the local parks-department workers, and check the town dump if it's nearby and you're allowed in. Your neighbors' backyards and gardens may also yield a considerable supply.

But don't hoard more than you can use. I've seen too many woodturners with piles of what was once wonderful material lying spoiled by the weather and sun, split and scarcely fit for a fireplace. If you grab logs, do something with them: Rough-turn bowls or convert them to boards and waxed billets—anything rather than waste them through neglect.

If you cut defect-free lumps, wax or paint the ends—chances are the wood will dry without splitting. Then the longer you leave it the better it becomes. Wood is said to gain its maximum workability after a few hundred years, and material of that age certainly is wonderful to work.

As an amateur or budding-but-penniless professional, you could do worse than approach a going concern about their offcuts. When I began to turn, I worried that I would never collect a good stock of wood. A few months later, I had a storage problem. I went around local yards buying up cheap odds and ends—almost doing the lumberyards a favor by taking what they wanted to get rid of anyway.

I cut everything to the maximum diameter possible for discs or square lengths for centerwork, keeping all the offcuts. Soon, I had filled a dozen sacks. Small blanks became a major storage problem when I began to concentrate on turning larger pieces. (On two occasions, I have sold several tons of small blanks.) You should be able to accumulate all the wood you need without any problem—apart from complaints and comments from those who share your space.

INDEX